JOHN

HIS INNER LIFE

DR. ZENO, CAPUCHIN

JOHN HENRY NEWMAN

HIS INNER LIFE

IGNATIUS PRESS   SAN FRANCISCO

Cover photograph:
John Henry Newman
by Robert White Thrupp
© National Portrait Gallery, London

Cover design by Roxanne Mei Lum

© 1987 by Ignatius Press, San Francisco
ISBN 978-0-89870-112-8
Library of Congress Control Number 1986-81424
Printed in the United States of America

CONTENTS

INTRODUCTION

The history of this book is a history of more than forty years.
When in 1935 I had to take two subjects subsidiary to my
studies in English language and literature at the University
of Nijmegen, I chose philosophy and theology in connection with English philosophers and theologians, starting on
Newman's *Essay on Development*, *Grammar of Assent* and
Apologia and writing the required theses on those books as
a preparation for what is called in Holland the doctoral
examination. For the title of a doctor, the Dutch universities
demand an original study on a special subject, resulting in a
rather lengthy dissertation. So for five full years I studied
Newman's doctrine on the illative sense, and in 1942 I defended
my book before the assembled professors and a select audience
in the University Hall. These studies had fascinated me to such
a degree that I could not stop there. When a Dutch publishing
firm wanted me to translate the *Grammar of Assent* and to write
explanatory notes and a thorough introduction for it, I gladly
availed myself of this opportunity. This took another five
years and served as a kind of recreation from other, more
pressing tasks.

All these studies, however, made me wish to know more
about Newman's personality, his inner life, his motives, his
contact with the invisible world. On the one hand he appeared
to me as a great, heroic soul, but on the other hand I met
people, especially in England, who could not praise him
unreservedly. I read books on him which were full of appreciation but others, too, which imputed unworthy motives
to his words and acts. Had he been a great man with many
foibles as several authors insinuated? Or was he misunderstood, and had his motives and his inner life never been
brought into full daylight? His books suggested a man of high
ideals, but did he always live up to them? So I began reading
the immense amount of material in the Newman archives,

which were put at my disposal by the kindness of the Oratorian
Fathers. It took me, all in all, fifteen months to examine the 430
files of letters in the Archivium and the formidable collection
of papers, journals and memoranda in the cupboards of the
Cardinal's room. (Most of these documents have recently been
published.) Studying the forty-five volumes of Newman's
works which had up to then been published also required
much time. While I read and copied out what threw light on
his inner life, the outlines of Newman's soul gradually became
clear to me: the following pages are the result of this labor of
love.

Glanerbrug, July 29, 1979

CHAPTER ONE

LATELY COME FROM GOD'S PRESENCE

1801–1815

> When I was a child, I was instructed in religious knowledge
> by kind and pious friends, who told me who my Maker
> was, what great things He had done for me, how much I
> owed to Him, and how I was to serve Him. All this I learned
> from them, and I rejoice that they taught it me: yet they did
> more; they set me in the way to gain a knowledge of
> religious truth in another and higher manner. They not only
> taught me, but trained me; they were careful that I should
> not only know my duty, but do it. They obliged me to obey;
> they obliged me to begin a religious course of life. . . .[1]

My story begins a few years after the French Revolution.
Napoleon was the rising sun in Europe and threatened both
England and the whole Continent. England was at war with
France and at the same time suffered from the effects of the
Industrial Revolution. More and more working-class people
moved from the country to the towns. They were worked to
death in the mines and the "dark Satanic mills". By an Act
of Parliament their unions, called Combinations, had been
declared illegal. Communication between villages and towns
was hampered by bad roads and slow means of travel. Neither
railways nor the steam engine had been invented, and the first
iron ship had been launched only ten years previously. A horse
was still the fastest means of travel on land. There was no
welfare state, and the fear of epidemics was prevalent.

In several respects the Anglican church resembled a body
asleep. Nor was there much life in the University of Oxford,

where the Anglican clergy were trained. Many ministers of the church lived a worldly life, devoid of religion, and their damp and musty churches were not opened except on Sundays. Many a bishop acted like an official and not like a clergyman. The so-called "old religion" had all but died out, and there were only a few timid Catholics, who did not venture to show themselves in public life. In recent times, however, some of their civic rights had been restored to them. As a reaction against this measure Lord George Gordon, foolishly and irresponsibly, instigated an anti-Catholic riot. There was nevertheless a feeling of sympathy emerging, and French priests who fled from the Revolution discredited various prejudices cherished by the people against the Roman Catholic Church, the Pope and the few remaining Catholics.

It was into these conditions that John Henry Newman was born on February 21, 1801. His parents, John Newman and Jemima Fourdrinier, were middle-class people who lived in comfortable circumstances in the heart of London. John Newman's ancestors had been small farmers and tailors in Cambridgeshire, but his father had left the county for London and obtained there a better position so that his son John could become a partner in a banking firm. The Fourdrinier family, however, were French émigrés who had escaped to England when Louis XIV repealed the Edict of Nantes. They had become paper manufacturers.[2] John Henry was the eldest of their six children, three boys and three girls. He was baptized a few weeks after his birth.

He did not, in later life, doubt the validity of his baptism as Lucy Pusey, his friend's wife, did hers (he himself rebaptized her).[3] The grace of the sacrament developed without difficulty in the child because he was educated by pious relatives in quiet, favorable surroundings. They taught him what duties he had toward God, and they trained him to obey the Commandments.

Among the "kind and pious friends" who instructed him in religious knowledge were his paternal grandmother and his great-aunt, with whom he often stayed during his childhood.

At his brother Frank's coming-of-age John Henry mentioned his grandmother's influence in a poem, dedicated to his brother as a birthday offering:

> Ah! brother, shall we e'er forget
>   Her love, her care, her zeal?
> We cannot pay the countless debt,
>   But we must ever feel;
> For through her earnestness were shed
> Prayer-purchased blessings on our head.[4]

After he had learned to write, John Henry frequently sent letters to his grandmother. They were full of affection, gratitude and religious thoughts. When he had grown up he still trusted in the efficacy of her prayers.[5] He called her his earliest benefactor.[6] And in 1825 he wrote to his aunt: "That we are living together in peace, harmony and affection, and that we have (as I trust we have) the fear of God before our eyes, is under God owing to my dear grandmother and yourself."[7] In the same letter he ascribed his call to the ministry and his success in parish work especially to the fact that from his youth Providence employed his kind relatives as instruments to turn his thoughts to religion.

This does not imply that his mother's influence did not leave a mark on his character and religious sentiments. From her letters it appears that she possessed a balanced mind, enjoyed life and had a deep insight into the characters of her children. She made the home into a happy place by her cheerfulness and affection, her unselfish care of her family, even in the most distressing times.[8] The children found every kind of happiness in family life and wanted neither friends nor visitors, who appeared to them to be intruders.[9] Simplicity was another distinguishing trait of Mrs. Newman's character. A friend testified to this when writing about her eldest son, stating that his admirable simplicity was inherited from his mother.[10] He never wrote a superfluous word. He was never driven to showing pride in his extraordinary talent, his high gifts, his cultured mind. Mrs. Newman was not sentimental, though very sensitive and sometimes overanxious. This is evident from the fact that even those children who were dearest to her and of whom she was extremely proud could hurt her painfully.[11]

Above all she had a deeply religious mind, which showed itself especially by a genuine and practical trust in God's Providence and great resignation in trials. These were virtues of which she was sorely in need since she had to bear many heavy crosses in her married life. The war with France caused a financial crisis in her husband's business and undermined his health. Her youngest daughter Mary died before she was twenty. Her son Charles proved a constant burden to the whole family up until his death. Her third son Frank had strange ideas and wild plans and caused great anxiety. But she always remained patient, full of trust in God, resigned.[12] "I can only repeat", she once wrote to John Henry, "that in the midst of so many and great troubles, I have ever had so many blessings to be thankful for, that I have even at the worst been full of hope."[13]

John Newman, her husband, was quite different. He called himself a man of the world and was of an independent turn of mind; he looked at things from his own point of view but could listen to other people's opinions and appreciate them. It was small wonder that he should be somewhat sceptical. At any rate he seems to have felt shocked at some Bible texts and unable to agree with those who were certain about the historic foundation of Christianity. Hence his son Frank states that he learned his morality more from Shakespeare than from the Bible. But whatever he was, he was not irreligious. He believed in God and admired certain religious books.[14] He warned his eldest son against "enthusiasm in religion", a feature of the Evangelicals of the time.[15] When on his deathbed, he showed through his trust in God and his gratitude for God's gifts how genuine his belief was. He had a more than common sense of justice, and this made him forget personal interests. His financial troubles did not prevent him from securing a university education for John Henry. His son often remembered his father's generosity and called him in many respects his guide and instructor from youth.[16] He taught his son to read and write,[17] imbued him with a love of music and gave him riding lessons. His advice was always prudent and seriously given. In his old age John Henry mentioned that his father's praises were the source of a sunny serenity of mind and a soothing, satisfactory delight.[18]

It has often been said that the Newman parents gave their happy and somewhat self-sufficient children an Evangelical upbringing. It is, however, beyond doubt that they themselves were normal moderate Anglicans, neither High Church nor Evangelical, and that they educated their sons and daughters as the mass of Anglicans did in those days, that is, with the Bible, the Catechism, the Sunday services in church and the morning and evening prayers, said together on their knees. The children received, however, little or no instruction in the doctrines contained in the Bible and the Catechism. Much attention was paid to the simple moral precepts, which were after all more intelligible and had a more immediate bearing upon life.[19] Hence John Henry was very fond of the hymns which formed part of his prayers as a child, such as the evening hymn:

> And now another day is gone,
> I'll sing my Maker's praise,
> My comforts ev'ry hour make known
> His providence and grace.

The hymn closes:

> With cheerful heart I close my eyes
> Since Thou wilt not remove;
> And in the morning let me rise
> Rejoicing in Thy love.

His love for the other evening hymn which was said on Sunday evenings demonstrates how deeply his piety had already taken root in his heart:

> O Lord, how delightful 'tis to see
> A whole assembly worship Thee,
> At once they sing, at once they pray,
> They hear of heaven, and learn the way.

And the last stanza:

> With thoughts of Christ and things divine
> Fill up this foolish heart of mine;
> That hoping pardon thro' His Blood
> I may lie down and wake with God.[20]

Most children would repeat such prayers without any realization of what they said. But John Henry loved to say them. No wonder that he could recount in 1843: "God put it into my heart, when I was five or six years old, to ask *what* and *why* I was."[21]

All these things seem to point to the fact that as a child he already lived in the invisible world. Of course, many of these early experiences can be explained as coming quite naturally to a sensitive, intelligent, imaginative child. But his natural qualities did not develop apart from grace, divine influences working through the lessons and examples of his mother and his pious relatives. He used to think of life as a dream and he an angel and all this world a deception, while perhaps his fellow angels concealed themselves from him and deceived him with the semblance of a material world.[22] We may even say in his own words that he seemed "to have come lately from God's presence". Hence his incapability of understanding the language of the visible scene of things, and his considering this world a temptation. Hence the simplicity of his ideas, his ready belief in everything he was told, his artless love, his frank confidence, his confession of helplessness, his ignorance of evil and his inability to conceal his thoughts. Hence, too, his contentment, his prompt forgetfulness of trouble, his regarding the things about him as wonderful, as tokens of the One Invisible.[23] While still very young he frequently heard an inner voice. It warned him and told him what to do and what to leave undone. It gladdened him when he had acted well. It made him feel ashamed and sad when he had done something wrong, though his faults came and went like little clouds in a blue summer sky and did not take away his innocence. He knew then that he offended One to Whom he was responsible, One Whom he did not see but Who saw him. When he had grieved his parents and noticed their displeasure, his child's soul turned spontaneously to this Voice and begged Him to set him right with them. This implied, as he himself inferred, that he possessed an impression on his mind of an unseen Being Whom he could address whenever he chose, of Whose good will toward him he was assured, Who was even dearer to him and loved him better than his parents.[24]

As an elderly man he copied down a story which had made a special impression on him because it fully complemented his own ideas and confirmed the reality of his own early experiences. The story concerned a small boy of four years of age who saw a spotted tortoise. He had a stick in his hands and lifted it up to hit the animal. But then a new sensation came over the child, so awful and so unexpected that he at once hurried home and asked his mother: "What was it that told me I was wrong?" The mother was touched by this question and took the boy in her arms and said: "Some men call it conscience, but I prefer to call it *the voice of God* in the soul of man. If you listen to it and obey it, then it will speak clearer and clearer. . . . If you turn a deaf ear or disobey it, then it will fade out little by little."[25]

Newman has written much about this voice. He starts with it in demonstrating the existence of God because conscience is clearly "the echoes of the voice of a Master, living, personal and sovereign".[26] Obedience to this voice brings inward peace, lightness of heart, self-approval; disobedience brings distress and apprehension, embarrassment, compunction and regret.[27] It is the voice of a beloved Friend, a voice more real than the sun, moon and stars, more real than a living man's voice.

Of course, as he said himself, the seed of evil was also in him. This is exemplified by a few minor incidents which occurred during these first years. For example, an instance of self-will: his mother forcibly prevented him from getting his own way, but he gloried in having tried very hard.[28] He was greedy when eating fruit in the garden: "How difficult it was to leave off, when once one got among the gooseberry bushes in the idle morning."[29] On another occasion he told his nursemaid that when in Brighton he had seen four different kinds of fish, among them a shark and a whale. This was sheer bragging.[30] From his later "journals" it appears that as a boy he was quick-tempered. But the only conclusion we may infer from such trifles is that he was a normal, healthy child.

When John Henry was seven he was sent, much to the distress of his mother, to a private boarding school at Ealing, run by Dr. Nicholas.[31] Here he received not only his primary but secondary education up to university level. As he was quick of intellect and had already learned many of the primary subjects at home, John Henry finished the so-called Little School in one year and began his classics and other grammar school subjects by June 1809, at eight years old.[32] When twelve he could read Virgil, Homer and Herodotus. Soon after he was fifteen he had finished the entire course.[33]

   John Henry, who, like many other intellectually talented boys, was not a sportsman, had no liking for games. Nevertheless, he was a normal schoolboy who had other interests than reading. He paddled in a swimming pool, but according to his brother Frank he never swam.[34] He learned to play the violin, danced and played billiards; he flew kites; he even edited a magazine for the boys and founded a secret club. He enjoyed the holidays, and when at home he knew how to amuse his brothers and sisters. Even as a child he showed a great liking for literary composition and the theatre. At eleven years of age he wrote a mock drama; at fourteen a burlesque opera. Once, when his master had introduced a new book for use in class, he could not refrain from reading it right through: "Instead of keeping it for school time as a lesson, I put myself in the large window, my legs hanging out or along it, and read it right through, or at least as far as time would allow, one half holiday."[35]

It is not difficult to trace in the documents he himself preserved the religious education he had received. There is still extant a pocket diary in which he wrote his thoughts and the ordinary events of everyday life. As a boy of nine he writes: "He is wise who curbs his passions." This is a reminder to himself of the duty of fighting against his temperamental nature. Hardly ten years old, he jotted down as an attempt at poetry:

> Into the palace of the Lord
> Those who do right and keep His word
> Will surely go; but those who don't
> I am quite certain that they won't.[36]

In his own book of verse, inscribed in a beautiful schoolboy hand, he wrote solemn religious truths: "The aethereal Father fills Heaven and earth and the wide sea. Whithersoever thou lookest, all things are full of God."[37]

However paradoxical it may sound, it appears to be true that the last years of the Ealing period were in a sense the darkest period of his life. The bitter memory of these years always haunted him and in 1844 he confessed to his friend John Keble that as a boy of fifteen he lived "a life of sin, with a very dark conscience and a very profane spirit".[38] Referring to the Ealing period when he was nearly fifty-nine, he spoke about himself as having been "more like a devil than a wicked boy".[39] And ten years later: "Among the ordinary mass of men, *no one* has sinned so much, *no one* has been so mercifully treated, as I have; no one has such cause for humiliation, such cause for thanksgiving."[40]

In his books we find many more allusions to this life of sin and this profane spirit. In the *Apologia* he tells us that during the Ealing period he found pleasure in Paine's objections against the Old Testament. He read some of Hume's *Essays*.

He copied out some French verses in denial of the immortality of the soul and thought this doctrine dreadful but plausible.[41] We know, too, that he later recollected how in 1815 he did not like to be religious; he only wanted to be virtuous. Nor did he realize the meaning of loving God. He had an argument with a master in favor of Pope's *Essay on Man*. The master seems to have shown disapproval of the poem, but John Henry considered it unobjectionable because it expressly inculcated the truth: virtue alone is happiness below.[42] In his *Meditations and Devotions*—true echoes of his inner life—he complains about having lifted up his hand against the face of Christ: "Turn back in memory, and recollect the time, the day, the hour, when by wilful mortal sin, by scoffing at sacred things, or by profaneness, or by dark hatred of this Thy Brother, or by acts of impurity, or by deliberate rejection of God's voice, or in any other devilish way known to thee, thou hast struck the All-holy one."[43] And never did he retract his statement that he had been a great sinner. On the contrary, he repeated it in his old age: "Was any boyhood so impious as some years of mine?"[44]

We might ask how it could come to pass that at Ealing he lost his religious sense.

To begin with, the religious atmosphere in the school was apparently not very high. When one of the masters, a fervent Evangelical clergyman, wished to give some religious instruction to the boys he was not encouraged. He was considered singular.[45] So it is quite natural that there should not have been much supervision of the boys' reading. John Henry read everything he could lay hands on. His father, something of a free-thinker, most probably stimulated this random reading, as is shown by some of John Newman's books, still preserved in Birmingham. There is, too, the period of adolescence to be considered, when the flesh frequently fights against the spirit. At the same time, the success of his studies gave him an elevated idea of himself. All these factors made him pray less and less and in an automatic and superficial way. Thus the sense of God's presence in his soul was dimmed, grace became less operative and the end was extreme spiritual weakness. It is notable that in his works Newman described at least four times a boy falling away from religious feeling into unbelief.[46] In his *Idea of a University*, for example, he pictures how for the first time a boy comes across the arguments and speculations of unbelievers. They throw new light on what he has hitherto considered sacred. And gradually he gives in and discards as so much prejudice the truths he had held previously. As if waking from a dream he begins to realize that there is now no such thing as law and the transgression of law, that sin is a phantom and punishment a bugbear, that he is free to sin, free to enjoy the world and the flesh. And still further, when he does enjoy them, he reflects that he may think and believe just what he will.

John Henry was soon to return from this path.

CHAPTER TWO

GOD'S LOVE TOOK ME CAPTIVE

1815–1822

O Almighty Lord, . . . Thou, in Thy inscrutable love for me, hast chosen me. . . . I should have lived and died in darkness and sin; I should have become worse and worse the longer I lived; . . . I should have got yearly more fit for hell, and at length I should have gone there, but for Thy incomprehensible love to me. O my God, that overpowering love took me captive.[1]

When John Henry had finished his course of study at Ealing and knew more than enough to enter university, his parents were in great financial distress. As a consequence of the war with Napoleon, the bank was forced to close its doors. But John Newman, scrupulously honest, wished to keep his reputation unstained and tried with every means in his power to prevent bankruptcy. The Headmaster of the Ealing school, when told of their situation, realized at once how difficult it would be for the parents to have John Henry at home and to pay board and lodging for his brothers Charles and Frank. So he generously suggested the school keep the three boys till things were settled.

For this reason John Henry stayed on at Ealing, though he no longer attended classes. He had plenty of time now. He worried not only about the anxieties of his parents but also about his own inner life. Moreover, he became seriously ill. It was a keen and terrible illness "with experiences before and after, awful, and known only to God". He felt "terrified at the heavy hand of God". And this was the beginning of a great change, which as he himself said, made him a Christian.[2]

Under these circumstances, the pious Master of Classics, Walter Mayers, began to influence the boy. Mayers would have preferred to devote himself entirely to pastoral work, but his financial position made it impossible. However, he led a life of prayer, and his example showed that "the unseen things of the spiritual world were always uppermost in his mind".[3] So he availed himself of the opportunity of talking to John Henry on religious subjects. In great earnestness the tormented boy listened to the comforting words about God's mercy and the healing power of Christ's Blood, about the forgiveness of sin and the hope of eternal salvation. These conversations were made more profitable still by the sermons and Evangelical books his master lent him. And then God's love touched his hard and unbelieving heart and took possession of him. After a time he seemed to be quite another person.[4] "Before I was blind, now I see", he said.[5] It was the beginning of a new life.

However complete this change might have been, an element of his former inner life had returned. He tells us that the principles which he had felt and acted upon when young regained their place in his mental makeup.[6] The invisible world became reality again. The presence of God was no longer dimmed by the shadows of profanity and unbelief. It was as though innocence had been recovered by the divine influence of God's mercy.

Although this conversion had much to do with the Evangelical school, which did not place much value on dogma and theological speculations—because faith was "not an acceptance of revealed doctrine, not an act of the intellect, but a feeling, an emotion, an affection, an appetancy"[7]—he nevertheless received "impressions of dogma" which, through God's mercy, were never to be lost or obscured. He accepted the doctrine that conversion implies eternal salvation; therefore he became convinced that he belonged to the elect.[8] But this conviction did not make him neglect his spiritual life. It did not tend to make him careless about pleasing God, but his soul and his Creator were the two things that occupied his thoughts continually, made him quiet and happy, isolated him still more from the material world, from persons and things, even from the troubles at home.[9] He also accepted as truths the dogmas of the Holy Trinity and the Incarnation and the Lutheran doctrine of justification by faith only.[10] A religion without dogma seemed to him a dream and a mockery.[11] He could not accept the idea that God does not mind whether we do or do not believe in the Son of God and His becoming man and dying for mankind.

Even in his old age Newman saw this inner change as one of the most important events of his life. When he wrote his *Apologia* in 1864, he was still certain of it, more certain even than of the fact that he had hands and feet.[12]

It was in the last months at Ealing that he began to write the memoranda about his inner life which give an insight into the nature and the effects of this change of heart. His notes, often in the form of prayers, are spontaneous. They reveal his deep sincerity and a great fear of falling again. They display a total confidence in God's help. They portray a profound conviction of his own weakness and imperfection but also a quiet happiness because of God's protection. They are prayers for the grace to find his contentment in God alone, and his wish to please his Creator appears in every page. Both here and in his sermons and letters we find innumerable proofs of this, the leading motive of his life: "Lord, what wilt Thou have me to do?"[13] These notes make it clear that the conversion was not only a "change of thought"[14] but a change of heart.

If I may give an example, I should like to quote the spontaneous prayer written at the end of the year 1816, in what he himself called doggerel verse:

> Let me always, my God and King,
>   In Thy dear Name rejoice
> And daily to Thy praises sing
>   With ever grateful voice.
>
> I am a worm, and Thou art good
>   To save a wretch like me,
> Who always has Thy grace withstood,
>   And turned his back on Thee.

O grant that I may persevere
  And finally obtain
A glorious crown, purchased for dear,
  That ever may remain.

Purchased for dear, for by the Blood,
  of Jesus it is given
Who suffered death, the Just and Good,
  That we may live in heaven.

O may I scorn each mundane joy,
  And meditate on Thee,
May heaven all my thoughts employ,
  Then happy shall I be.[15]

The style and language of this "poem" betray the influence of the Evangelical school—as do many of his early writings—but the thoughts express his real feelings, the feelings of a clever boy of fifteen who wishes to lead a truly Christian life.

He dated the period of this change from August 1 to December 21, 1816, and he resolved to do a work of charity every year on these two days.[16] This feeling of gratitude remains to the end, as well as the conviction of his sinfulness. No wonder that as an old man he could not burn "the record of God's great mercies to me, of the wonderful things He has done for my soul".[17]

In December 1816 John Henry was going to leave Ealing for Alton, where his father was manager of a brewery. He gave considerable thought to the way in which he should behave at home, because he was afraid of the dangers to his soul which worldly amusements would pose. He felt that the devil would certainly attack him again. "Give me strength", he prayed. . . . "Above all keep me from yielding to the enticements of the world, from preferring gatherings, dances and pleasures to my God. . . . Further, guard me against the temptations of the flesh. Alas, wretch that I am! I have sinned."[18] He decided to speak frankly to his parents of these resolves and, should the family be invited to dances and other social functions, to make it clear to them that he himself would consider all such amusements as definite temptations. For himself he could not and would not enjoy what, outwardly, appeared beautiful. For to him the dancers were instruments of sin and servants of the Evil One. But he would present his "scruples with humility and a due obedience, open to conviction and ready to obey". On the other hand he did not wish to judge others because he "who tries to act well, is on the right way" even if this meant going to a dance. But he himself was weak and could only conquer through God's grace.[19]

In the autumn of 1818 he came to believe that he was to make a great and uncommon sacrifice. It had nothing to do with his education or Evangelicalism. "It would be the will of God", he thought, that he "should lead a single life".[20] This was the outcome of two things: his feeling of isolation from the visible world and his conviction of a call, comparable with the call heard by a Catholic boy, to lead a life of total dedication to God by becoming a priest.[21] Young though he was, he realized that this would entail the sacrifice of his deep need for affection, but youthful enthusiasm—in the true meaning of the word—helped him to follow God's will. How genuine this call was will appear from the faithfulness with which he followed it till the end of his life.

On December 14th John Newman took his eldest son to Trinity College, Oxford. An old Admission Book may still be seen there in which John Henry himself wrote that on that day he had been entered as a Junior Member under the tutorship of the Masters Ingram, Wilson and Short. But it was only in June of the next year that rooms became vacant and he could take up residence.

During the half year he still had to stay at Alton. He read several Protestant books, one of them the *Private Thoughts* of Bishop Beveridge, a copy of which had been given him by Walter Mayers, who exhorted him to form his opinions from the Bible and not from his own reasonings. He reminded him: "We are candidates for eternity, and should live as such; if we do not, we shall bitterly lament our folly." He ought, however, always "to rejoice in the Lord". "No book was more dear to me", Newman remarked nearly sixty years later.[22] Although it did not influence the development of his religious opinions, it incited him to piety and occupied his thoughts so that he began writing short sermons after Beveridge's example. He destroyed them, however, and only kept the titles. They dealt with the worthy reception of the Eucharist, eternal punishment, fasting, the incomprehensibility of God's works, the avoidance of sin and the vanity of human life. Lastly, there was a remarkable title that betrays his innermost feelings: "Let no one despise thy youth." His religious earnestness and fervor urged him to "witness for truth" and to live up to his principles, while his natural timidity tried to prevent him from doing so. What would people think? What would my parents, friends, relatives say? He felt the need of inner encouragement and sought it in writing this sort of meditation.[23]

Another author John Henry studied deeply was Thomas Scott, the saintly clergyman of Aston Sandford, a village not far from Oxford. This man had been converted to Evangelicalism and a very pious life, and he had written several spiritual books. John Henry was extremely fascinated and influenced by them. In later life he stated that humanly speaking he almost owed his soul to Thomas Scott. Scott had accepted Calvinism but not in its entirety. For instance, he denied and abjured the Calvinistic doctrine that some men were predestined to eternal death and others to eternal salvation irrespective of their virtues and sins. John Henry could not accept this dreadful doctrine either. As a consequence the assurance of his own election to eternal glory gradually faded from his mind.[24] Scott's writings probably helped to preserve Newman from subjectivism in religion, for gradually the tendency to dwell upon his feelings and emotions instead of upon the objective truths of revelation vanished.[25]

With extraordinary industry John Henry began his university studies. He hated the noise made by his fellow students; how dearly he loved quiet and silence appears from his poem:

> There is in stillness oft a magic power
> To calm the breast. . . .

This stillness filled him with divine feelings and thoughts and enabled him to devote long hours to his studies. Other students did not understand this:

> Alas for man! he knows not of the bliss,
> The heaven that brightens such a life as this.[26]

They laughed at him. They tried to include him in their boisterous gatherings and to make him play the violin. The first time this occurred, wishing to be courteous, he complied with their request. But when they tried to make him drunk, he left and decided never to go to their parties again. Shortly afterward, however, two students rushed into his room while he was studying and in a wild manner pressed another invitation on him, but he ordered them to go so resolutely and so calmly that they went. The following day one of them returned in quite another mood and apologized. After this episode they left him alone.[27]

At Trinity he received his first communion as an Anglican. He never forgot how he had to tear off his new silk gloves and spoil them because they would not come off when he was to receive the bread in his hands.[28] Though he did not then believe in the Real Presence, to which a friend later led him,[29] he was filled with awe and anxiety. The very words—the Sacrament of the Lord's Body and Blood—sufficed to make him deeply reverent. He felt shocked by the conduct of other students, who after having received communion behaved like "true sons of Belial", getting thoroughly drunk.[30]

However industrious he was, he did not neglect to take sufficient recreation in order to relax from the strain of hard work. He had early formed a close and lasting friendship with John William Bowden, who studied with him, dined with him, walked and rowed with him. Indeed they seemed inseparable. In their spare time they wrote together a long romantic poem on "St. Bartholomew's Eve". They published it and each day went to the publishers to find out if any copies had been sold.[31] When he was dying, John Bowden remembered how Newman would pull such faces while joking as to make his friend roar with laughter.[32]

Thomas Short, who became John Henry's tutor, soon recognized his talents, his assiduity and his knowledge of mathematics[33] and the following year advised him to sit for the examination for a scholarship. Competition, he told Newman, would be stiff, and, as he was by far the youngest of the candidates, he must not count on success. Newman was very nervous,[34] but, thinking of his parents and their increasing financial troubles—the Alton brewery had proved another failure—he realized that a scholarship carrying a grant of sixty pounds a year for a period of nine years would be a great relief to them. But what about his inner life? He hoped for success, but he feared that he had set his heart too much on it. He was still confident of his eternal salvation, but his conscience had become scrupulously exacting; he was so keenly aware of his weakness and so overwhelmed by God's infinite goodness to him that he trembled at the thought: Might not success turn me away from God? Therefore he prayed that the Almighty would not grant him what he so eagerly wanted if it was to make him ungrateful. God knew better than he himself what was good for him.

Notwithstanding four formidable rivals, and to the immense joy of his parents, he was successful. The day after the examination he wrote in his journal: "Yesterday, out of his infinite loving-kindness He gave me the scholarship. O praised be the Lord of Israel who only does wondrous things! Give me grace, make me holy."[35]

Two years later he prepared himself for his final examination. He hoped to pass with "honors". And in his notes he started analyzing his feelings. He blamed himself for not having been grateful enough after getting the scholarship because since that time he had become indifferent in watching and praying, and he fell into temptations and sins. What would happen when he was successful again? And now he prayed: "Lord, give me content and confidence in Thee, and, above all, grant me not my heart's desire by any means, if the price be transgression in consequence. . . . Give me not fame, or learning. I will accept of none of these, without bargaining that sin is not included in the gift." He foresaw that God would answer this prayer, but he kept on flattering himself with the certainty of gaining honors. As a matter of fact nobody doubted but that he would succeed. How bitter the disappointment would be and how very humiliating if he should fail. He asked his brother Frank to pray for him that he might succeed if it were possible, but on the other hand that he might bear failure with calmness and resignation.[36]

He was living much more in God's presence now. The quiet of the last long vacation preceding the examination proved profitable both to his studies and his inner life. But at the same time he had doubts about his sincerity: "I am acting the part of a very hypocrite; I am buoyed up with the secret idea, that by thus leaving the event in the hands of God, when I pray, He may be induced, as a reward to such proper a spirit, to grant me my desire. Thus my prayer is a mockery."[37]

His moods varied incessantly. On some days he felt very happy, but at other times he was depressed and anxious. Full of gratitude he repeated: "Give me good" and "Thy will be done." He thought of his former sins, and he reproached himself that he had not studied as religiously as he ought. "Yet," he writes, "through the thick cloud of heaviness which is on my heart, the gracious Lord at intervals . . . shows that He has not forsaken me."[38]

In November 1820 he sat for his examination, which he failed. There were several causes: he was overworked; he was called up a day sooner than he had expected; and his College had not given him the guidance he wanted. So he obtained his Bachelor of Arts degree but without any distinction.[39] He considered this as the answer to his prayers and mentioned it as "his most happy failure in the Schools".[40] To his sister

Harriett he wrote: "I could enlarge and tell a long story to show many reasons why I so happily failed in the Schools, and point out, how that disappointment was at once a chastisement for former offences, and a kind preventive of future."[41] He suffered, of course, especially because of his parents: "What I feel on my own account is indeed nothing at all, compared with the thought that I have disappointed you", he wrote to them.[42] His father's wish to let him study for the Bar had now become a dream. He could stay at Oxford for several years more, however, on account of his scholarship. And so he decided to take pupils and earn enough to pay for his brother Frank's university studies.[43]

The time following the disappointment was a period of great austerity and intense spirituality comparable with the first months after his conversion. Much time was spent in collecting Bible texts on theological problems.[44] He felt cheerful and generous. In later life he realized that a sanguine temperament and other natural causes had helped him to lead such a life, but at the same time he recognized that it was God's grace, too, that worked in his soul.[45]

This grace led him to pray for the divine favor of becoming a "minister of Christ". One evening in January 1822 his father remarked that he had better decide what kind of career he wished to follow. "So I chose and determined on the church", John Henry wrote in his journal. "Thank God, that is what I have prayed for."[46] According to the advice of his spiritual guide, Walter Mayers, and against common practice, he wanted to receive the diaconate as soon as it was allowed.[47] In a fervent prayer he gave utterance to his idealistic wishes: "Lord, Thou hast blessed me with all goods, but make me Thine. Melt me down, mould me into the Divine Image. Let me be spent for Thee. Let me go through sickness, pain, poverty, affliction, reproach, persecution, anything of worldly evil, if it is to promote Thy glory. O save me from a useless life, keep me from burying my talent in the earth."[48] We shall see how literally God answered this prayer in the course of his further life.

More than ever he worked for perfection. One of the means he used was a thorough and often repeated examination of conscience. His Evangelical books guided him. He discovered many deficiencies in his daily life, he noted them down, he accused himself with the same humble self-reproaches as good Catholics who acknowledge their little sins in the confessional. He saw his faults in a light which became clearer and clearer. What he later analyzed in the pulpit applies fully to himself: "The best men are ever the most humble; for, having a higher standard of excellence in their minds than others have, and knowing themselves better, they see somewhat of the breadth and depth of their own sinful nature, and are shocked and frightened at themselves. The generality of men cannot understand this."[49]

Thus he often complained about coldness and listlessness in his prayers;[50] about temptations, especially of impatience,[51] unbelief,[52] and pride;[53] about faults of insincerity.[54] Now and again he observed that for long periods he was troubled by bad thoughts.[55] A few times he had differences of opinion with his parents and he showed "great want of meekness and of gentleness."[56] In the lessons given to Frank and other pupils he suffered from bad temper and was sometimes violent.[57]

His self-accusations were often followed by good resolutions. He would try to pray better;[58] he would fight against temptations;[59] he would "redeem his character" regarding his parents;[60] and he made an arrangement with Frank in order to prevent attacks of bad temper.[61]

At the same time he led a life of prayer. His heart was full of God during the day, especially when he was walking alone.[62] Sometimes God's presence became palpable, and he felt "the peace and love of God diffused on his heart".[63] Even in his dreams he now and again seemed to be thinking of God. Once he dreamed that a spirit came to him and talked with him about the other world and the mystery of the Holy Trinity. It said that it was absolutely impossible for the reason of man to understand this doctrine, and it was therefore vain to argue about it. But in the other world everything was so very, very plain that there was not the slightest difficulty about it. And he dreamed that he instantly fell on his knees, overcome with gratitude for so kind a message.[64]

His prayers not only expressed thankfulness. They were also supplications "for all friends, and for all mankind", supplications, too, for self-improvement and sometimes for financial help.[65] Since he wanted to pay all Frank's expenses he was often in financial difficulties. On one occasion bills were long overdue. The patience of his creditors distressed him, and he prayed: "O Lord, Thou doest all things well. . . . I am fully confident Thou wilt relieve me—how mercifully I have been delivered hitherto." On the very same day, entering his room, he found a letter containing thirty-five pounds. This had happened at another time also.[66]

His care of his brother Frank proved that his introverted nature and his apparent self-centeredness did not prevent him from thinking of others. He carried tracts on religious subjects about with him in order to do some good to his fellowmen.[67] He tried to convert his brother Charles from his strange religious ideas and to make him more generous in the fulfillment of his religious duties.[68] He practiced charity by giving alms in spite of his poverty and blamed himself for not giving more.[69] He helped a friend with revision work while walking.[70] He sent two articles to the *Christian Observer*, encouraging students to a religious disposition toward study. One article was to prove that "no science perhaps is more adapted to confirm our belief in the truth of Christianity than that of mathematics, when cultivated with a proper disposition of mind." The other dealt with the question of how religious students can show that they do not seek honor for its own sake. They should not postpone their devotions—prayer, meditation, self-examination, the reading of Scripture—to the last half hour of the day. He warned them against indifference and formality in the College Chapel. They ought especially to observe Sunday and never forget the awfulness of the mystery of Christ's Body and Blood.[71]

John Henry's father, however, showed some uneasiness concerning these articles. He thought his son was "on dangerous ground", carrying religion too far. He did not like the ideas and practices of the Evangelical school or the strong conviction and energy with which his son followed them up. These articles were "more like the composition of an old man than of a youth entering life with energy and aspiration", he said. John Henry humbly accepted his father's warning and jotted down in his journal: "O God, grant me to pray earnestly against any delusion, heat or fanatic fancy, or proud imagination of fancied superiority, or uncharitable zeal. Make me and keep me humble and teachable, modest and cautious."[72] A few years later he admitted that his father had been right regarding his mistrust of the Evangelical principles.[73]

He gradually got rid of the "critical peculiarities of Evangelical religion" but kept what was good and true. Thus he gave much time to the study of the Bible and often learned complete books of it by heart. This study filled him "with good and holy thoughts".[74] Mainly for religious reasons he declined a tutorship with a Parisian family, although he would have received a salary of 200 pounds a year.[75] But this withdrawal from extreme Evangelicalism was a slow process. Again and again we find traces of its influence. A year after his examination, for instance, he complained that he did not venture to show his Evangelical principles without reserve. "O that I were known to hold those opinions I *do* hold!" he exclaimed. "How intolerable is the constraint which is now upon me."[76] But gradually he found courage to tell his friends what he had concealed from them, namely, that he wished "to keep Sunday holy" and declined all invitations for Sunday evenings. When he became acquainted with Edward Pusey, a religious-minded and modest young man, he at first showed a somewhat patronizing manner, as though it were he who wished to lead Pusey. But very soon Pusey's noble character and sincere piety made him feel that he had thought too highly of himself. "What importance I think myself of! My deeds, my abilities, my writings! Whereas he is humility itself, and gentleness and love, and zeal, and self-devotion."[77] Together they discussed missionary work among the heathen, and John Henry enthusiastically called such work the highest privilege from God, but he thought he himself was neither worthy nor capable of it. He could only pray to God to make him a missionary.[78]

Not long after his painful failure, he "conceived the audacious idea of standing for a fellowship at Oriel, at that time the object of all rising men in Oxford, and attainable only by those who had the highest academical pretensions". Almost all his friends considered it unwise,[79] although Thomas Short, his former tutor, encouraged him. Convinced that Newman was not going to succeed, he judged that he would nevertheless show what was in him and would honor his College.[80] So he decided to stand. From his private journal we learn that he was afraid and upset about it. "How active still are the evil passions of vain glory, ambition etc., in my soul! After my failure last November, I thought they never would be unruly again. . . . Alas! no sooner is any mention made of my standing for a fellowship, than every mound and barrier seems swept away. . . . And without Thy help, o Lord, what will be the end of this? . . ."[81] At times he was full of hope, at other times certain of disappointment. How could God grant his wish when he was not humble and religious enough to bear the consequences of success? Moreover, he was poor now; God was "feeding him by the ravens". What would happen if he became independent in money matters? Nevertheless he kept praying for success, and he finished his prayers with the words: "O Lord, dispose of me as will best promote Thy glory—and, after that, as will best advance my sanctification—but give me resignation and contentment."[82]

The examination lasted five days. He suffered in body and mind from the strain. Sometimes he was kept busy nine hours and more a day.[83] In the hall where the examination took place can still be seen, high in one of the stained glass windows, a coat of arms with the motto: *Pie repone te*, which he translated: Keep quiet in mind as well as body.[84] These words comforted and calmed him. When on the point of going to sleep the day before the results were to come in, he noted: "Thank God I am now going to bed, and have been very calm the whole evening. How can I sufficiently praise Him! Before I look at this book again, it will be decided. God grant grace!"[85]

The next day, April 12, 1822, he wrote in a jubilant mood: "I have this morning been elected Fellow of Oriel. Thank God, thank God."[86] And later: "Now I have a home and every comfort about me. It is God's gift."[87] He hoped to live and to die a Fellow of Oriel, and he would always consider this event the turning point of his life. "It raised him from obscurity and need to competency and reputation." And till his old age he always thanked God's Providence in a special way on the twelfth of April.[88]

CHAPTER THREE

I AM CHRIST'S SOLDIER

1822–1828

> Lord! I pray thee for Jesus Christ's sake, continue to me
> Thy benefits. . . . Bless me, O Lord Jesus! . . . Bless my
> parents. . . . Bless the whole family! Make us all good by
> Thy Spirit. . . . Bless the King of this country and all in
> power. Bless my native land! Lord, show Thyself to the
> whole world, and turn all to thy truth! Sacred Trinity in
> Unity, hear my prayer.[1]

At the Oxford of that time many a student and graduate,
destined for the church, did not worry about purity of intention or of spiritual formation. True, John Henry's journal
seldom gives actual thoughts of his future ordination and care
of souls, but his ascetic life and the subjects of his studies show
how seriously he wished to prepare himself. Not only did he
follow theological lectures,[2] he also looked into his Bible for
texts referring to the duties of a minister of Christ, and one of
them made him feel "much struck and humbled".[3] Shortly
before his ordination as a deacon, every text came home to him
"with tenfold force",[4] and he made a great effort to live up to
them. Thus a few months before his ordination, he tried to
fast. At first he did not succeed because he considered fasting in
the same austere light as did the Fathers of the desert. But
eventually he appears to have imitated them.[5] On his twenty-
third birthday he wrote: "I quite tremble to think the age is
now come, when, as far as years go, the ministry is open to
me."[6] But am I worthy, he murmured, am I prepared? The
step is irrevocable and the words "for ever" are so terrible.[7]

Thoughts like these sometimes made him consider withdrawing.[8] But in spite of anxiety, doubts and listlessness he continued his way and prayed: "Let me, living or dying, in fortune and misfortune, in joy and sadness, in health and sickness, in honour and dishonour, be Thine."[9]

On Trinity Sunday 1824, John Henry was ordained by the Bishop of Oxford in the old church of Saint Frideswide.

Except for the oath about the sovereignty of the King—excluding any influence of the Pope—the Anglican rites of ordination still bear strong resemblances to the Roman Catholic ordination ceremonies and prayers. Touching in their earnestness, gravity and piety, they awoke deep though conflicting feelings in the young man. During the *Veni Creator* his "heart burnt within" him. But now and again the fear of lifelong responsibility prevailed; the idea of giving up everything for God made him feel melancholy. In his generosity he asked for holiness, not for comfort. And he wept "most abundant and most sweet tears". No longer was he first and foremost a Fellow of Oriel, but above everything else he was a Minister of Christ, dedicated for ever and consecrated to the service of Almighty God.[10]

Before the ordination took place he had accepted the curacy of Saint Clement's. The old rector wanted an assistant. It was no easy task. Most of the two thousand parishioners went to chapels or alehouses on Sundays, with the excuse that Saint Clement's was too small and the rector too old. At once Newman began to collect money for a new church, gave ten guineas himself and had the satisfaction of receiving more than 4000 pounds in a few months.[11] At the same time he began to work with extreme zeal and energy for the spiritual welfare of his flock. At first it was with an anxious heart. How could he, young and inexperienced, trust his own judgment if it concerned immortal souls? His despondency was made more painful still by the great number of unimportant matters that had to be decided. But after a time "through God's mercy the prospect cleared", and everything became easier.[12]

From a little book, written for the "parochial minister's assistant", he learned that "the readiest way of finding access to a man's heart, is to go into his house".[13] So a month after his ordination he started visiting the parishioners one by one, and he omitted none of them.[14] They generally received him very civilly and often showed their gratitude. They explained why they did not go to their parish church but expressed no unwillingness to come back.[15] Above all, the sick had his constant attention and help. The prayerbook he took with him[16] shows signs of frequent use, especially at the prayers to be said before visiting the sick. As a matter of fact he often prayed for them and for the whole parish and its spiritual needs, as is shown by a long list of intentions for every day of the week. Thus on Tuesdays he prayed for his flock at Saint Clement's, churchmen, dissenters, Romanists, those without religion, and so forth, for the pious and the worldly, for the rector and the churchwardens, for the old and the young, for expectant mothers, for the rich and the poor and for the school. And lastly, showing an ecumenical spirit, he prayed for unity.[17]

There is still in existence a large exercise book in which he recorded his experiences with the sick. The notes indicate that in the beginning he was still influenced by his Evangelical ideas. He still tried to distinguish between the elect and the nonelect. He still clung to the Evangelical idea of conversion. He still wanted to make people rely on Christ only and ignored the value of meritorious acts.

After two weeks of visiting he remarked that he was becoming "more convinced than ever of the necessity of frequently visiting the poorer". They seemed delighted and praised him. He often helped them with wine, loaves of bread, books, money, and on one page of his journal he recounts that he gave a poor woman "an ink prescription for her boy's ringworm".[18] He succeeded in helping a family who were threatened with eviction.[19] He wanted to open a Sunday school and tried to find out whether it would be possible to have the shops closed on Sundays, observing: "I fear I shall have much trouble and much opposition; my trust is in God."[20]

Sometimes he felt his deficiencies, complaining that he was very incapable and shy.[21] He considered himself to have been too gentle to a man who was dangerously ill, showed signs of repentance but was a drunkard. And he sighed: "God pardon me."[22] In his sermons, however, he was bolder. At first they were more or less in the Evangelical style, but gradually they changed their mildly Evangelical tone.[23] In summer he gave two sermons each Sunday.[24] He prepared them with the greatest care and founded them on the Bible as much as possible.[25] He did not like to flatter his audience: "The doctrine of Christ crucified is the only spring of real virtue and piety, and the only foundation of peace and comfort", he said. Of this he was firmly convinced. Here on earth we must toil and struggle. "Comfort is a cordial, but no one drinks cordials from morning to night."[26]

Very soon he saw the results of his energetic and incessant work. The parishioners admired his generosity, his munificence, his inspiring sermons, his edifying example. The number of churchgoers and communicants increased. Several sick people bore their crosses with more resignation.[27] Sinners became repentant. When visiting an old, rich farmer of bad character who was very ill, he noticed that he was not welcome. But he went on calling, not without difficulty, till at length the man asked him to pray for him. A few days later the farmer attained "great comfort and peace" and expressed "the utmost abhorrence of his sins". And Newman finished his account with the words: "He grew weaker and weaker and at length departed (as I trust) in the Lord."[28] Another sick person, too, did not wish to see him at first. She was afraid of dying. Newman called again and again. His persistence and goodness won her confidence, and she agreed that he should pray with her and read for her from the Bible. Finally she felt so resigned that she did not mind whether God took her or not. He is all-merciful, she said. On her dying day her eyes were shining, and Newman felt a thrill, which he could not describe better than with the words: "It was like the gate of heaven."[29]

Another sick woman told him that she thought of a picture of Our Lord whenever he entered her sickroom. He made a note of it and added: "I should not have put this down, did not Saint Paul say to the Galatians: Ye received me as Jesus Christ. And though ministers are now immeasurably below Saint Paul, yet Christ is infinitely above Paul as well as us. I am indeed a sinner."[30]

Of course he also met with the everyday disappointments of every zealous worker for souls. Behind his back he was called a Methodist.[31] He had a dispute with his choir, which ended in their leaving the church.[32] He failed in converting a drunkard. He was apparently deceived by a dying man.[33] But perhaps his greatest disappointment was his inner life. He complained that his successes promoted an "empty vanity of mind". He had discontinued his self-examination and had "little opportunity for devotion or private study of the Scriptures".[34] He was too busy. Apart from parish work he was always coaching one or two pupils. When in March 1825 he became vice principal of a small college, it meant still more work.[35] Sometimes he was "seduced to neglect morning prayer, either from forgetfulness or excess of work".[36] But he saw his good points as well: he still constantly prayed during his walks; he was not so bad-tempered, was more pure in his intentions and not attacked by grievous temptations.[37] But the extreme austerity of former times had disappeared, although he never relaxed in doing a great deal of good.

At this time he lost his father.

John Newman's financial difficulties had risen to such an extent that he was not only forced to leave the brewery and declare bankruptcy, but he also had found it necessary to accept the management of a public house in an unfashionable district of London.[38] All these years of failure had undermined his health, and at fifty-nine he was dying. John Henry was called home, and he left Oxford on the night coach. It must have been a miserable journey.[39] The grief and anxiety of his mother, sisters and brothers, the problem of their future but most of all the spiritual state of his father must have tortured his mind. He knew and admitted the many excellent qualities of his father; he was full of gratitude for them, but the differences concerning religious ideas and convictions pained him. He remembered his father's remark about his visiting the parishioners; he had questioned the wisdom of this method; an Englishman's house was his castle. Sometimes there had been a strained atmosphere between them, which resulted in bitter words on both sides. Once he alluded to this in his journal when he wrote: "So cold a veil does not seem to separate me from my Father. I am not so distant from Charles. . . ."[40] When he reached home his father recognized him. He tried to put out his hand and said: "God bless you." John Henry read to him three chapters of the Bible, words of confidence in God and exhortations to repentance. After a few days the sick man died "in great peace of mind", and John Henry himself performed the last sad duties. He wrote in his journal: "That dread event has happened. Is it possible! O my Father, where art Thou?"[41] In the months that followed, the often recurring thought of his father was accompanied with feelings of regret and remorse: "I might have softened his afflictions much by kind attentions which I neglected. I was cold, stiff, reserved." Moreover he had hurt him and not said how much he owed him. "O for a moment to ask his forgiveness," he wrote.[42]

From this time onward he filled the vacant place. He lightened his mother's financial difficulties and other burdens. He enabled her to live according to her condition—she was the daughter of a manufacturer—and he gave her children a suitable education. Nothing was too much for him. For her he would even go house hunting. His mother called him her guardian angel, her greatest comfort in all her trials and her joy in all circumstances. The family afflictions were changed into blessings through her eldest son, and his sermons did her much good.[43]

Very early in life John Henry's brother Charles became a great trial to the family and developed a growing antipathy for religion.[44] Out of brotherly love but still more out of love for his soul, John Henry made numerous attempts to cure him of his dangerous opinions. Charles was a talented young man. At Ealing he had received a thorough classical education; he spoke French and German and had a special gift for philosophical research. He was upright, sensitive, honest, generous, open-handed and affectionate, but at the same time possessed of "preposterous pride and want of common sense". He entertained "an ever-present, vivid notion that he was all men's equal, that the employee is in no sense inferior to the employer and that what are called benefits are really duties and do not deserve the gratitude of those who receive them". But he could not always control himself, and he used to break out wildly to relieve the fierce indignation which he felt at "his own distressing impotence of mind". Once he received a book from Frank as a present. He returned it in a very mutilated state, leaves torn out in parts, insulting remarks on several pages, the cover cut.[45] Not long after his father's death, John Henry started a correspondence with him since, as appeared from his blasphemous letters, he had lost all faith in religious doctrines. All the sorrow in the world was unnecessary and to be deplored, he wrote; it could be remedied by knowledge. "It is religion immediately or obliquely", he added, "that brings evil most abundantly into the world."[46] Full of gentle pity and unfeigned love, John Henry sent him a long and elaborate answer. He had insight into Charles' difficulties and partly explained them by referring to his mental instability and his sensitive character and the treatment he had received at the hand of his employers.[47] But everything was in vain. Charles tried to convert him to his way of thinking and at one time thought he had partially succeeded.[48] One wonders how John Henry could afford the time to write down for him complete essays filling almost eight large exercise books. The refrain of his elucidations lay in his statement at the end of one of the letters: "Till you have recourse to the Author of Nature himself for direction, humbly, sincerely, perseveringly, can you expect to possess real knowledge and true peace? For the fulfilment of that joyful event I offer for you, my dear Charles, continual prayers."[49] But John Henry had to give up his exhausting attempts and to leave everything to God, who has his own time for all things.[50]

Almost a year after his ordination as a deacon, Newman was ordained a priest. In those days an everyday atmosphere prevailed around the Anglican ordinations. No retreat or other special preparation seems to have been required. The great day, Trinity Sunday, 1825, was—apart from the ceremony itself—quite an ordinary Sunday for Newman. In the morning he finished the sermon he was going to preach in the afternoon, and then he went to the cathedral where the bishop ordained him together with some other deacons. In the afternoon he gave his sermon in Saint Clement's, churched two ladies, baptized and buried a dead parishioner. Then he dined in his room. No mention was made of any guests being present.[51]

The Anglican ordination service is a beautiful ceremony with wonderful prayers and exhortations. A Catholic will at once recognize the order, progress and sometimes even the very words of the old Catholic Ritual; it omits, however, the parts relating to the Sacrifice of the Mass. Newman wrote on that day: "I have this day been ordained priest. What a divine service is that of Ordination. The whole has a fragrance in it; and to think of it is soothing and delightful." Then he describes how he observed the working of the Holy Spirit in the souls of his fellow deacons, and, unlike his attitude toward them at the ordination of the year before, his thoughts regarding them were full of charity. And he prayed, "Perfect that, O Lord, what Thou hast begun in us."[52]

His changed opinion about the same persons is to be explained by his gradually changing ideas. His experience as a minister had undermined his belief in the Evangelical theories. He could no longer heartily believe in the evident separation of the elect and the nonelect. He could no longer deny that baptism meant more than the Evangelicals taught. He began to suspect their subjectivism. One evening he felt distressed about it, and the thought even struck him that he might be forced to leave the church.[53] But gradually he saw things in a clearer light, and the doubts about the Anglican church and its doctrines vanished. He gave up all tenets peculiar to the Evangelical school and accepted those dogmas the Evangelical party does not acknowledge. In this way his love and anxiety were bound more and more to the church.

After two years of direct pastoral work, Newman was appointed a tutor.[54] This implied the end of his curacy, though he did not give up his ideal of working for souls. So he wrote in his journal: "O Lord, I am entering with the new year into a fresh course of duties. . . . May I engage in them in the strength of Christ, remembering I am a minister of God, and have a commission to preach the gospel, remembering the worth of souls, and that I shall have to answer for the opportunities given me of benefiting those who are under my care."[55] He hated to imitate other tutors who considered their function as an ordinary, secular task and a means to earn a living. As a matter of fact, the University Statutes ordered the tutor "to instruct the pupils committed to his care, in a religious way of life, and to teach them the doctrine of received authors, especially the principles of divinity and the articles of faith."[56] This statute had been neglected for a long time, but Newman appealed to it and made up his mind to look after the morals and religion of his students.[57] Unless he should find

opportunities of doing spiritual good to those over whom he
was placed, it would become a grave question, he said, whether
he ought to continue being a tutor.[58]

He acquired the assistance of two colleagues who had the
same view of their task as tutors and then started work. At that
time the college was filled with young men of high birth and
wealth, and considerable profligacy existed among them. He
tried discreetly to improve the situation and especially fought
against the scandal of compulsory communion, because some
students got drunk after communion at a champagne breakfast.[59] Of course there were other well-behaved and promising
undergraduates. For them, he was like a father or rather an
elder and affectionate brother. He hated "the martinet manner
then in fashion with college tutors". And his own pupils
quickly found out that he really cared for them. In this way he
gained first their attachment and then their affection, which
very often lasted their whole lives.[60] So great and many-sided
was his success that he began to consider his talent for giving a
well-rounded education a special gift of God which he should
not leave unused.[61]

In these years Newman's missionary ideals were fading away.
Before he became a deacon he had written to the Church
Missionary Society, and in July of the same year he had gone to
its headquarters in London to put questions about the necessary
qualifications. He had learned there that his bad eyesight, his
weak voice, his nervousness and his susceptibility to cold
would be no obstacle.[62] After his father's death he had written
in his journal: "When I die, shall I be followed to the grave by
my children? My Mother said the other day, she hoped to live
to see me married; but I think I shall either die within a College
walls, or a Missionary in a foreign land—no matter where, so
that I die in Christ."[63] The first public speech he ever made had
been to beg money for the missions.[64] But after eighteen months
of toiling in Saint Clement's parish he began to forget his ideal.
He perceived it himself and feared that "notions of theological

fame, desire of rising in the church, etc." counteracted his early wish. For a long period, however, he remained an active member of the Church Missionary Society.[65]

All this is not difficult to understand. As a pastoral worker he saw how much there was still to be done in his own surroundings. As a tutor he experienced how strongly his influence could work for good. As a man of many talents, he was asked for assistance and advice on every side. But perhaps another factor was already active, the tendency of what he calls Liberalism. The learned members of his College overrated logic, that is, the intellect thinking along mathematical lines in the field of faith. Though by no means irreligious they tried "to determine on intrinsic grounds the truth and value of propositions which rest . . . simply on the external authority of the Divine Word". Newman became infected with this mentality and began to prefer intellectual excellence to moral and practically gave up his principle "Holiness rather than peace".[66] He began to think of the dogma of the Holy Trinity in a way reminiscent of the Arian heresy. He criticized the Athanasian Creed and showed a certain disdain for the Fathers of the Church. In an article, he enumerated a long series of miracles which he could not admit because they seemed to him incompatible with God's wisdom, for example, the exorcism in the Book of Tobias, in which the evil spirit, enamored of Sara, was driven away by the smell of a certain perfume. He had doubts about the claims to supernatural power in the primitive Church because Jews and Gentiles performed the same exorcisms and cure of diseases. His fellow tutor Richard Hurrel Froude had warned him but in vain.[67]

He was rudely awakened from this dream, as he puts it, by two great blows, illness and bereavement.[68]

Illness struck him in the autumn of 1827, when he was a University examiner. Too much exertion and anxiety about an aunt caused extreme fatigue and a terrible headache. He had taken the task of an examiner too seriously and begun preparations at least two months earlier. At the same time he had been looking for means to pay the heavy debts of his beloved aunt Elisabeth. The news that the Head of the College had been promoted to a bishopric, so that there was anxiety about a successor, made things worse, and during the examinations he found he could neither think nor remember, and he was obliged to leave.[69]

He was still at home in the early days of 1828, not yet entirely recovered, when his sister Mary died. It was a very painful loss. John Henry was full of loving affection for his brothers, but more so for his sisters. He seems to have bestowed on his relatives and especially on his sisters the love a young man cherishes for his fiancée and afterward for his wife. His letters were full of manly tenderness, and he always looked forward to their answers.[70] "You always understand about everything and always make me happy when I am uncomfortable", wrote his sister Harriett.[71] Addressing God, he wrote in his journal: "O how I love them. So much I love them that I cannot help thinking: Thou wilt either take them hence, or take me from them, because I am too set on them."[72] This love, however, was influenced and strengthened by the doctrine of Christ's Mystical Body. Thus he wrote to his mother: "Since, as we may humbly trust, we are in Christ, we are both safe, and with each other, wherever we are."[73] Harriett, the eldest of his sisters and nearest to his age, was the one who understood him better than the others, and at one time he told her that he continually thought of her and prayed for her; he would think it his greatest cross if he were to lose her love and confidence.[74] As for his second sister Jemima, he admired her for her sweet character and called her a blessing wherever she went.[75] But Mary seems to have been the most beloved of them all. She was a "joy of sad hearts and light of downcast eyes",[76] not only because she was young and beautiful but much more because she was highly intelligent and singularly good. Moreover, she owed a great part of her intellectual and religious education to him. Because of her unearthly loveliness he had had a presentiment that they were going to lose her.[77] All these things made her death "the heaviest affliction with which the good hand of God had ever visited him". He could not forget her for a moment. Not long before she died she had visited him at Oxford, and he had delighted in showing her the grounds. And now Oxford was full of Mary: "Everything reminds me of her. . . . Every building, every tree, seems to speak of her."[78] Even five months after her death he observed that not one half hour passed but Mary's face was before his eyes.[79] When he was sorting his letters during the long vacation, his eye was caught by Mary's handwriting, and he had to lock the letters up and turn his thoughts another way.[80] His journal speaks of his deep sorrow but also of his resignation: "O my dearest sister Mary, O my sister, my sister, I do feel from the bottom of my heart that it is all right—I see, I know it to be, in God's good Providence, the best thing for all of us; I do not, I have not in the least repined—I would not have it otherwise—but I feel sick, I must cease writing. . . ."[81] Some of his most touching poems were written about Mary. They prove that he considered the suddenness and circumstances of her death a merciful favor from Providence: her pain was short; nobody could help her; the suspense did not last long. Her image would always be associated with youth and loveliness.[82] Everything seemed a sure sign to him that her heart was prepared for heaven. Such thoughts made him write to his mother: "What a series of ills is human life, compared to that real and living life to which she has been translated. For her I do not grieve . . . and it quite gladdens the room to me in which I am writing that her prayerbook is always on the table. . . ."[83]

Newman has never said either in his letters or in his works how exactly it came to pass that his illness and Mary's death opened his eyes to the danger of Liberalism. But it is not difficult to guess. His illness gave him time to think. He was no longer kept from self-examination through an excess of work. Thus he began to compare the state of his inner life with the fervor and ideals of his stricter days. He employed to the full his powers of analysis and his wonderful insight into the future and discovered what would be the end if the principles of his incipient Liberalism were carried out to their logical ends. He enjoyed the quiet and the rest, necessary for hearing the inward Voice he had known so well. When at the same time death crossed his path and made him suffer as never before, the Voice became louder and louder. He saw the vanity of intellectual excellence, because death would be the absolute end of it. He realized again the paramount value of holiness, because holiness alone would last into eternal life. He knew that he, too, might be taken away suddenly and without warning. So he concluded with certainty that the one thing which lay before him was to please God. What gain would it be to please the world, to please the great, to please his intellectual friends, in comparison with that one thing: not to be disobedient to the heavenly vision?[84]

From this time onward he studied "the heavenly vision" in the writings of the Fathers of the Church. As a boy he had read a church history and felt delighted by the extracts of the Fathers he found there.[85] While this early devotion was returning,[86] a friend taught him the great value of Tradition.[87] Not only by means of Scripture but especially by oral tradition did the Ancient Church possess the original doctrine of Christ and the apostles, his friend had said. In 1826 Newman thought of studying the Fathers in their original writings,[88] but this was apparently no more than a wish. It was only in 1828, after the two blows, that he set out to read them chronologically.[89]

CHAPTER FOUR

I Have a Work to Do

1828–1833

> Lead, Kindly Light, amid the encircling gloom
>   Lead Thou me on!
> The night is dark, and I am far from home—
>   Lead Thou me on!
> Keep Thou my feet; I do not ask to see
> The distant scene—one step enough for me.[1]

The years just described had been years of preparation for an important mission, although John Henry did not seem to have realized it. Only when illness and bereavement led him to a life of deep spirituality, and this for the second time in his life, did he become aware of a special call. At that time the Anglican church began to be a living reality to him, and he grew more and more enamored of her. As early as 1825, in a sermon on the visible church, he had started preaching high church principles.[2] The Anglican church seemed to him to surpass any other because she possessed "the most formally correct Creed".[3] The systematic reading of the Fathers not only gave him a deep impression of her beauty but made him all the more concerned about her poor, defenseless position. The stream of opinion and "the talent of the day" were against her. In a letter to his mother he drew up a long list of her enemies.[4] He feared that the church was going to be deprived of her wealth[5] and that unworthy ministers would be given high places.[6] What was far worse, her internal state seemed alarming, for she showed an extreme worldliness that involved innumerable dangers for souls.[7] It was one of the consequences of what he called the national sins: the increasing influence of wicked men in the government; the profanation of Sunday; the profane mocking of holy church and her rulers, the bishops; the love of money; the many secret sins, particularly the sin of unchastity; the heresy and scorn of those who were in authority.[8] True, on the face of society a general decency prevailed, but it was not founded upon revelation.[9] Moreover, reason was usurping the province of morals and religion.[10] Several societies had been established which, as he said, gradually led "to an undue exaltation of the Reason" and formed an unconstitutional power, advising and controlling the bishops.[11] Many of these prelates allowed heretical principles without knowing it; they held that the rule of divine government is nothing but benevolence; evil is but remedial and temporary; sin is of a venial nature; the moral sense is substantially an instinct of benevolence.[12] True seriousness and strict conscientiousness were despised as the marks of a gloomy or a narrow mind. There was no discipline in the church, and her rulers did not make themselves heard.[13] Among the English people the spirit of Saul prevailed, showing itself in open resistance to constituted power, irreverence to antiquity, unscrupulous violation of the commands and usages of the forefathers, sceptical objections to the Creed, criticisms of the liturgy. It was all the result of trusting one's own will more than God's word. Even the good could not altogether escape the infection.[14]

These were the thoughts that haunted him. While his spiritual life concentrated on his Maker, he desired to be totally dependent on Him. As God's will and wishes had been revealed in the visible church, the Church of England, he wanted to use his many talents for her welfare. He wished to prevent the high ecclesiastical places from falling into the hands of worldly men. He wanted to destroy the influence of a government that had supreme power in ecclesiastical matters and considered progress in knowledge and prosperity to be of higher value than truth and morality. But what could he do? How to begin and how to accomplish it? Therefore he prayed for guidance from the kindly Light that in the dark night led the Israelites from Egypt, not knowing where it took them. He, too, felt guided without being able to see, and he only asked that he might be able to take one step farther on his way.

It is from this viewpoint that we should judge Newman's fierce action against Sir Robert Peel, who worked for the emancipation of Catholics. In 1817, Oxford University had elected him as its Member of Parliament especially because he was against this emancipation. Although his antipathy never abated, Peel changed his mind in 1828—and this for the sake of expediency, because he preferred emancipation to an Irish civil war. So in the early part of 1829, he resigned his seat in Parliament out of loyalty to his Oxford electors, and he offered himself for reelection, as he wanted to know whether the University approved of his policy or not. But Newman and several of his friends started a fierce campaign against reelecting Peel. He considered Catholic emancipation a fruit of Liberalism, "one of the signs of the times, of the encroachment of Philosophism and Indifferentism in the church". There was a spirit at work which called all doctrine the fruit of bigotry and discipline and the instrument of priestcraft, and its consequence was emancipation.[15] Newman and his friends succeeded: Sir Robert Peel was not reelected.

"We have achieved a glorious victory", he wrote to his mother. "It is the first public event I have been concerned in, and I thank God from my heart for my cause and its success. We have proved the independence of the church and of Oxford."[16]

It was during this period that he cut the last ties with the Evangelical school. Although in his sermons he had done away with Evangelical teaching, he was still a secretary to the Oxford Branch of the Church Missionary Society, an institution of the Evangelicals.[17] This Society was nominally connected with the Anglican church, but a committee in

London exercised the supreme direction, independent of ecclesiastical authorities, the bishops having no means of control. It sent out missionaries in its own name, and there was a
tendency among the members to detach the Society from the
church altogether.[18] Newman thought of it as a real evil. The
church was "the pillar and ground of the truth", the divinely
appointed means of salvation. And in this important matter
the church had no say. So, as a remedy, he wrote a pamphlet
suggesting that the clergy should "take upon themselves the
management of the Associations in their own neighbourhoods".
In this way they might be able to direct its movements,
exclude unauthorized speakers and even influence the London
committee. Thus gradually the Society would be submitted to
the church authorities.[19] Newman knew that he was doing
something unsafe; it might place him in a vulnerable position.
But "one must take risks to do good", he observed.[20]

Of course, the Evangelicals felt greatly hurt by the pamphlet.
Five weeks after its publication Newman noted in his private
diary: "Turned out of the Secretaryship of the Church Missionary Society because of my pamphlet."[21] His magnanimity
and the purity of his motives may be gathered from the fact that
seven months later he preached for the Society without any
rancor and collected about sixteen pounds for the missions.[22]

He took a similar line with regard to his membership in the
Bible Society, and this for the same reason. As early as 1826 he
had begun to doubt the propriety of the Society,[23] but he had
hoped to lessen the great evils by remaining a member. He
knew it made churchmen liberals; it caused people to under-
value the guilt of schism; it made them feel a wish to conciliate
dissenters at the expense of truth. He thought it was preparing
the downfall of the church.[24] So he withdrew his name.

This disgust at Evangelicalism became one of the causes of
estrangement between John Henry and his brother Frank. In
former years John Henry had done everything possible to earn
the necessary money for Frank's university education. He had
been proud of Frank's great successes, and Frank always

showed his gratitude for the way John Henry had helped him. But while the former was losing his faith in the Evangelical School and the latter still lived up to its principles, "a most painful breach" occurred between them. "The church was to him everything," Frank wrote, "while the church (as viewed by him from the day of his ordination) was to me *nothing*. Hence we seemed never to have an interest nor a wish in common."[25] The first remembered conflict took place as early as 1824. When Francis went up to Worcester College, John Henry decided to give him some pictures for his rooms and sent him two engravings. One was Correggio's "La Madonna col Devoto". It can still be seen in the room where Newman died. The engraving represents Saint Jerome and another saint sitting at a table while the latter presents a monk to the Blessed Virgin and the Divine Child. It took Newman's fancy as a work of art and in no sense as a devotional picture. It was the best engraving he had been able to find. Frank, however, was indignant, refused the present and sent it back to his brother.[26] In the same way Francis showed his religious fanaticism when he became one of the "Plymouth Brethren" and travelled to Persia with a group of them on missionary work. It was a wild enterprise, useless from the beginning, bringing death to several of them.[27] The same fanaticism makes it clear that Frank could not follow his brother's developments. He felt "a growing distaste" for his society.[28] Moreover, he suspected John Henry's humility and feared growth in pride, for he was so well spoken of, especially as an examiner.[29] Frank could no longer consult him on practical matters, he said.[30] At one time when Frank endeavored to press his own wrongful opinions concerning infant baptism on his sisters, John Henry came to feel a dread of his influence. He therefore wrote a long treatise about the subject so that they should not be disturbed by Frank's ideas. While writing he prayed continually for wisdom and a sound judgment, and he introduced his explanations with the words: "May He to whom I surrender myself as an instrument and minister, bless what I shall say to His glory."[31]

This growing estrangement may have been furthered by the problem of Maria Giberne, who has been called "the prima donna of the Oxford Movement". She had admired the rare beauty of Newman's sister Mary, and after Mary's death she became fascinated by the extraordinary asceticism, the refined character, the genuine piety of John Henry. On one occasion she had listened to a sermon of Newman's out of mere curiosity, but she had felt so impressed that for a long time she could think of nothing else. In the meantime Frank fell in love with her. On two occasions, at least, he proposed to her. But she refused, remaining under the spiritual influence of his brother.[32] It is quite possible that her interest in John Henry was a source of jealousy for Frank and so another cause of estrangement.

Just after Newman's illness, Edward Hawkins, a friend of his, was elected by the Fellows as Provost or head of Oriel College. He gave Newman the post of Vicar of Saint Mary's.

This event was the beginning of new life in the Church of England. In this church, Newman preached his famous sermons which reawakened the religious spirit and which even now influence many people. It is impossible to count the numerous eulogies written about these sermons and their preacher. There seemed to emanate an almost electric influence from him, first from his appearance, more still from his way of praying and reading the Bible, but most of all from his words in the pulpit. He did not use tricks to keep the attention of the audience. He read his sermons and never looked up from his papers. His high-pitched voice was not powerful. He had a strange way of pausing a long time after every quickly spoken sentence. Nevertheless, he kept his congregation spellbound. One witness wrote: "I can never forget the first time I heard him preach in Saint Mary's, and the electric thrill which ran through the audience as sweetly soft and tender sentences were uttered with his divinely melodious voice. I remember an awestruck whisper that came from a long and lean young man at my side: It is like the opening of Paradise."[33] And another student wrote about the sermons: "They spoke of God, as no man, I think, could speak unless God were with him; unless he were a seer, like the prophets of old and saw God. . . . It was to many of us as if God had spoken to us for the first time."[34] These sermons even changed the atmosphere of Oxford and gave the old university a spirit of piety and purity.

There is a continuous tone of earnestness in all those sermons. "A tone, not of fear, but of infinite pity runs through them all", said Anthony Froude.[35] This is something different from the anxiety, fear and pessimism which some people ascribe to them. Many passages reveal tender joy in God's goodness and love and a peaceful confidence in God's mercy and omnipotence. The preacher, however, knew the great superficiality of most of his hearers. He warned them against the spirit of the age, namely, the desire for earthly goods, ambition and covetousness, upon which would follow "influence, power, enjoyment, and the lust of the flesh, and the lust of the eyes, and the pride of life".[36] In a world of progress and wealth, of "enlightened" views and the march of progress of the mind, it was necessary that a powerful preacher should try to isolate his hearers from their surroundings and bring them face to face with the two great realities, God and their souls. People had lost their sense of sin. "Newman saw a religion prevalent all around, which was secular and mundane, soft and self-indulgent, taking in that part of the gospel which pleases the flesh, but shrinking from its sterner discipline and higher aspirations."[37] Never before Newman did preachers touch on the essential immorality of impurity. The schools which prepared young men for the University "were such that it was rare, indeed, if any innocent youth passed through them without being stained; too often he was utterly corrupted". No wonder if for such young men Newman's sermons came like a new revelation.[38]

It is not only the religious and moral condition of the English people of the time that accounts for the deep earnestness of those sermons but also the factor of his character and temperament. From the beginning of his life to the end, we recognize his great dedication. Since his first conversion he was filled with thoughts of the exceeding holiness of Almighty God and his own unworthiness in His presence. His own sinfulness was always before him. Hence there was no superficiality, no conceit, when he appeared in the pulpit, nor did he make a show of sublime and highbrow ideas.

If there seems to be "fear and trembling" in some of his sermons, it is the fear of the Lord, the beginning of wisdom. He reminded his audience: "Christ . . . desires your salvation, has died for you, has washed away your sins by baptism, and will ever help you; and this thought must cheer you, while you go on to examine and review your lives, and to turn to God in self-denial."[39] These words reveal clearly the light and shadow of his own inner life.

True though it may be that he often spoke of judgment to come and warned his hearers against that day, the passages that speak about becoming saints, about fulfilling God's will as the only way to true happiness, about God's presence in our hearts, about the immense love of our Savior, are just as numerous. "God has loved us before we were born. He had us taken into His Church in our infancy. He by Baptism made us new creatures, giving us powers which we by nature had not, and raising us to the unseen society of Saints and Angels. And all this we enjoy on our faith; that is on our believing that we have them, and seriously trying to profit by them."[40]

The character of Newman's "fears" is further to be discovered in the following passage, in which he urges us not to fear unreasonably: "God's grace is sufficient for us. Why, then, should we fear? Rather, why should we not make any sacrifice, and give up all that is naturally pleasing to us, rather than that light and truth should have come into the world, yet we not find them? Let us be willing to endure toil and trouble."[41] So everything in his sermons may be reduced to a deliberate preference of God's service to everything else, a determined resolution to give up all for Him, being led by a love that is not passionate and fanatic but like that which a child bears toward his parents: calm, full, reverent, contemplative, obedient.[42]

Although he performed his duties as a parish priest with great zeal, Newman did not neglect his function as a tutor, and his success was remarkable. Nevertheless, within a few years circumstances forced him to bury his educational talents. At first the new Head of Oriel College had cooperated with him as a friend, but after some time he could no longer agree with the new methods of the three young tutors. When he found that they had carried out their wishes in spite of the existing customs, he began to oppose them. The system of the time had proved a great advantage to the College, he maintained, and it should not be put aside without his direct sanction, which he did not choose to give.[43] Both parties presented their views and gave their reasons orally and, even more, in writing, but the arguments on the one side had no effect whatever on the other. Newman hated fighting a man who was once his friend and to whom he owed so much. Provost Hawkins had taught him to weigh his words and to be cautious in his statements. He had given him a great reverence for Tradition and thus stimulated his desire to study the works of the Fathers.[44] Newman could never forget this, but neither could he give up the pastoral work which the Statutes prescribed. He felt disappointed that Hawkins did not believe in the sincerity of his motives, suspecting him of love of money; Newman attributed his conduct to irritation and ill health.[45] In his innermost heart he continued to love and respect Hawkins, but outwardly he became cool and reserved. Hawkins behaved like a dictator and grew more and more angry with Newman.[46]

For more than a year the quarrel went on. When at last Newman sent a kind of ultimatum to his Provost, Hawkins decided to put an end to the affair. He had no right to dismiss his tutors, but he would give them no more students. This would put an end to their work. So by the summer of 1832, all

Newman's students had taken their degrees, and that was the end of his tutorship.

This fact, so disappointing and humiliating, would prove a new turning point in Newman's life. It would give him leisure to devote himself to a task much wider and much more fruitful.

It was in these circumstances that he accepted an invitation from his intimate friend and colleague Richard Hurrell Froude to accompany him and his father on a journey to the South of Europe. Newman had just finished his first book, the history of the Arians of the fourth century, a result of his studies of the Fathers of the Church. He felt exhausted by the work and found it necessary to look after his health.

The ship left Falmouth on December 8, 1832. The travellers visited Gibraltar, Greece, Malta, Sicily, Rome and Naples. When Froude returned to England, Newman went back to Sicily, attracted by its strange beauty. In the midst of the trip he became ill, and his life was despaired of. But he experienced a rapid recovery and wanted to go home as quickly as possible. At Palermo, however, he was forced to wait for a vessel. After more than a fortnight of misery a slow cargo boat carrying oranges was to take him to Marseilles, but it was becalmed for a whole week in the Straits of Bonifacio. Finally, in July 1833, he arrived at his mother's house near Oxford.[47]

From the numerous letters and verses written during this journey, we learn a great deal about his inner life.[48] Uppermost in his mind was the sad state of the Anglican church. To his indignation, the government wanted to suppress several Irish bishoprics. He called it a crime, the "crime of demolition".[49] A sad presentiment took possession of him that the gift of truth was going to be lost for ever: Rome had lost it long ago, England was now on the way to losing it.[50] He considered the atrocious bill about the Irish bishoprics a humiliation for the Anglican church, nay, a sacrilege. Although the end would be victory, the church should be prepared for disasters.[51] The anguish of his soul found an echo in his poetry. He saw the time coming when the Church of England would disappear. Christ would "call the Bride away" so that Christmas would eventually be celebrated without Christ.[52] Though he felt a natural thirst for peace and rest, he wished to forget that selfish desire and to fight for the church.[53] He thought of the attacks and successes of Liberalism, which halved the truths of the Gospel and liked to preserve the cultural influence of religion without troubling about sanctity and grace.[54] He compared the dogmas of religion to leaves of the tree of life, fallen in autumn, neglected and forgotten, and he looked at each exquisitely colored leaf with reverence and, for the sake of it, endured the cold sleet and the rain.[55]

For the first time in his life he saw Rome. But he looked only at the surface and did not search for the essence. He visited Catholic churches only to admire their architectural beauty or to hear the fascinating music or to get rid of his restlessness, his homesickness, his weariness.[56] He could appreciate Rome's majesty and glory;[57] he recognized gratefully that England owed to her the blessing of the Gospel, but he lamented the "superstitions" which she taught as the essential part of Christianity.[58] He could not stand "the wretched perversion of the truth" which he believed he saw there.[59] "O that Rome were not Rome! but I seem to see as clear as day that a union with her is *impossible*. She is the cruel Church, asking of us impossibilities, excommunicating us for disobedience and now watching and exulting over our approaching overthrow."[60] It was not Rome only: all the southern countries made him shudder. They were full of "infidelity and profaneness". And he hoped that after all England would be the "Land of Saints" and her church "the salt of the earth".[61]

For several years Newman had been hoping for a deliverer. One of his 1831 sermons had even been prophetic in tone. "Perhaps we see not God's tokens; we see neither prophet nor teacher. . . . Darkness falls over the earth, and no protesting voice is heard." Nevertheless, "the worse our condition is, the nearer to us is the Advent of our Deliverer. Even though He is silent, doubt not that His army is on the march towards us".[62] In the same year he had made up his mind never to leave Oxford for good. It would "want hot-headed men and such I mean to be".[63] When in the following year cholera had broken out, he knew that he would escape. His time had not yet come; he felt destined for a work as yet undone.[64] During the journey he got a more explicit presentiment that he had a mission regarding the necessary "second reformation".[65] Such thoughts and moods were supported and intensified by his trials during the journey.

There were lesser troubles, "inconveniences which become great as soon as they are dwelt upon but shrink to their proper size when the mind is occupied by any more important object".[66] The disagreeable consequences of seasickness; the discomfort of the boat; the sleepless nights at Malta; a very bad cold,[67] a dirty house, people who did not understand his language and were cheating him;[68] the difficulties in Sicily; biting fleas, a strained leg, the impossible food:[69] all these things kept him thinking of the psalm: "I will lift up mine eyes unto the hills, from whence cometh my help."[70]

But all this was nothing in comparison with his illness in Sicily and his constant homesickness. In the wild center of the island a dangerous fever took hold of him. At first no medical help was near. He felt like Job, entirely in the power of the devil, while God was fighting against him. He saw his faults in a clear light. He thought he had been very self-willed in going to Sicily alone. He remembered his conduct in the tutorship affair and considered it, too, as very willful. He seemed to perceive more and more his "utter hollowness", his "great want of love and self-denial". Yes, he could enlarge beautifully on his principles, but they were only intellectual deductions from a friend's convictions. He saw he had some good qualities: he had no vivid love of the world; he had some firmness and dignity of character; he loved the truth; he had some faith. But his sins were so many and so serious that he needed all his faith to gain forgiveness. It seems that God wished him to go through an intense purification, a very dark night. Once a beam of light dispelled the darkness for a moment when "a most consoling, overpowering thought of God's electing love" seized him. He knew he was His. This dark night prepared him to follow willingly "the kindly Light", step by step. That was what he kept praying for and what made him say with tears: "I have not sinned against the light."[71]

There was another trial, which perhaps many of us now can hardly understand but which finds an explanation in his sensitivity and the circumstances of the times. It was his homesickness. From the very beginning of the journey he had been full of thoughts of home. He yearned for letters, but after three months' waiting he had received only two.[72] He could not be reconciled to the length of time he was to be away; it made him despondent.[73] He dreamed about his relatives, and in these dreams letters would arrive, but when he tried to read them either he could not decipher them or he would wake up.[74] His good sense helped him not to give in to that nostalgia and return; he hoped to benefit his health, to increase his usefulness and influence.[75] Notwithstanding the pleasure he enjoyed in seeing beautiful sights, the wonders of the pagan times, the indescribable scenery, he missed something: "*aliquid desideravere oculi mei*", he said, and he made up his mind never to leave England again.[76]

Especially after his recovery, in the weeks at Palermo, his homesickness tried him extremely. He could not leave the town for a long time lest he should miss a boat. The thought of home brought tears to his eyes.[77] He found himself weeping in the dark, cool churches.[78] But he understood the ways of Providence: "God is giving me a severe lesson of patience, and I trust I am not altogether wasting the opportunity of discipline. It is His Will."[79]

During all these trials he kept musing and worrying about the Anglican church and the souls of his countrymen and even of all Christians, nay, about all mankind. Among a group of foreigners, whose language he did not understand and whose religion he did not share, he noticed that their conversation turned on religious subjects, and he wished he could act as a witness for truth.[80] But at other times his contemplative soul hungered for peace and rest. Then he urged himself to fight. If Saint Paul had not done his work, he, John Henry Newman, would have been a heathen.[81] He was aware that he could save not only his own soul but the souls of others by praying and fasting, by patience under trials, by chastity, by charitable deeds, by faithfulness to truth and zeal for God's honor.[82]

His trials, however, did not make him earthly-minded. His soul continued to dwell in the invisible world. The angels kept their place in his thoughts. His first poem, written during the journey, was a moving tribute to his guardian angel. He was convinced of his presence when conversing with others, when in grief or hidden dangers and even in his dreams of the future.[83] He invited the angels to share his joy while admiring the magnificent beauty of the Sicilian scenery.[84] And he wistfully remembered the smiling angels in the visions of his boyhood.[85]

The saints, too, played a great part in his inner life, especially those of the Old Testament. Once he dreamed that he was longing for the company of a saint, and a saint came. It was Saint Paul himself.[86] Visiting the Palermo churches he even dedicated a poem to the relics of the saints.[87] While fallen nature might feel secretly pleased by sensual desires, he prayed God for Mary's help:

> Thou, who didst once from Mary's breast
>   Renew from day to day,
> Oh, might her smile, severely sweet, but rest
>   On this frail clay!
> Till I am Thine with my whole soul; and fear,
> Not feel a secret joy, that Hell is near.[88]

He felt small and sinful in God's sight. He regretted the waywardness and indifference of his early years. When he heard an old tune, cherished in his youth, he was pleased at first, but soon it became painful to him, and he was tormented by fear, disgust and remorse.[89] He wished to accept seasickness and homesickness as penances.[90] He begged God to determine how best he might be punished for his sins.[91] And in his poems he often admitted that he was "frail clay", charmed by evil, "full of unlovely thoughts and rebel aims".[92]

But in spite of all these gloomy expressions of sinfulness, Newman enjoyed peace because he was full of confidence. His humility and his repentance had not sprung from wounded pride. He did not suffer from Byronism.[93] He hoped to feel the burden of his sins fall from his soul so that he might start a new life.[94] He hoped that when the world passed away, he might enter the gates of the long-lost paradise. And nothing could destroy his confidence, because once Christ had said, and still said now to him: "It is I, be not afraid."[95]

At the end of his long and tedious journey home by the dark and quiet sea, he wrote his poem of blind unconditional surrender:

> Lead, Kindly Light, amid the encircling gloom,
>   Lead Thou me on!
> The night is dark and I am far from home—
>   Lead Thou me on!
> Keep Thou my feet; I do not ask to see
> The distant scene—one step enough for me.
>
> I was not ever thus, nor pray'd that Thou
>   Shouldst lead me on.
> I loved to choose and see my path, but now
>   Lead Thou me on.
> I loved the garish day, and, spite of fears,
> Pride ruled my will; remember not past years.
>
> So long Thy power has blest me, sure it still
>   Will lead me on,
> O'er moor and fen, o'er crag and torrent, till
>   The night is gone;
> And with the morn those angel faces smile
> Which I have loved long since, and lost awhile.[96]

It seems to have been the heroic act for which God had been waiting. Purified by illness and sorrow, by contrition and penance, there was no further danger that his extraordinary gifts, the admiration of his followers, the tremendous powers of his rare eloquence, the devotion of his countless friends, would make him proud. He was prepared; he could start on his mission.

CHAPTER FIVE

THE HAPPIEST PERIOD

1833–1839

In behalf of Christ, our Saviour and Lord, who yielded up His precious life for us, and now feeds us with His own Blood, for the sake of the souls whom He has redeemed, and whom, by a false and cruel charity, the world would keep in ignorance and sin, we cannot refrain; and if his Holy Spirit be with us, as we trust He is, whatever betides, whatever is coming on this country, speak the truth we will, and overcome in our speaking we must; for He has given us to overcome.[1]

The change wrought in Newman by the Mediterranean journey was so conspicuous that at first sight some of his friends did not recognize him. His health had been restored, exuberance and energy animated him, and the joy of being in England again made everything light and easy.

A few days after his return, John Keble preached his famous sermon on "National Apostasy", which impressed Newman so deeply that he always mentioned it as the starting point of the Oxford Movement.[2] In this sermon Keble drew the attention of his hearers to the miserable state into which the Church of England had fallen. Many people had turned their backs on her, and he compared her condition to an infectious disease which affected the whole nation. In the same month, James Hugh Rose, an influential clergyman, organized a meeting at Hadleigh and made plans for an association in support of the church. After the suppression of the Irish bishoprics he expected other drastic governmental measures and gave consideration to what future policy should be, should worse come to worst. This meeting resulted in an association of "Friends of the Church", and Newman became a member at once.[3]

But he saw too well the great disadvantages of organized action to give his assent and support wholeheartedly. "Living movements do not come of committees", he used to say.[4] Hence, in his own way, and with the help of a few friends, he tried to impress upon the clergy their duty "to maintain the doctrine of the Apostolic Succession and save the Liturgy from illegal alterations".[5] He would not hear of party motives, financial purposes and political aims. The state might take every penny from the church if only the bishops remained elected by the clergy and the liturgy not be changed by a government without faith.[6] As the bishops were the legitimate successors of the apostles, they and only they were the inheritors of the supreme ecclesiastical authority.

Newman used every expedient to achieve his purpose. First, of his own accord, he wrote pamphlets intended to rouse the clergy from their lethargy. Very soon friends followed his example. Eventually these pamphlets grew into long tracts, the "Tracts for the Times", which appeared at irregular intervals. He insisted on their being personal and concrete, and he excluded all organized criticism: every contributor should write according to his own viewpoint and not be checked by committees and censors.[7] As another expedient he began a series of articles in an Evangelical review and even in poems gave utterance to his ideals. Besides the press, he adopted other means of propaganda. First, there was the address to the Archbishop of Canterbury, signed by nearly 8000 clergy, declaring that His Grace could rely "upon the cheerful co-operation and dutiful support of the clergy in carrying into effect any measures" that might "tend to revive the discipline of ancient times; to strengthen the connexion between the bishops, clergy and people; and to promote the purity, the efficiency and the unity of the church".[8] He wrote a book to give a doctrinal basis to Anglican theology, in which he argued that the essential note of the true church was the preservation of theological truth; that Rome had added to it and Protestantism had subtracted from it; but that Anglicanism had kept the *via media*, the middle way. He also wrote another book, dealing with justification, against Lutheranism. Meanwhile he continued preaching in Saint Mary's while crowds of undergraduates listened. They spread his ideas—practical conclusions from his doctrines, full of the spirit of the Movement—all over the country. Later his sermons appeared in book form, which greatly enhanced their influence. "It was as if a trumpet had sounded through the land", one of his former pupils wrote.[9] Lastly, he organized and presided over informal meetings of undergraduates and graduates in which theological discussions were held so that many intellectuals were imbued with the ideals of Newman and his friends.

The results of his activities surpassed all his expectations, and at times he was frightened by them.[10] The printer could not keep pace with the demand for the Tracts.[11] Long neglected religious practices were reintroduced. In many places the churches were again kept open on weekdays. Religion was no longer a formality. The Fathers of the Church became objects of study. The Liberals lost ground and sadly remarked that the principles of the Movement were spreading in the venerable establishment with an unexpected and astonishing rapidity. The government became cautious and did not venture to appoint as a bishop the liberal headmaster of Rugby, Thomas Arnold. Surely, God's blessing rested on the work. This remarkably swift progress went on for six full years, years in which Newman was overwhelmed with work and care but which—from a human point of view—were nevertheless the happiest years of his life.[12]

It is in this period especially that he began to enjoy

> Blessings of friends, which to my door
> Unasked, unhoped, have come.[13]

God gave them to teach him His way more perfectly, he said.[14] Chief among these friends was Richard Hurrell Froude, who influenced him more than any other person during the whole of his life. Froude "had a high severe idea of the intrinsic excellence of Virginity; and he considered the Blessed Virgin its great Pattern. He delighted in thinking of the Saints; he had a vivid appreciation of the idea of sanctity, its possibility and its heights. . . . He embraced the principle of penance and mortification. He had a deep devotion to the Real Presence, in which he had a firm faith." And Newman was gradually led to think what Froude thought and to believe what Froude believed.[15] He considered Froude to be a saint.[16]

Another friend whom Newman viewed in the same light was John Keble, a man who in later life reminded him of Saint Philip Neri, the founder of the Oratorians. Both were "formed on the same type of extreme hatred of humbug, [and] playfulness, nay, oddity, tender love for others, and severity".[17] In 1828 Newman had suddenly become conscious of his own congeniality of mind with Keble. Previously he had considered him "an angel" and admired his "childlike purity".[18] It was Froude who brought Newman and Keble to understand each other.[19] It was Froude who communicated to Newman Keble's ideas and feelings about religion and the church, his reality of thought and purpose, and his transparent and saintly simplicity.[20] This explains why Newman called him "the true and primary author" of the Oxford Movement.[21]

The man who first named the Movement, Edward Bouverie Pusey, had been Newman's friend since he became a Fellow of Oriel. Newman had an enthusiastic admiration for him. His great learning, his immense diligence, his simple devotion to the cause of religion[22] made Newman turn to him in many trying circumstances. And even during his lifetime he could write about him: "Never was a man in this world on whom one should feel more tempted to bestow a name which belongs only to God's servants departed, the name of a saint. Never a man who happened unconsciously to show, what many more (so be it!) have within them, entire and absolute surrender of himself, in thought, word, and deed, to God's will."[23]

One wonders, however, whether Newman's love of his

friends was not surpassed by his friends' affection and admiration for him. They enjoyed his conversations because he was always imaginative, original, instructive; he could enter wholly into their thoughts and feelings and could understand them better than they could understand themselves; he drew them upward, out of the visible into the invisible world; they seemed to speak with "a better kind of self".[24] When they felt sad, he knew how to comfort them. Thus, at the death of Pusey's child, he spoke so beautifully and consolingly that the bereaved father called his visit the visit of an angel.[25] They considered it a privilege to have a man who showed such extraordinary gifts for a friend. As a result, their tokens of love and admiration were many; they were tender, enthusiastic, exuberant.[26]

But in spite of his tenderness Newman could also be severe toward them. It was to be a trait of his character during the whole of his life. When a friend, however intimate, had pained him and did not give an explanation, Newman showed a certain "flintiness" which puzzled and grieved the offender. Though remaining correct, he appeared touchy and unchari-table. Frederic Rogers, a very close friend, told us that this attitude arose from a sense of duty and justice, and that it was exceedingly difficult for Newman to maintain this severity as he was not angry nor had he any desire for revenge. But as soon as the guilty friend "came to a frank explanation, there came from the rock a gush of overpowering tenderness".[27]

Although these years were very happy years—his mother believed that everything was going well with him[28]—they, too, brought their greater and lesser trials, keenly felt by his sensitive nature. He spoke about "sharp distresses underneath the visible garb of things"[29] and a hair shirt invisible to the world. In 1833 his work on the Arians was refused by the editors of the theological library, for whom he had written it; the circulation of the Tracts caused various difficulties, and the *Record*, in which he had published several articles, politely refused him publication in its columns. His books and articles were a type of "mental childbearing". The Provost of Oriel thwarted him in his plans about Littlemore, the hamlet near Oxford, whose inhabitants were in his charge. His sisters Harriett and Jemima married, and both these marriages caused him anxiety. A controversy with a French priest resulted in difficulties with a friend. Occasionally his health gave him trouble, and he frequently suffered from toothache.[30]

It is no wonder that from the early days of the Movement he experienced hours of discouragement. But they soon passed away and did not influence his lively activity. When a friend fiercely attacked his Tracts and he was hurt because the criticism came from a friend, it was only with difficulty that he could continue his work. In a letter to Maria Giberne he complained that from all parts he heard of nothing but failures. Several people called him a Papist to his face although he continually attacked Roman doctrines. His friends did not flatter him but informed him of his "mistakes" and "absurdities". He himself had predicted that his action would cause difficulties, yet he was treated as if he were quite unconscious of them and thought himself a fine fellow. It was all very humbling. But he closed a complaint about his experiences with the words: "It is a good discipline and I will gladly accept it."[31]

All these things, however, were of no importance when compared with the heavier trials which befell him.

The first concerned the question of a marriage. When asked to marry two people who were previously unknown to him, he discovered that the woman did not belong to the Anglican church, had not been baptized and had explicitly refused baptism. Newman was surprised and, having no time to consult the bishop, refused to comply with their wish. He could not in good conscience recite the beautiful prayers of the marriage service over such a person. This fact became widely known. The *Times* printed indignant letters. Newman wrote to his mother that there was apparently no one to support him. In his distress he went to the old schoolmistress at Littlemore and had a talk with her by way of consolation.[32] An encouraging note from his bishop would have comforted him, but, although Dr. Bagot wrote about the case to the Protestant minister, he did not answer Newman's long explanatory letter.[33] Newman, however, could not be sorry for what he had done. "I am determined", he wrote to his friend John Bowden, "that, as far as I am concerned, the church shall not crumble away without doing in my place what I can do to hinder it."[34]

In 1836 the whole Liberal camp was against him. A new Professor of Divinity had been appointed, the "liberal" Dr. Hampden, who had undermined the faith by his rationalistic Bampton Lectures. In order to prevent further harm to the church, Newman and his friends managed to exclude him from preaching in the University. On account of this action, Newman was called a conspirator, a fanatic, a heretic. He and his supporters were said to be like "the zealots of the circumcision and the ceremonies of the law, . . . the slanderers and persecuters of Saint Paul, . . . the doters upon old wives' fables and genealogies, . . . the men of soft words and fair speeches". They were even accused of being "blinded by wilful neglect of the highest truth" and "corrupted by the habitual indulgence of evil passions".[35] But Newman quietly carried on his gigantic work, seemingly unperturbed, but in reality finding strength in God's presence and his ideal motives: "I know well that there is no pain but may be borne comfortably, by the thought of Him, and by His grace, and the strong determination of the will."[36]

Then another blow fell upon him. His friend Richard Hurrell Froude died. Above all others, including John Bowden, Froude was his most intimate friend. Never had he met a man of such amiable disposition and great talents. Everything about him was bright and beautiful.[37] But his health had been impaired when he spent a night sailing in the Channel. He had developed tuberculosis, for which no cure existed at that time. Newman realized that Froude was to die young. A few days before Froude's death he had preached a sermon on the "Ventures of Faith", that is, on the duty of relying on Christ's words unconditionally. He gave many examples of people who possessed the faith to do this and spoke, too, of a man "who has friends or kindred, and acquiesces with an entire heart in their removal while it is yet doubtful; who can say: 'Take them away, if it be Thy will, to Thee I give them up, to Thee I commit them'; who is willing to be taken at his word".[38] After the Almighty had really taken him at his word he consoled himself with the thought that Hurrell had become a foundation stone of the City of God and that he himself would be able to fight to greater advantage because of that.[39]

At this time Newman felt intensely harassed by his relatives. Charles, with his continual financial difficulties, his outbursts of rage and his unbelief, was a constant source of anxiety. Frank was developing heretical opinions. He denied the personality of the Holy Spirit and the duty of praying to Christ. He was, in fact, originating a schism and organizing a new sect. According to the injunction of Saint Paul, John Henry objected to meeting him in a familiar way or sitting at table with him.[40] Even worse was the fact that his mother and sisters no longer understood him. John Henry had done everything possible to bring them to live nearer to him. He had succeeded, and they had a house close to Oxford. But because of the pressure of work, it was as though he were still far from them, and, "as it was not a distance of the body, it seemed to be one of the mind". When they tried to overcome this invisible obstacle, however, their affectionate manner troubled him. Moreover, their views concerning the principles and methods of the Movement often differed widely from his, so that he lacked his mother's sympathy and praise although he esteemed nothing as more precious. Certainly, she felt grieved when she learned that he was considered a Papist, but she rejoiced at his great influence. She noticed with gladness that he was humble and sought guidance and aid where it could be given, but she could not follow him in the development of his ideas. This was a considerable trial to him.[41]

In the midst of all his work, he received news that his

mother was dangerously ill. In a letter to his beloved aunt he wrote: "If it be God's will to take my dear Mother, most bitter as will be the loss to me, the acutest I can conceive, yet it will be so inexpressibly her gain, that one must not murmur."[42] He went home and stayed with her till the end. They were anxious hours. Her mind wandered in a frightening manner, and, although her death when it came caused him great pain, yet it brought relief. "Nothing but sure faith can bring us through", Newman wrote.[43] Up to the time of the funeral he was completely dejected, but afterward he started working again and succeeded by a resolute effort to overcome his grief. "I trust I shall get on very well," he wrote to Harriett, "and, after all, this life is very short, and it is a better thing to be pursuing what is God's will than to be looking after one's own comfort."[44]

More difficulties, anxieties and troubles were caused by his publication of Froude's papers. The first two volumes were received with a storm of disapproval. Godfrey Fausset, a Professor of Divinity, felt himself called to preach a sermon and publish it against the *Remains* as tending "to depreciate the principles of Protestantism" and palliating "the errors of Popery".[45] Fausset had written with great bitterness, but Newman calmly and deliberately refuted his charges in a pamphlet of his own, winding up with the words: "O that we had the courage and generous faith to aim at perfection. . . . Thousands of hungry souls in all classes of life stand around us; we do not give what they want, the image of a true Christian people. . . ."[46]

But this attack, however painful, was nothing in comparison to the blow dealt to him by his bishop a few months later. It had its origin in the reaction caused by the publication of the *Remains*. In August 1838 Bishop Bagot read his "charge" or diocesan directions to his clergy and informed them that he had received many anonymous letters accusing the writers of the *Tracts for the Times* of Romanism. He added that he felt disturbed by some of the words and expressions used, considering them likely to lead others into error. He feared more for the disciples than for the masters, and he advised them not to go too far.[47]

This unexpected reproach filled Newman with bitterness. Why publicly attack the Tracts without first speaking privately to the responsible leader? Why fling an indefinite suspicion over them if in the main they were orthodox? He had been working five full years for the Anglican church, and the thanks he got amounted to a painful rebuke. "It seems hard", he wrote to Keble, "that those who work, and who while working necessarily commit mistakes, instead of being thanked for that work, which others do *not* do, are blamed. It is very comfortable to do nothing and to criticise".[48] He himself had always shown the deepest respect and obedience toward his bishop. "I can truly say", he wrote to Pusey, "that I would do anything to serve him. Sometimes, when I stood by as he put on his robes, I felt as if it would be such a relief if I could have fallen at his feet and kissed them." His bishop was his pope. But never during these five years did the bishop support him. He had nothing to appeal to in justification but his conscience, which told him that in the main he was right. His sole comfort had been that the bishop had not spoken against him personally.[49]

All this troubled him, and he decided that it would be wiser to propose stopping the Tracts altogether and to withdraw those existing from circulation because he saw no way of finding out to which passages the bishop referred. But his words, for Newman, revealed God's will. To withdraw would involve a considerable loss of money because he had republished the Tracts in four volumes, and the fifth was shortly due to appear. He considered, however, that withdrawal would make people realize that he and his cooperators were sincere and not ambitious.[50]

Before carrying out his plan he let the bishop know, in a very respectful manner, how pained he felt that the first notice of his writings the bishop had taken should be so public and so negative. He inquired which Tracts contained the passages to which reference had been made. Bishop Bagot, a kindhearted man, was distressed at the idea of having grieved Newman.

This had not been his intention. Newman must have misunderstood him. He had indeed approved very much of what Newman and his friends had done, had censured nothing, merely warned. He entreated Newman to do nothing before the charge had appeared in print.[51]

In fact, everything turned out in Newman's favor. The printed edition of the charge contained a note disclaiming any wish to pass a general censure on the Tracts. There were no opinions carried into extremes or mooted in a spirit tending to schism. Interference was not called for.[52]

As Froude's *Remains* had led Fausset to preach against Newman, and the bishop to charge against the Tracts, so again the *Remains* were the chief cause when, later, Newman got into difficulties over the translation of the Roman breviary, "that most wonderful and most attractive monument of the devotion of saints",[53] a translation which he himself had instigated. Friends warned him that he showed little regard to the state of information, the feelings and the wants of people in general.[54] In some cases this appeared to him to savor of suspicion, jealousy and discontent. And he wrote to John Bowden: "I am so bothered and attacked on all sides by friends and foes, that I had much rather say nothing. . . . I mean I mistrust my judgment, and I am getting afraid to speak. It is just like walking on treacherous ice: one cannot say a thing but one offends some one or other—I don't mean foe, for that one could bear, but friend."[55] He was referring specifically to John Keble's brother, and when Newman wrote to Keble about his thoughts and feelings in the matter, Keble tried to bring about a better understanding between the two men. He did not succeed. Newman sought to know what God's will would be. He wrote to Keble: "I put myself entirely in your hands. I will do whatever you suggest. . . . Is it to stop writing? I will stop anything you advise. . . ."[56] In the end Newman stopped the printing.[57]

This meek docility, however, did not result from weakness of character. There are plenty of instances proving the reverse. At times Newman could be fierce and even apparently harsh.

The examples he gave in the *Apologia*[58] may be multiplied. "If I were a Bishop," he wrote indignantly to a friend, "the first thing I should do would be to excommunicate Lord Grey and half a dozen more, whose names it is almost a shame and a pollution for a Christian to mention."[59] Such sayings are characteristic of him. He knew that nothing would come of his labors for the independence and purity of the church unless he acted strongly and severely. He was to continue his efforts without fear, not considering the necessary hurt to others. He and his friends should be "cautious, longheaded, unfeeling, unflinching Radicals", as he expressed it.[60] And in a protest against the admission of Dissenters to the University he said with apostolic firmness: "You cannot join together Truth and falsehood, Light and darkness. If they are forced upon us, we will draw ourselves within the lines of our church, and cut off absolutely all communication even of fire and water with those whose souls we love too well to be kind to their bodies."[61] Words like these are more understandable when we consider that his enemies called him and his followers "a sect of damnable and detestable heretics of late sprung up in Oxford; a sect which evidently affects Popery, and merits the heartiest condemnation of all true Christians. . . . We shall show them up, and demonstrate that they are a people to be abhorred of all faithful men. . . ."[62]

We should like to know more about Newman's inner reactions to all these events and try to discover his deepest motives. As he could not afford the time to jot down autobiographical notes or write spiritual journals, we have to search the sermons of those years in order to discover what were his deepest feelings. Considering that preachers in the pulpit and on paper often may put forward sublime thoughts which astonish and move their audiences but which do not correspond with their acts in everyday life, the question might be asked: What about Newman? A study of his public life shows clearly that he was always consistent. He first put into practice what he was about to preach. His hearers again and again testified to this. The sermons can therefore serve as clear windows on his spiritual life.

In the first place we gather from them what he thought about troubles and pain. He was convinced that God sends trials as the portion of good Christians. "He brings them into pain, that they may be like what Christ was, and may be led to think of Him, not of themselves. He brings them into trouble, that they may be near Him." He was convinced that afflictions consecrated him "as a minister of God's mercies to the afflicted". Taught by his own pain, his own sorrow and even by his own sins, he had a heart and mind exercised for every service of love. His word and advice, his very manner, voice and look were gentle and tranquil. He knew that man should make up in his body what was wanting in the sufferings of Christ. Therefore he considered bodily pain as the medium of God's choicest mercies. It led to the contemplation of Christ's Passion and taught him to forget self, seeing only Christ's resignation and His love for him. Thus he was compelled to strive after a cheerful and ready concurrence of his own will with the will of God. [63]

Newman's habitual state of mind is expressed in a sermon of 1834: "What is nobler, what is more elevating and transporting than the generosity of heart which risks everything on God's word, dares the powers of evil to their worst efforts!" He called it an infinite mercy that sinners like himself were privileged to act the part of heroes rather than of penitents. He did not wish for sight. He would enjoy the privilege. He would triumph in the leave given him to go forward though he knew not whither he went. It was enough that his Redeemer lived. [64] A year later he expressed the same idea in a still more concise way: "Let us not fear opposition, suspicion, reproach, or ridicule. God sees us; and His Angels, they are looking on." [65]

Nevertheless Newman, on the whole, seemed to live in another world, a world of spiritual joy, especially at the end of this period. How he enjoyed getting up early in the morning! Day after day, quietly and calmly, he knelt down before his Maker. And "all things, light or darkness, sun or air, cold or freshness, breathed of Him, the Lord of glory, who . . . gave Himself . . . and poured forth milk and honey" for his sustenance though he saw Him not. And he thought of Saint Paul, who "did not look on this life with bitterness, complain of it morosely or refuse to enjoy it . . . but . . . felt that if he had troubles in this world, he had blessings also." "We must live in sunshine, even if we sorrow" was his principle.[66] It was the peace of mind which he had preached about in 1833, "the constant abiding peace of those whose minds are stayed on God, a peace which ever remains to them in the bottom of their soul, in spite of all the occasional grievances of life which for an instant seem to agitate its surface".[67]

In the years before the great turning point, when doubt would overcast his sky, we even hear a triumphant note. He speaks about God's love and God's presence, of God's mercies and the Gospel Feast. Sins and vices, the corruption of the world, the crimes of its rulers have lost their prominent place. God is not the object of fear and trembling, but He is the God of love, of holiness, of blessedness. God is a God of peace.[68] When he mentions mortifications, trials and sufferings, it is in a cheerful tone, in joyful resignation and sincere gratitude. He rejoices because the church is in peace and mercifully leads great numbers to the full truth. "We have had enough of weariness and dreariness, and listlessness, and sorrow, and remorse. We have had enough of this troublesome world. . . . But now there is stillness; and it is a stillness that speaks. . . . Calm and serene days have begun; and Christ is heard in them, and His still small voice, because the world speaks not."[69]

It was this voice that led him on. His successes had not affected the pure motives of the beginning. Ambition and pride, love of fame and a craving for influence might easily have crept into his mind, and he would have been able to conceal those unworthy ends from his friends, indeed even from himself. True, he hoped for the Moral Professorship, although another man was appointed. He was put on the list of candidates for the important Chair of Divinity, but it was Dr. Hampden who obtained the honor. He lived and prospered under the sun of an ever-widening circle of admirers and frankly confessed that he wished for influence among the undergraduates.[70]

But all this has nothing to do with ambition or other selfish motives. He was only concerned with the ideals of the Movement. The professorship would enable him to fight the "Liberals" with more success.[71] As he told Keble before the appointment of Hampden took place, the simple question was what was God's will. If the professorship were offered to him, he thought it a duty to accept it because it would be a great gift to be used for the welfare of the church. But he could say with a clear conscience that he had no desire for it. Had he his choice, he would decide that the offer should not be made to him. He felt too indolent, and he liked his own way too well to wish for it.[72] If he had been ambitious, he would hardly have taken advice from his friends as he did, and remarks such as the following are frequent in his letters: "I do so fear I may be self-willed in this matter of the tracts. Pray do advise me according to your light."[73]

Moreover, he greatly disliked the idea of being a leader. In the first weeks of the Movement he expressed his wish that Keble should become its head.[74] He was not attracted by this task, and he did not think himself the right man. "I do not wish to put myself forward. I find extreme pleasure in reading and study, and should be rejoiced to be let alone in such occupations. . . . But if others who ought do not lead, such as I will make a row."[75] And in several letters he spoke about his wish for retirement and the possibility of taking a small living somewhere in the country as Keble had done.[76] All this is in keeping with the fact told us by one of his pupils: "When strangers were daily coming to Oxford and making it their first business to see the abode of the man who seemed to be moving the Church of England to its foundations, they were surprised to find that he had simply an undergraduate's lodging."[77]

The sermons which allow us a deeper insight into his inner life and his great spiritual ideals exclude all ambition. Thus in one of them he gives us a fine description of Christ's self-abasement and quotes the beautiful texts that can inspire us to cultivate all kinds of humiliations. And he adds: "Instead of loving display, putting ourselves forward, seeking to be noticed, being loud and eager in speech, and bent on having our own way", we should be content and even rejoice in being made little of, in performing servile offices, in being hardly suffered among men, in being patient under calumny. We should take pleasure in insults. We should return good for evil, win over an enemy and oppressor with love, by being kind, gentle and calm.[78]

No wonder, then, that in these sermons the old self-accusations turn up again but in a most natural way, excluding all affectation and mock humility. He describes

> how weak the governing principle of his mind is, and how poorly and imperfectly he comes up to his own notions of right and truth; how difficult it is to command his feelings, grief, anger, impatience, joy, fear; how difficult to govern his tongue, to say just what he would; how difficult to rouse himself to do what he would, at this time or that; how difficult to rise in the morning; how difficult to go about his duties and not to be idle; how difficult to eat and drink just what he should; how difficult to fix his eyes on his prayers; how difficult to regulate his thoughts through the day; how difficult to keep out of his mind what should be kept out of it.[79]

The more his soul became one with Him Who deigned to dwell within him, the more he would be enabled to see with His eyes. True it was, he had a double duty, to repent as well as to work; but even so, he might pray without fear. "I know He is of purer eyes than to behold iniquity; but I know again that He is All-merciful, and that He so sincerely desires my salvation that He had died for me."[80]

Anyone who has ever lived for some time among people exerting themselves for a great spiritual object will have observed how easily religious zeal and apostolic labors "eat up the spirit of prayer". Even very pious apostles may feel an

impulse more and more to shorten the time of intimate intercourse with God. At first they will suffer and sigh about this
unavoidable necessity, as they call it, but gradually they will
get accustomed to it, and they never return to their former
contemplative habits; indeed, it would be impossible without
painful efforts. And this will especially be the case if selfish
motives claim a part in their busy life. But Newman was never
caught in that snare.

As early as 1830 he had started Saints' Day services in Saint
Mary's,[81] and in the summer of 1834 he even began daily
services[82] although the congregations were small. One single
soul, he said, if but one, was precious enough for Christ's
love.[83] Shortly afterward he explained the reason for this
practice to students and parishioners. This sermon is a panegyric on continuous and united prayer.[84] It was in the same
year that he wrote some of the very few poems he composed
during that period of activity, and all of them bear witness to
his spirit of prayer. As the book of devotions, written by
Bishop Wilson, had formerly convinced him of the excellence
of prayer and had taught him to have his "heart always
devoted to God as the sole Fountain of all happiness", he soon
published a new edition of it and loved to use it.[85] In 1836 he
inherited Froude's Roman Catholic breviary and from that
date he used it almost every day,[86] even if it took several
hours.[87] In imitation of the breviary prayers, he composed
Latin prayers for the Movement.[88] And in his volumes of
sermons we find numerous passages and several entire sermons
on prayer, on living in the invisible world, on uninterrupted
communion with God, written with such unfeigned earnestness and undeniable reality that we must exclude all "hollowness", all "preaching without practising". He evidently spoke
from experience. True Christians cast in their lot with saints
and angels, he said, not with the visible world.[89] He knew
himself to be a citizen of the world to come. Why should he be
anxious for a long life or wealth or credit or comfort, knowing
that the next world would be everything which his heart could

wish for? Why should he rest in this world when it was but the token and promise of another? Everything he saw spoke to him of that future world. The very glories of nature, the sun, moon and stars and the richness and beauty of the earth were as types and figures witnessing to and teaching the invisible things of God.[90]

Notwithstanding the many troubles and anxieties connected with the Movement, the loving contact with God and the saints and angels was still intensified by his realization of the doctrine of the Communion of Saints and the Mystical Body of Christ. He saw God in the church, in the members of the church and in all good men. He loved the words of Hooker, the great Anglican divine, whom he venerated as a Father of the Anglican church: "The church is in Christ as Eve was in Adam. Yea, by grace we are every one of us in Christ and in His church. . . . Christ is therefore both as God and as man that live vine, whereof we both spiritually and corporally are branches."[91]

It was by mortification that Newman supported this life of prayer, this unity with Christ, this living in the invisible world. He believed that a man of prayer should show his earnestness of purpose by mortifying his flesh.[92] In the early years of the Movement he set apart days of prayer and confession. He wanted to try "sufferances of cold". He attempted to practice every mode of fasting.[93] He knew that great deeds were impossible for him, and that he could not carry Christ's Cross literally or live on locusts and wild honey, but what he could do was to avoid display and to be suspicious of luxuries and comforts.[94] Therefore, as soon as possible he wanted to dispense with a servant and serve himself.[95]

How can we account for the fact that in spite of his immense labors and his overwhelming success Newman led such a well-balanced spiritual life? The answer is to be found in his effective desire to obey God's commandments, to do God's will, to please God. This desire is conspicuous in almost every sermon and in many of his letters. The perfect Christian state, he said, is "the state in which the Angels stand; entire subjection to God in thought and deed is their happiness; an utter and absolute captivity of their will to His will, is their fulness of joy and everlasting life".[96] Therefore he exhorted his congregation to surrender their hearts to the guidance of God's Holy Spirit.[97] He wished them to be "wholly Christ's in will, affections and reason".[98] Good Christians, he said, prove "themselves not to be their own, but bought with a price, set on obeying, and constant in obeying His will".[99] Our whole duty and work is made up of these two parts: faith and obedience, looking to Jesus and acting according to His will.[100]

Thus we may read sermon after sermon and volume after volume, and in each of them, from the first to the last, we observe this fundamental, ever-recurring theme. What fascinated his hearers and caused so many to improve their lives was the fact that he preached what he had felt and practiced himself. So the inner cause and motive power of his keen activity and his beautiful inner life must have been his great desire for the fulfillment of God's will and not, as is sometimes said, his fear of God's justice. Among his hitherto unpublished papers there is a list of sermons, conceived for a course on the Epistle to the Romans. Three of them deal with the reasons for obedience and give far nobler motives for pleasing God than judgment and punishment.[101] He appears full of gratitude toward his Maker; he admires God's greatness and mercy, His infinite beauty and measureless perfection, His unfathomable love of men. He delights in speaking about God's love of His creatures and tries to lead his congregation to a grateful requital of this love. He calls the church "a pledge and proof of God's never-dying love".[102] He gives an enthusiastic description of God's love, which is shown in the redemption of mankind, and he exhorts us to praise God "for His surpassing loving-kindness in taking upon Him our infirmities to redeem us, when He dwelt in the innermost love of the Everlasting Father".[103] His sermon on the indwelling

Spirit is a hymn about God's merciful love: "We can but silently adore the Infinite Love which encompasses us on every side."[104] Nothing is more touching than his wonderful sermon about the tears of Christ at Lazarus' grave. Here he tries to change our abstract love of Christ into real, concrete, practical love.[105] He wishes to distill everything into that divine attribute, but the Evangelicals and Unitarians had abused the scriptural words on God's love to such a degree and discarded so many other sacred truths as superfluous that he dared not speak too long of that heavenly subject.[106] In a moving sermon on God's tenderness for each individual soul, he gives an insight into his own spiritual life: "What is man, what are we, what am I, that the Son of God should be so mindful of me? What am I, that He should have raised me from almost a devil's nature to that of an Angel's? that He should have changed my soul's original constitution, new-made me, who from my youth up have been a transgressor, and should Himself dwell personally in this very heart of mine, making me His temple?" And when he went to his daily duties these thoughts were still his inward strength.[107]

After all this we cannot doubt that the motives, described above, were accompanied by real joy. "While He is with us," he said, "we cannot be but joyful, for His absence only is a cause of sorrow."[108] His former sins did not take away this happiness, though he was not able to wipe them altogether from his memory. He knew that sins were destroyed by baptism absolutely and once for all, but he had sinned after being baptized. Nor does faith by itself wash them away. There is repentance—but is repentance the work of a day? he asked. Even the "Sacrament of the Lord's Supper" and the absolution pronounced in it did not give certainty that his sins had been forgiven. But it was his consolation that God would bring him on the way if only he trusted in Him. He felt around him the proofs, in which he could not be deceived, of God's present love toward him. He knew he had really desired to do God's will. He was convinced that God had not cast him out of

His sight, whatever his sins had been. In spite of the trials that came upon him, there was peace and joy.[109]

In September 1838, when the rebuke spoken by his bishop had not yet been retracted and the Movement was at its height, Newman wrote his sermon on the remembrance of past mercies. It was his "Magnificat", in which as in that of Our Lady no mention was made of the sword and in which the fearful piercing of the heart was not even foreseen. He remembered the many sins that had been forgiven, the many prayers God had answered, the many mistakes He had corrected, the many dangers He had averted, the many warnings, the great light, the abounding comfort which He had from time to time given. How he was cherished as a child! How he was guided in the dangerous time when his mind began to think for itself and the heart to open for the world! How His sweet discipline restrained his passions, mortified his hopes, calmed his fears, enlivened his heaviness, sweetened his desolation and strengthened his infirmities! How he was gently guided to the narrow gate! How he was allured along His everlasting way, in spite of its strictness, in spite of its loneliness, in spite of the dim twilight in which it lay! God had been all things to him.[110]

CHAPTER SIX

AFTER A ROUGH SEA INTO THE PORT

1839–1845

> I adore Thee, O Almighty Lord, the Paraclete, because
> Thou in Thy infinite compassion hast brought me into this
> Church, the work of Thy supernatural power. I had no
> claim on Thee for so wonderful a favour over any one else in
> the whole world. There were many men far better than I by
> nature, gifted with more pleasing natural gifts, and less
> stained with sins. Yet, Thou, in Thy inscrutable love for
> me, hast chosen me and brought me into Thy fold.[1]

When six years of blessings and successes had passed, another
six years followed in which perplexity and dismay weighed
heavily upon Newman and the stars of his lower heaven went
out one by one.[2] The decline of his powerful action set in, the
Movement appeared a mistake and even heaven seemed to line
up against him. His enemies were doing their worst, and he
had to put into practice what he had preached after the anxious
hours of the bishops' displeasure: "What is it to us how our
future path lies, if it be but His path. . . . What is it to us what
He puts upon us so that He enables us to undergo it with a pure
conscience, a true heart, not desiring anything of this world in
comparison of Him."[3]

"Slowly advancing, not knowing whither"[4] and studying
the history of the Monophysite heresy in the long vacation of
1839, he was suddenly frightened by the mysterious shadow
of a hand on the wall: he saw clearly that if the Monophysites
were heretics, the Anglicans, too, should be considered as
such, because they followed the same middle path. History

repeated itself.[5] At the same time he read an article on the Donatists, written by Dr. Wiseman, and a friend drew his attention to a few words in it, quoted from Saint Augustine: *Securus judicat orbis terrarum*—the Christian world judges with security[6]—that is, when all Christians agree in a judgment against a small group, it is a sure warrant that the judgment is right so that they need not go back to Scripture or antiquity in proof of the point in dispute. This was a refutation of the Anglican idea that nothing is true unless it be found in the doctrines of the first three centuries.[7] The Anglicans were considered by the whole Christian world as a sect, so they must be a dead branch, cut off from the tree. The *via media* was absolutely brought to nothing.[8] Rome would be right after all.[9]

In his consternation he mentioned his terrifying discovery and consequent perplexity to two intimate friends, Henry Wilberforce and Frederic Rogers. Fear fell on Wilberforce like a thunderbolt, and he expressed the hope that his friend might die rather than leave the Anglican church for Rome. Newman replied that should the danger arise, he would ask his friends to pray that he might indeed die before taking such a step unless it were God's will for him.[10] Rogers felt such a shock that his own friendship with Newman lost its affectionate and intimate character, and after some time he formally made an end to all confidential relations.[11]

But what was Newman to do? He promised Henry Wilberforce never to take the great step unless Pusey and Keble agreed with him that it would be his duty.[12] He decided to be guided by his reason, not by his imagination.[13] He wished to have absolute certitude before he left the Anglican church. He wanted to know that he knew, as he expressed it.[14] So he made up his mind to study the problem thoroughly and to write down the results in an article. From the practical point of view he resolved to go on, doing day by day what he was convinced to be God's will.[15] As far as the future was concerned, in his heart of hearts he blindly surrendered himself beforehand to God's Providence and wrote: "If I have any view opened to

me, I will not try to turn from it, but will pursue it, wherever it
may lead. I am not aware of having any hindrance, whether
from fear or clamour; or regard for consistency, or even love
of friends, which could keep me from joining the Church of
Rome, if I were persuaded to do so."[16]

So he studied Saint Augustine's words and found so much
against this maxim that for the time being he thought there
was no need to worry. He published his conclusions in an
article on the catholicity of the English church. And he vehemently blamed Rome not so much for her corrupted doctrines
as for her political conduct, her controversial bearing and her
social methods and manifestations.[17]

In spite of the soothing effect of his study,[18] he became
despondent about the state of things.[19] Was it because he had
become afraid of Rome? He was not certain that the good
principles, which had shot up all over the country, were not
tending Rome-ward. He had strong apprehensions that only
Rome would be able to withstand Liberalism.[20] Moreover the
great speciousness of Saint Augustine's argument made him
fear for those young Tractarians who were inclined to hasty
conclusions, wild excesses and impetuous acts.[21]

One of the questions that came up continually concerned the
Articles. What did he think about the Articles? They appeared
to have been drawn up against Rome, but on the other hand
the doctrine of primitive Christianity must live and speak in
them because the Anglican church was the continuation of
antiquity. He realized that it was a matter of life and death to
show this. And when in 1840 he went up to Littlemore to keep
Lent he took with him the notes he wanted for a thorough
study of the problem.[22]

This stay at Littlemore marked the beginning of a very strict
period of his life that was to last for six years. He had asked
himself why he was so frail and feeble and languid, so dim-
sighted and fluctuating and perverse. Why was it that, day
after day, he served God so poorly, why did he grovel in the
dust instead of mounting with wings like an eagle? He thought

he lacked the real, simple, earnest, sincere inclination and aim
to use what God had given him. God had abounded in His
mercies to him. He knew he had a depth of power and strength
lodged in himself.[23] So he was led not only to fasting, praying
and enduring hardships but to teaching the ragged children
of Littlemore. This self-abnegation filled him with deep
happiness.[24] He began to think of a monastic house. It was the
beauty of a perfect spiritual life which fascinated him; it was
a conclusion from the doctrine and the example of the Fathers;
it was a revival of what he thought so sublime in the Roman
Catholic religion. So he bought ten acres of ground at Littlemore and began planting.[25]

In the latter part of 1840 he unconsciously gave a survey of
his inner state, full of calm serenity and resignation in spite of
all misgivings. This was in a letter to one of his spiritual
children: "Be assured that I have my doubts and difficulties as
other people. Perhaps the more we examine and investigate,
the more we have to perplex us. . . . We must resign ourselves
to doubt as the *trial under* which it is God's will we should do
our duty and prepare ourselves for His presence. Our sole
question must be, *what* does a merciful God, who knows
whereof we are made, wish *us to do* under our existing ignorance and doubt?"[26]

In this way he began the year 1841. He considered, as he
wrote to Pusey on the first day, that every new year was "but
one continued movement from first to last of God's loving
kindness and tenderness".[27] It was to be a year of great
importance.

In February he published his Tract on the Thirty-nine Articles. In it he showed that the Articles, although usually taken as
an unqualified condemnation of Catholic doctrines and opinions,
bore a truly Catholic interpretation. This declaration aroused
great consternation, the upshot of a long-smoldering animosity
against the Tractarians and especially against their leader. An
old pupil successfully exerted himself to incite everybody
against it. The Heads of the Colleges assembled, and Newman's
request for the necessary time to explain and defend himself

was refused. A condemnation was published accusing him first of dishonesty and secondly of wantonness. This condemnation was posted up at the buttery-hatch of every College, the same action used to denounce a dishonest cook.[28]

He felt this to be an insult, an injustice, a humiliation. It utterly undermined his authority so that not only he but the Tractarian principles and even the Anglican church herself were sure to suffer from it. The violence of the outbreak startled him. "In every part of the country and every class of society, through every organ and opportunity of opinion, in newspapers, in periodicals, at meetings, in pulpits, at dinner-tables, in coffee-rooms, in railway-carriages", he was spoken of "as a traitor who had laid his train and was detected in the very act of firing it against the time-honoured Establishment". He realized that this would be the end of public confidence. It would be impossible for him to say anything more to good effect.[29] A public letter,[30] proving how much the Heads misunderstood him, did not change the situation. The condemnation had done its work.

What was his inner reaction?

It would have been quite natural if he had used his unrivalled powers of irony and mastery of language to expose the authorities. They had unjustifiably taken advantage of their high position to crush his energetic endeavors and had betrayed him in an arbitrary and hasty act. But his reaction was so dignified and meek, so courteous and humble, though he did not give up one line of what he had said, that the minds of many people were softened, and Hawkins, Head of Oriel, a fierce opponent, could not but praise his "excellent spirit under trying circumstances".[31] He had known long before that he would incur the dislike and opposition of his adversaries, "unkind censure, carping, slander, ridicule, cold looks, rude language, insult, and, in some cases, oppression and tyranny".[32] No one ever did a good thing without suffering, he wrote to his sister.[33]

It was a great consolation that the Tract had not been condemned by his bishop. Heads of Colleges did not speak in the name of God: the bishop did.[34] Dr. Bagot had only written a kind letter, expressing his anxiety that the Tract should tend to increased disunion. He had asked him therefore, for the peace of the church, that discussions on the Articles should not be continued in the Tracts.[35] Newman answered at once that he would gladly comply with his desire. The bishop was grateful for this ready acquiescence[36] and Newman replied: "The kindness of your Lordship's letter of this morning brought tears into my eyes. My single wish . . . is to benefit the church and to approve myself to your Lordship. . . . I think of the text: Keep innocency, and take heed to the thing that is right, for that shall bring a man peace at the last." He proceeded to explain how it came to pass that he had been obliged to write the Tract. If he had kept silence, he would have seemed underhanded, and he did not like to lead people to false notions about his opinions.[37]

However, since Newman appeared to be so submissive, authorities in London, among whom was the Archbishop of Canterbury, approached Dr. Bagot to make Newman suppress Tract 90 and stop the issue of further Tracts entirely.[38] An action such as the suppression of the Tract would be without precedent in the Anglican church. It would mean both a self-condemnation and abnegation of the principles of the Movement. It would imply that he was acting against his conscience. Newman could only obey if he could find a way of showing that his action would be one of mere obedience and not an assent to contrary statements. But this would involve retirement from Saint Mary's and the diocese. In his perplexity he wrote to Pusey: "I cannot deny that I shall feel this suppression very much. My first feeling was to obey without a word: I will obey still; but my judgment has risen against the measure ever since. If I have ever done any good to the church, I would ask the Bishop this favor as a reward for it, that he would not insist upon a measure from which I think good will not come. However I will submit to him."[39]

When the Bishop heard of Newman's anxiety he was moved and changed his mind. He expressed the wish that a public letter be written by Newman announcing the cessation of the Tracts and expressing his attachment to the church, his disapproval of the errors of Rome and his submission to spiritual authority. This would finish the matter as far as the bishops were concerned.[40] Newman could do so conscientiously and honestly. Therefore he most willingly obeyed and wrote his letter of March 29th, an example of reverence, humility and generosity, ending with these words: "May God be with me in time to come, as He has been hitherto! and He will be, if I can but keep my hand clean and my heart pure. I think I can bear, or at least will try to bear, any personal humiliation, so that I am preserved from betraying sacred interests, which the Lord of grace and power has given into my charge."[41]

Spring and summer of the year 1841 passed peaceably. He had made up his mind to put aside all controversy and set himself down to his translation of Saint Athanasius. He did not worry about his doubts but entrusted himself to God's good guidance when between July and November the vehemence of the trial returned and three blows came down upon him and broke him.

First there appeared again the mysterious hand on the wall. In the history of Arianism, so strongly bound up with Saint Athanasius, he discovered the same phenomenon he had found with the Monophysites, and he saw clearly that the pure Arians were the Protestants, the semi-Arians were the Anglicans, and Rome alone was now what it had been then.[42]

While he was in the misery of this new disturbance the bishops, one after another, began to attack Tract 90, entirely against their promise. It was the English church officially condemning the Movement, officially repudiating her connection with the Ancient Church, the Church of the Apostles.[43]

"As if all this were not enough, there came the affair of the Jerusalem Bishopric."[44] For political reasons, a Prussian minister had induced the Archbishop of Canterbury to appoint and consecrate a Bishop of Jerusalem. This bishop, a converted Jew, was to take care of all Anglicans, Lutherans, Calvinists,

Nestorians, Monophysites, Jews, and so on who would care to join the English church and place themselves under his authority, while no abjuration whatsoever of their beliefs was required.[45] "This was the third blow, which finally shattered my faith in the Anglican church", Newman observed. "That church was not only forbidding any sympathy or concurrence with the Church of Rome, but it actually was courting an intercommunion with Protestant Prussia and the heresy of the Orientals." This fact, like several others he had encountered, led him to the suspicion that the English church had all along never been a church at all.[46] Many of his followers, too, began to despair. He warned against dangerous measures, quoting Cowper's lines:

> Beware of desperate steps. The darkest day,
> Live till to-morrow, will have passed away.[47]

He decided to write a public protest. He knew that people might call him a fanatic, but how could he remain passive?[48] Accordingly he carried out this plan, hoping that all the miserable confusion would turn to good and that his prayers and alms would "come up as a memorial before God".[49] In a letter of comfort to a lady in distress he revealed his own spiritual attitude: "Let this be your simple and engrossing prayer: to know God's Will and to do it. Who are you to covet with James and John the right and left of your Lord's throne? Know your place. . . . Be the English church what you fear it is, not a legitimate branch of the true Church, yet surely, it is good enough for you; surely, it has excellences and graces, it has saints, it has gifts, it has lessons, which are above you and me. No—the sole reason we can have for leaving the church in which God's Providence has placed us is a call from God."[50]

In his anxious desire for a sufficient intellectual basis, he expanded these words in four sermons. God in His judgment had obscured the visible and public notes of His Kingdom, but in His mercy He had not deprived the church of personal and private notes. There was still the presence of Christ.[51] "O! pause ere you doubt that we have a Divine Presence among us still . . . though our brethren tell us it is all a dream."[52] God had been with the English church in the past; would He leave her now? God showed her members mercies unfathomable and wonderful Providences. God gave them real answers to their prayers. Were not the awful sacredness of the sacraments and ordinances other proofs of Christ's presence? Did not the edifying, holy deaths of so many Anglicans show the same? And must not that be a church which contained men so saintly in their lives, so self-denying, so obedient? And was it not true that Christ's presence is the very definition of the Church?[53] He reminded his hearers that the Anglican church resembled the people of Samaria. They had lived in schism, but God continued to send them prophets and showed them His mercy. In the same way, He had not left the Anglican church though she had lost her visible notes of catholicity and apostolicity and lived in schism.[54]

These ideas would prove untenable in the long run, but at the time they supported him. He was quite clear about his duty to remain where he was.[55] He did not feel any anxiety about his own person, but the pain of unsettling others began to make itself felt. Robert Wilberforce had heard rumors that Newman's ideas were changing. He wrote to his revered friend and hoped he was going to answer: "How absurd", as he used to.[56] Newman kept him waiting for more than a month, then gathered courage and revealed to him his real state of mind, namely, that he had earnest misgivings as to whether he belonged to the Universal Church. Wilberforce was shocked by the news. He could not sleep. He could not tell his wife. He could not even write anything against it except to make those points which Newman himself stressed far more strongly.[57] This is only one example, but the fact that he was causing severe conflict in others was one of the reasons why he went up to Littlemore for good, providing Saint Mary's with a curate.

In that little village he had furnished a range of farm buildings, turned into cottages, as a quiet house of retreat, with a dining room, small bedroom/sitting rooms and an oratory. It was not his purpose to revive the monastic orders in the Roman Catholic sense of the word; this was meant to be a house where he could retire and where he could offer hospitality to those who felt inclined to leave the English church or who longed for a more regular and more religious life. He himself yearned after a life of quiet meditation, of living more actually in God's presence, of doing penance for his sins, of praying for light and guidance in his perplexity. There was no question of vows, however, nor of simple obedience to a superior, nor of stability, nor of liturgical exercises.[58] Very soon, however, rumors began to spread that he was building a "popish monastery". There grew a hostile interest, which manifested itself in a kind of espionage. People from Oxford University kept an eye on the building and checked whether he entered at the back door or at the front. They wanted to know who his visitors were. Journalists came, and in the newspapers they asked what he was doing at Littlemore. Indignantly he answered: "Why will you not let me die in peace? Wounded brutes creep into some hole to die in, and no one grudges it them. Let me alone, I shall not trouble you long."[59] The bishop, too, heard the reports and called him to account. Newman let him know that he only wished to give himself a life of greater religious regularity but that it was very unpleasant to confess such a wish to the general public and even to his bishop, for the plan might seem arrogant or come to nothing. He felt it very cruel that such delicate matters were made a subject of public talk.[60] He was not at all attempting any revival of the monastic orders in "the Romanist sense of the term".[61]

In April 1842 he slept for the first time at the Littlemore parsonage, as the house was to be called, and two days later he was joined by a young graduate, Dalgairns.[62] They started to say the daily office from the Roman breviary; they observed silence for the greater part of the day; they tried to live in a very simple way. He knew, as he said in a sermon of the time, that we have, in a certain sense, to detach ourselves from our bodies if our minds are to be in a state to receive divine impressions.

"A smooth and easy life, an uninterrupted enjoyment of the goods of Providence, full meals, soft raiment, well-furnished homes, the pleasures of sense, the feeling of security, the consciousness of wealth—these, and the like, if we are not careful, choke up all the avenues of the soul, through which the light and breath of heaven might come to us."[63]

Thoughts like these led him to rise at midnight for the recitation of Matins and Lauds. Later on he and his companions —for others had joined him—rose at three. Their fasts were very strict, especially in Lent and Advent. Three days in the week they had no meat. At one time they took their first meal at five in the afternoon. Each one made his own bed. When they had breakfast, they took it standing and in silence. Newman tried to dispense with servants, and he seems to have succeeded. For some time he tried not to sleep in a bed, but he found this impossible. All these rules were, however, subject to variations, and as soon as a member of the community was away he was free from them.[64]

Since the Tract 90 affair, the cry had been raised all over the country that Oxford University was "Popish". This made the state of affairs critical. "People up and down the country, clergymen, squires, and the like, demand that the University should not be a place where Popery is imbibed", Newman observed.[65] Nobody, however, went over to Rome, and again he made up his mind to ask for prayers that he might die rather than take a wrong step himself.[66] A very devout Catholic had sent him the *Paradisus Animae* in the belief that Newman was likely to join the Roman Catholics soon. But he answered: "I must assure you then with great sincerity, that I have not the shadow of an internal movement, known to myself, towards such a step. While God is with me where I am, I will not seek Him elsewhere."[67] When at the anniversary of Littlemore Chapel he preached on the forlorn state of the Anglican church, and this in such a touching tone that even the modern reader is saddened, he all at once turns round and begins to enlarge on Christian joy:

Yet . . . cheerfulness is a great Christian duty. Whatever be our circumstances, within or without, though "without be fightings and within fears", yet the Apostle's words are express, "Rejoice in the Lord always". That sorrow, that solicitude, that repentance, is not Christian which has not its portion of Christian joy; for "God is greater than our hearts", and no evil, past or future, within or without, is equal to this saying that Christ had died and reconciled the world unto Himself. We are ever in His presence, be we cast down, or be we exalted; and "in His Presence is the fulness of joy".[68]

Although he heard no inward call to join the Church of Rome, his affection for her had grown to such an extent that he felt ashamed for what he had written against her. So in 1843 he collected his most violent anti-Catholic statements, printed at different times and in different publications, and withdrew them publicly. It was a solemn act of reparation and self-humiliation, in obedience to his conscience, drawn up without a single word against the Anglican church. Some prominent Catholics wrote telling him how thrilled they were by his splendid example of Christian simplicity and generosity, his self-effacing honesty and humility.[69] But he considered this act simply a matter of justice and piety and was of the opinion that they thought too well of him and gave him higher praises than he deserved. Moreover he warned them not to conclude that there was any movement on his side to their Church.[70]

He felt, however, more and more troubled about his position. So many people placed too much confidence in him. So many undergraduates were trusting him more than they should. He called it an "evil conscience", and it haunted him.[71] They were attracted by Rome, and he could no longer attack Catholicism in order to keep them from her. Besides which, the bishops continued to condemn Tract 90, which he considered the foundation of his faithfulness to his church. The number of persons who came to him for spiritual guidance was continually increasing. Was he not in a false position? Should he not resign his office as Vicar of Saint Mary's? A few years before, Keble had given a negative answer to those questions, and at this moment he again put the question to his revered friend and requested him to take the time for a reply.[72]

In the meantime—in the spring of 1843—Newman kept his "strictest Lent". No food before five o'clock in the afternoon. Less sleep than ever, the last days of Lent little more than four or five hours. Every day a meditation of at least one hour. Finally he made a retreat, without any guide except some books, among which were the *Spiritual Exercises* of Saint Ignatius.[73]

In his notes we find the general rules he followed. They are highly characteristic of Newman and reveal his habitual state of mind: 1. The person under exercise should surrender himself wholly to his Maker. 2. No one should interfere between him and his Maker; God must deal with His creature and he with God. 3. His aim should be, not consolation, but to know God's will concerning him and to learn to love Him. 4. He should not be set on any point which he is not willing to relinquish.[74]

In the personal annotations he applies these maxims but at the same time gives us a remarkable description of the outer and inner circumstances under which this retreat was made. Thus he tells us how long the hour of meditation sometimes appeared to him; how grateful and joyful he was when it had seemed short; how he had to fight against wandering thoughts, against sleep, against feelings of misery; how difficult it was sometimes for him to meditate on the subjects of the book and to exercise the affections in the way of colloquy. We observe his honesty when he writes down that he told a little lie to one of his companions and what lie it was and how he wished to repair this fault by confessing it to the very friend. We learn that he felt a great aversion even to the word of penance. When he meditates on humility, he thinks it an absurdity to give praise to a person who is humble, because the Word humiliated Himself so very condescendingly. However, he appeared to himself to be unwilling to pray the words: "Give me utter obscurity", and he ascribed this partly to a desire for post-humous fame, partly to a dislike that others should do the work of God in the world and not he himself. Generously he gave himself up to God to do what He would with him, to make him what He would, to put what He would upon him. He realized what this meant and wrote down what would be great trials to him: bodily pain and hardship, the loss of his library, a general confession to someone in the Anglican church and the duty of joining the Church of Rome.[75]

On reading the notes one feels in a sense disappointed, though in another sense grateful for his honesty. They are so full of fierce self-accusations. He often speaks about his sins, mortal and venial, about judgment and hell, about fear of his own weakness, and he even calls himself an odious monster in the sight of the angels. Everything is so intensely introspective. But we should not lose sight of the circumstances. He lived in doubt and perplexity. Was it not possible that God should have forsaken him on account of his secret pride, his many imperfections and sins? In his first meditation he had realized how human his motives still were. Had he ever acted purely for God's glory? Had he not used his gifts for himself? Perhaps this was "the sovereign sin of his heart".[76] This frame of mind explains much. Apart from this, we should never forget that the higher men aim with their ideals and the nearer they try to approach God and show generosity in fulfilling God's will and create silence in their hearts, the more they are illuminated by God's light and the clearer they see their imperfections and utter misery. The prophet Jeremiah and the Apostle spoke in the same violent way about their shortcomings. They measure the purity of their intentions against God's infinite purity, which they know better than we do. And so, from this point of view, Newman was right when he wrote to a lady who admired him for his spirituality: "Never were you more mistaken than when you fancy that a person like me is without innumerable infirmities."[77] But at the same time one of his companions was no less right when he wrote about this period at Littlemore: "I have not forgotten this brilliant and shining example of true holiness, piety and self-denial which for more than twelve months I beheld with an inward feeling of wonder."[78]

Almost a month after this retreat, Keble's answer to Newman's suggestion about resigning Saint Mary's arrived: he had a duty neither to give up his office nor to keep it; if he resigned, however, he should keep Littlemore in order to avoid showing dissatisfaction with the Church of England.[79]

When Newman took steps to act on this advice he could not obtain leave to keep Littlemore. It was a great disappointment.[80] Again he wrote to Keble for advice and in the same letter revealed his secret that in 1839 it had suddenly become clear to him that the Anglicans were in a state of schism, and now he feared he considered the Roman Catholic Church to be the Church of the Apostles. Hence the charges of the bishops distressed him as protests against his secret unfaithfulness and as a sign of how far the English church was from even aspiring to Catholicity.[81] It seemed to him safer to retire from Saint Mary's.

In a very hesitating manner Keble dissuaded him from retiring.[82] In the meantime Newman saw a new reason for it and wrote again.[83] Keble answered that he might go on at Saint Mary's without sin, but on the other hand that he could equally well retire.[84] Submissively, Newman put the subject aside for some months. Then Keble advised him to find a confessor with a strong hand, giving him full leave to demand absolute obedience.[85] The next morning Newman began a journal,[86] in which he put down "not only infirmities but temptations", even when he did not feel them to be more than external to him. He also described how every day passed.[87] This self-humiliation brings to mind the holy Capuchin, Saint Fidelis of Sigmaringen, who for some time revealed his faults twice a day in confession. After ten days Newman sent the journal to Keble, who did not, however, discover anything that might be the cause of an illusion.[88]

The last straw came with young William Lockhart's sudden conversion to the Church of Rome. A year before, Newman had admitted him into his little community. He had made him promise, as a condition of his stay at Littlemore, to remain in the Anglican church for at least three years. While on holiday and without saying a word to Newman, he had become a Catholic, writing afterward that the call had been so very strong that he felt he dared not disobey.[89] Newman was very much upset about this and did not hesitate any longer: "I am not a good son enough of the Church of England to feel I can in conscience hold preferment under her. I love the Church of Rome too well."[90] Only Keble might have induced him to continue as Vicar of Saint Mary's, but after all this Keble had no more objections to make.[91]

When Newman's sister Jemima learned of his plan, she wrote him a very sad letter, beseeching him to think of the effect upon his followers. "My dearest Jemima," he answered, "my circumstances are not of my making. One's duty is to act under circumstances. Is it a light thing to give up Littlemore? Am I not providing dreariness for myself? If others . . . suffer, shall I not suffer in my own way?" He asked her to pray that something might occur to hinder him if he were wrong.[92] And to his sister Harriett, whose husband he had been trying to keep back from following an impulse toward the Church of Rome, he wrote: "My dear Harriett, you must learn patience, so must we all, and resignation to the will of God."[93]

It was on September 7th of that year that he officially broke the news to his bishop by asking permission to resign Saint Mary's. He did not pour out bitter reproaches or take revenge in deliberate coolness or stilted commonplaces; neither did he conceal his displeasure in flattering words. When so many bishops had said such things of him and none of them had taken his part, he could not but resign. He thanked his bishop for his friendship and expressed his great sorrow insofar as he himself had been the occasion of his anxieties about the state of the church. But he could sincerely say that he had ever felt great love and devotion toward his Lordship, that he had ever wished to please him, and that he had labored hard to uphold the church and to retain her members. Now that he had lost or forfeited her confidence, he felt forced to retire from her service.[94]

On September 18th, after a sleepless night, Newman signed the document before a notary, and on the 25th he preached at Littlemore for the last time. It is the famous sermon on "The Parting of Friends".[95]

That day was the seventh anniversary of the consecration. The little church, decorated with flowers, was full of friends. So many people were present that chairs had to be put in the churchyard. When Newman mounted the pulpit there was complete silence. His sermon was a heartbroken expression of the most intense distress. It revealed how well he loved the church and how great was his sorrow to be torn away from her. It was a mournful lament that his work had been a failure. The whole was touchingly made more beautiful by wonderful passages and phrases from Scripture. One of his friends wrote: "The sermon I can never forget, the faltering voice, the long pauses, the perceptible and hardly successful efforts at restraining himself, together with the deep interest of the subject, were almost overpowering."[96]

And Pusey wrote to his brother on the same day: "I am just returned, half broken-hearted, from the commemoration at Littlemore. The sermon was like one of Newman's, in which self was altogether repressed, yet it showed the more how deeply he felt all the misconception of himself. It implied, rather than said, Farewell. People sobbed audibly, and I, who officiated at the altar, could hardly help mingling sorrow with even that Feast. However! The peace of God 'which passeth all understanding', closed all."[97]

This peace of God, passing all understanding, was expressed in these closing words, words of resignation, of gratitude for sincere friendship, of humility in asking for prayers, and especially of a great desire to do God's will at all costs:

And, O my brethren, O kind and affectionate hearts, O loving friends, should you know any one whose lot it has been, by writing or by word of mouth, in some degree to help you thus to act; if he has ever told you what you knew about yourselves, or what you did not know; has read to you your wants and feelings, and comforted you by the very reading; has made you feel that there was a higher life than this daily one, and a brighter world than that you see; or encouraged you, or sobered you, or opened a way to the inquiring or soothed the perplexed; if what he has said or done has ever made you take interest in him, and feel well inclined towards him; remember such a one in time to come, though you hear him not, and pray for him, that in all things he may know God's will, and at all times he may be ready to fulfil it.[98]

After this radical step, the return to the state of a layman, Newman was still far from Rome, much farther than we should expect. Much study and many graces were still necessary, for intellectual difficulties and other obstacles seemed to him insurmountable for the time being. As early as 1839 he had received "a deep impression" that "communion with the See of Rome was the divinely intended means of grace and illumination".[99] He seemed to be certain. But he had been certain about Evangelicalism, and it had proved an error. He had been certain about his *via media* and four words of a Father of the Church had pulverized this middle way. How could he be certain, certain with absolute certitude, that he was not in error again? He might be deluded by his secret sins. Next, there were so many exterior circumstances which made it impossible for him to follow the new light without the greatest circumspection and reserve. He was responsible for an immense number of souls, who had been brought to a life of great spirituality by his tracts, sermons and articles. How could he let them down by becoming a Catholic! How many of them would be puzzled, perplexed, deeply pained. Their unsettlement might lead them to Liberalism and scepticism, or to indifferentism. Religious souls would lose their piety and perhaps be lost for eternity. Moreover, he should have to leave his friends, to incur the reproaches and indignation of his sisters and brothers. He would lose his reputation with all non-Catholics; they would call him a fool, a traitor, and consider him inconsistent and wanton. He would have to face the triumph of the Liberals and confirm their worst expectations. Then, too, he would be poor again, without his fellowship, without a living, without the money from his books. He would have to leave Oxford for an uncertain and obscure future, among people he neither knew nor loved, people who did not have the refined culture of Oxford.[100]

Delay seemed to him God's will. "Our Lord tells us to count the cost", he wrote; "how can you tell whether it is His voice, or that of a deceiving spirit?" In spite of the treatment he suffered at the hands of the ecclesiastical authorities, he was on his guard not to be led by sensitivity, indignation, resentment. He wished to be led by prayer and penance, study and advice.[101]

When the news that he had resigned Saint Mary's became public, many reactions filled him with great grief. People began to realize that his submission to Rome might be expected any day. Thus an old schoolfellow wrote to him: "There are so many that love you and revere your character, and have been formed by your works, who will be utterly cast down, if you take this step, who will not know where to turn, that I conjure you not to do it, unless conscience makes it altogether unavoidable. My dear friend Clarke . . . is perhaps dying, and, if he is taken away, it will be an unspeakable loss to me, but that separation will be as nothing to my hearing that Newman, who rescued me from low views . . . had ceased to call himself my brother, and declared me to be in heresy. Oh! Newman, do do stop with us—what shall we do without you!"[102]

We should bear in mind the incalculable influence he had been in the English church. Thousands and thousands had become happy in a renewed religious life. Difficulties had been solved, despondency dispelled, temptations robbed of their strength. He had been the great "physician of souls", the great instructor and master, who had given light and comfort. For many people he had been as an angel, sent from heaven to reveal to them their spiritual state. Again and again he received letters from all kinds of persons who said that they owed more to him than to any other human being, and if they were to be saved they would owe their salvation to him. Women wanted to become nuns. A girl broke off her engagement and another made a vow of celibacy in Saint Mary's. Many dying persons finished their lives like saints. And Oxford itself had been transformed into a center of piety.[103] And now he was going to be a disappointment, a puzzle, a stumbling block, a cause of despair, for all these devoted souls. "None can know the dismal thing it is to me", he said, "to trouble and unsettle and wound so many quiet, kind and happy minds."[104]

This trial was so intensely felt that it made him forget his own perplexity. "It is the shock, surprise, terror, forlornness, disgust, scepticism to which I am giving rise; the differences of opinion, division of families—all this it is that makes my heart ache", he wrote to Jemima.[105]

How could he bear all this without losing mental and bodily health? It was only through his resignation, his supernatural trust in God and the influence of God's grace. "The great remedy of all uneasiness", he wrote, "is to feel that we are in God's hands, and to entertain an earnest desire to do His will."[106] So he could say hopefully: "I have a greater confidence in the love for them of Him who had made them what they are, to fear that He will abandon them."[107]

The end of Advent of the year 1843 was spent in a retreat with four companions. After the meditations, he used to write down his thoughts, his faults, the impressions that struck him, his difficulty in fixing his mind on God's presence, even his bodily reactions. Again we notice his deep humility and his sense of utter sinfulness. He remembered his youth. He felt sure he had been "all but damned" and was still in danger, just like somebody who was gliding down a steep descent and needed to take the greatest care lest he should fall into a chasm. He asked himself whether he had ever really repented of many of his grave sins. Once when he had nothing to think about during his meditation he turned to his "own venial sins, for example, impatience, impetuosity, rudeness, inaccuracy of speech sometimes approaching to lying", whereas he considered as his main faults: "indulgence of the appetite, self-conceited thoughts, and wanderings in prayer".

On the other hand, we find in these notes proofs of both stronger and unconditional self-surrender: "I begged that Christ would make of me what He would. . . . I tried to give up to Him, if for His greater glory, my fellowship, my Library, the respect of friends, my health, my talent, my reason but I added: 'Lord, be merciful.' "[108]

The year 1844 found him peaceably at Littlemore. Again he kept Lent in his austere manner, although it was less stringent than the years before. They had their first meal at twelve and their full meal at five in the afternoon. There was no restriction on tea at any hour.[109] He lived in a cheerful frame of mind, translating Saint Athanasius, happy in the company of young friends, sleeping soundly at night. And he trusted that God would overrule all painful things which he himself or others had to bear, to his and their good.[110]

But in September his great friend John Bowden lay dying. New grief overwhelmed him: "One forgets past feelings, else I should say that I never have had pain before like the present", he wrote.[111] The next day Bowden passed away, and Newman wrote to Keble: "And there lies now my oldest friend, so dear to me—and I, with so little faith or hope, as dead as a stone, and detesting myself." And later he added: "I sobbed bitterly over his coffin to think that he had left me still dark as to what the way of truth was, and what I ought to do in order to please God and fulfil His will."[112]

He had become extremely tender and sensitive. His weak health, his austere penances and the anxious feelings regarding his followers caused him a great deal of pain. This sensitivity made him write a distressing letter to his brother-in-law, Jemima's husband, because he felt disappointed by an apparent lack of sympathy on her part. He thought she had given him up. But Jemima answered that he was mistaken. His slightest act or feeling awakened her interest and anxiety. Some things that had been reported even caused her pain.[113]

Indeed, many reports about him had been circulating. Travelling from London to Oxford he heard a man in another compartment of the train say that he was a Jesuit.[114] Fantastic ideas were given rein to explain his conduct. Friends, admirers, well-wishers pointed to secret motives which actuated or deluded him. Keble suspected that Newman was driven by restlessness, though all his feelings and wishes were against change and the Roman Catholics did not attract him at all. Some thought that it was the Roman liturgy which had influenced him. But he hardly ever attended a Roman service. Nor could he hope for a dignified position in the Catholic Church,[115] though his sister Harriett believed the silly tale that Rome had offered a cardinal's hat and he had declined it in a "most triumphant and masterly answer".[116] But the general idea was that there was something wrong with him. He expressed it in these words: "A person's feeling naturally is, that there must be something wrong at bottom; that I must be disappointed, or restless, or set on a theory, or carried on by a party, or coaxed into it by admirers, or influenced by any of the ten thousand persuasions which are as foreign from my mind as from my heart, but which it is easy for others to assign as an hypothesis."[117] No, his only motive was that he believed the Roman Church to be true, he said; he realized that it might be his duty to join her if he would be saved.[118] The only thing that stopped him from moving at once was his fear of "some secret undetected fault".[119]

In a letter he told Keble that he took comfort in the words: Thine Hands have made me and fashioned me; despise not the works of Thine own Hands. He looked back to past years when he was a boy and asked himself: "Would He have led me on so far to cast me off? What have I done to be given over, if it be such, to a spirit of delusion?" And he described in a wonderful and touching way how God had guided him and trained him from his boyhood up to the day of his great trial. Since his conversion as a boy of fifteen, when he had lived "a life of sin with a very dark conscience and a very profane spirit", he had never forsaken Him, while God had upheld him. God had led him forward by a series of providences. He repeatedly and variously chastised him. He took from him a dear sister and at the same time gave him kind friends to teach him His way more perfectly. When he had gone to Sicily, he had had a strong idea that God was going to effect some purpose through him. Then came the great Movement, and while reading the Fathers he came at last to the strong conviction "that the Roman Communion is the only true Church". He fought and wrote against it and began to lead a stricter life. He humiliated himself and prayed and prayed. Of course, he was conscious of innumerable weaknesses, in heart and conduct, but he trusted they were not laid to his charge. He even could say that in many respects his heart and conduct had improved. Why should God have granted his prayers in these respects and not granted them when he had prayed for light and guidance? He had kept many people from going over to Rome, and he asked himself: "What if you are the cause of souls dying out of the Communion of Rome, who have had a call to join it?" Perhaps this had happened already. Others whom he had been keeping from Rome might have been led to a sort of latitudinarianism and Liberalism. What then was the will of Providence for him? "Has He led me thus far to destroy me in the wilderness?" he asked.[120]

Keble knew how to comfort him. He was sure Newman would not lose the divine guidance. Keble only suffered from the thought that he could have averted or mitigated Newman's anguish if only he had been different from what he was. He reproached himself that he could remain so calm at such bad news from his friend and that it did not even make him lose one night's rest.[121] Newman replied that this was the only way to be able to view things healthily and rightly: "Do not lament that you do not lose your sleep. I think sleep is the greatest of our ordinary blessings. Nothing goes well with the mind without it; it heals all trouble."[122]

A kind of quiet resignation had come over him: "As far as I can make out," he wrote to Jemima, "I am in a state of mind which divines call *indifferentia*, inculcating it as a duty to be set on nothing, but to be willing to take whatever Providence wills."[123] Therefore he remained indifferent to the many attacks made on him. There was only one exception: "The only thing which I feel, is the charge of dishonesty. Really no one but O'Connell is called so distinctly and so ordinarily a liar, as I am." It pained him very much not to be treated as a gentleman. But when friends tried to remove this pain through a private address protesting against such reports, it struck him that he would be trying to remove a cross and he might get a heavier one. "If there is a cross which is blessed from those who have borne it from our Lord's own time, it is this—and it is safest to be content with it."[124]

His spiritual indifference had made him so much detached from all that was connected with the Movement that he could live near Oxford without being interested in what was going on. Of course, he was distressed about the proceedings against his friend George William Ward, who was deprived of his title because of his Roman ideas. But generally he lived "as though a dead man", and the Oxford authorities could do him neither good nor harm.[125]

About New Year 1845 he decided to put an end to his vague misgivings and try to make his certitude habitual and absolute. He was going to write a book on the development of Christian doctrine. This development seemed to him the key to the solution of all intellectual difficulties. If only his conviction in favor of Rome were not weaker at the end of his study, he promised himself to take the great step and join the Catholic Church.[126]

He started in January 1845, and it proved a tremendous work. He had vastly more materials than he knew how to employ. Never had anything cost him so much hard thought and anxiety.[127]

By this time his state of mind had become fully known to his brothers and sisters. Harriett had tried to argue with him, attempting to show that he was in a false position. But he had refused to comply with her wish. She should have read what he had read. She had not, so she remained just as she was.[128]

She felt so greatly distressed about it all that she could not write to him any more.[129] Frank did not understand him either. He supposed that John Henry wanted to be a Catholic because he thought the Catholic Church "the most bearable of existing forms of religion", and he advised him rather to form a sect of his own.[130] But if by following his conscience he were to become poor, Francis offered him his house and every financial support.[131] Charles lived in Germany and was constantly in trouble. In January he let his relatives know that he had lost his money, his watch, his best clothes and that he was quarrelling with everybody.[132] Jemima understood John Henry best of all, so that the correspondence between them went on uninterruptedly. She knew he acted from conscience, but she thought his plan a grievous mistake. And she used all her power of eloquence to dissuade him from the step. In March 1845 he wrote to her a very long letter and repeated what he had told her already: that he thought he should offend God by not moving.

> What in the world I am doing this for . . . except that I think I am called to do so? I am making a large income by my sermons. I am, to say the very least, risking this; the chance is that my sermons will have no further sale at all. I have a good name with many; I am deliberately sacrificing it. I have a bad name with more. I am fulfilling all their worst wishes, and giving them their most coveted triumph. I am distressing all I love, unsettling all I have instructed or aided. I am going to those whom I do not know, and of whom I expect very little. I am making myself an outcast, and that at my age. Oh, what can it be but a stern necessity which causes this? . . . Suppose I were dying . . . I think I should directly send for a priest. Is this not a test of one's state of mind? Ought I to live where I could not bear to die? Again, I assure you it makes me quite uncomfortable travelling. . . . Is this a right frame of mind to be in? . . . What is the difference between me and a poor profligate? We both feel we have a work to do which is undone.

And he told her that in spite of this misery he never thought: Oh, that I had never begun to read theology; oh, that I had never

written the Tracts! He exhorted her humbly to take comfort in
the thought that so many persons were praying for him. Even
if he had done some irreparable thing that he could not remember, might he not trust that those earnest prayers would be
heard? He himself prayed continually to discover the delusion
if he were deluded at all. And then, the thought came to him
how many people before him had been in his case. It had often
happened that heretics or schismatics saw their state and had to
go through the same trials. "Have Jews never had to turn
Christians, and been cursed by their friends for doing so? Can I
shock people so much as they did? Is the Church of Rome, can
it be, regarded more fearfully than Jews regard Christianity,
than Jews regarded Saint Paul? Was he not the prince of
apostates?" It says in the Bible that Christians must quit
friends and relations, houses and goods, for Christ's sake.

> So, my dear Jemima, if you can suggest any warnings to me
> which I am not considering, well, and thank you; else do take
> comfort, and think that perhaps you have a right to have faith in
> me, perhaps you have a right to believe that He who has led me
> hitherto will not suffer me to go wrong. . . . His ways are not our
> ways, nor His thoughts as our thoughts. He may have purposes
> as merciful as they are beyond us. Let us do our best, and leave
> the event to Him. He will give us strength to bear. Surely I have
> to bear most; and if I do not shrink from bearing it others must
> not shrink. . . . May we not trust it will turn for the best?[133]

Two months later the fear of a delusion had not yet altogether
disappeared. "How can I be sure I have not committed sins
which bring this unsettled state of mind on me as a judgment?"
he wrote to Henry Wilberforce in April 1845.[134] But certitude
was very near, and he could write a few weeks later: "Certainly
I am not, except at times, in the state of distress I was in last
Autumn. My mind is a great deal more made up."[135] And after
one more month he seemed to have lost any fear: "It seems to
be want of faith to think that I am not being guided. . . . I trust
I am not deceiving myself when I say this is not the case."[136]
He knew that he knew with real and certain knowledge that

God had entrusted the Church of Rome with the revelation, and that no error had defiled it. He knew without a shade of doubt what God wished him to do.[137] As an everlasting memorial of God's mercy in giving him light and peace, he left his book unfinished and wrote as his conclusion:

> Such were the thoughts concerning the "Blessed Vision of Peace", of one whose long-continued petition had been that the Most Merciful would not despise the work of His own Hands, nor leave him to himself;—while yet his eyes were dim, and his breast laden, and he could but employ Reason in the things of Faith. And now, dear Reader, time is short, eternity is long. Put not from you what you have here found; regard it not as mere matter of present controversy; set not out resolved to refute it, and looking about for the best way of doing so; seduce not yourself with the imagination that it comes of disappointment, or disgust, or restlessness, or wounded feeling, or undue sensibility, or other weakness. Wrap not yourself round in the associations of years past, nor determine that to be truth which you wish to be so, nor make an idol of cherished anticipations. Time is short, eternity is long.[138]

A year before, Newman had made the acquaintance of a simple Italian priest who from his youth had heard a call to work for the conversion of England. The meeting had been very short, but the impression had been indelible. "When his form came within sight," Newman wrote in his ninetieth year, "I was moved to the depths in the strangest way."[139] Father Dominic, a Passionist, was to Newman "holiness embodied in personal form"[140] and fulfilled the ideal Newman had written about when he said of Catholics: "If they want to convert England, let them go barefooted into our manufacturing towns, let them preach to the people, like Saint Francis Xavier, let them be pelted and trampled on, and I will own that they can do what we cannot; I will confess that they are our betters far. . . . This is to be Catholics; this is to secure a triumph."[141]

A short time before, Father Dominic had received into the Church Newman's friend Dalgairns, who belonged to his Littlemore community. Dalgairns now asked Newman's leave to invite the Passionist on his way from England to Belgium. Newman saw in this an intimation from heaven: "What thou art going to do, do it now."[142]

On October the 8th Father Dominic was to arrive. When Dalgairns went to Oxford to meet his guest, Newman whispered to him: "When you see your friend, will you tell him that I wish him to receive me into the Church of Christ?"

It took a long time for Dalgairns to return. Meanwhile Newman wrote letters—many letters—which informed his friends in a few words of the step he was about to take.

At ten o'clock in the evening the coach that brought Father Dominic stopped at "The Angel" in Oxford. When he got off, soaked to the skin from sitting outside in incessant rain for five long hours, Dalgairns delivered Newman's message and the priest exclaimed with all his heart: "God be praised", forgetting the rain that had poured upon him.

After arriving at Littlemore, Dalgairns took him to a room where he tried in vain to dry his sodden habit near a fire. Then a knock at the door. It was Newman gliding in. He knelt down at the Passionist's feet, asked his blessing and begged him to receive him into the Church. On the Sunday before he had prepared himself, staying in all day. And now, in a general confession, he revealed all the sins he could think of, from his earliest childhood when he used to think himself an angel and life a dream, up to the last years at Littlemore. It was a long, moving story, and when he had finished Father Dominic in compassion suggested that the remaining and most important part of the admission might be well deferred till the following day.

In the evening of October 9, 1845, the historic event was completed. Newman and two young friends made the profession of faith. Then Father Dominic gave them absolution and baptized them *sub conditione*. Father Dominic was almost beside himself with joy.[143] He was amazed at Newman's intense fervor and piety. Dalgairns, who of course was present at the ceremonies, felt extremely impressed and wrote: "I have had no notion how firmly and entirely the Catholic faith was one with every power of his mind. I had been sometimes foolish enough to think that it was more so intellectually than in feeling and in heart; but I now see that the painfulness of his sacrifice consisted entirely in his love for his friends, which is unbounded."[144]

From that moment Newman possessed "perfect peace and contentment". He never had any further doubt or any anxiety of heart whatever. Although he did not experience more fervor, or any change, intellectual or moral, he felt as if he had come into port after a rough sea, and his happiness on this score remained for ever without interruption.[145]

CHAPTER SEVEN

A Saint Enters His Life

1845–1851

Philip, my glorious Advocate, who didst ever follow the precepts and example of the Apostle St. Paul in rejoicing always in all things, gain for me the grace of perfect resignation to God's will, of indifference to matters of this world, and a constant sight of heaven.[1]

Though Newman now lived "in the region of light, in the home of peace, in the presence of Saints"[2] and though day by day he seemed to gain a nearer approach to God,[3] yet after his reception into the Church, he did not experience a joyful enthusiasm. He felt exhausted,[4] which made joy impossible. The immense strain involved in writing his book, the stress of anxieties and uncertainty, the gradual separation from everything and everybody dear to him, had drained away his bodily and spiritual forces. He suffered too from the realization of the shock he had given to his Anglican friends. Keble had written to him about "so many broken hearts and bewildered spirits" and had blamed himself as if he were answerable for the "distress and scandal".[5] Pusey had poured out his heart in a public letter to an imaginary friend, complaining about the "intensest loss we could have had".[6] His veneration and love for Newman remained, but he gave up his walks to Littlemore. Other friends followed Pusey's example and with a few exceptions kept aloof and called no more.[7] Harriett reflected with pain on the man he had been and on what he was now, and the merest mention of him or his talents caused her profound grief.[8]

But Newman's own inner happiness may be guessed from what he wrote some years later: "While yet in the Anglican church, I recollect well what an outcast I seemed to myself, when I took down from the shelves of my library the volumes of Saint Athanasius or Saint Basil, and set myself to study them; and how, on the contrary, when at length I was brought into Catholic communion, I kissed them with delight, with a feeling that in them I had more than all that I had lost; and, as though I were directly addressing the glorious saints, who bequeathed them to the Church, how I said to the inanimate pages, 'You are now mine, and I am now yours, beyond any mistake.' "[9]

This was not the only joy he felt since his reception. When he entered a church he found there "a Treasure Unutterable, the Presence of the Eternal Word Incarnate, the Wisdom of the Father who, even when He had done His work, would not leave us". As never before he rejoiced that he was in the communion of saints; that he was allowed to address them and ask for their intercession; and above all that he was under the protection of the glorious Mother of God. He felt himself surrounded by God's light and love, the sacraments, the priest's benediction, the crucifix and the rosary, indulgences and the "whole armor of God". And he knew too that when he died he would not be forgotten. He would be sent out of the world with the holy unction upon him and be followed with Masses and prayers. He felt surrounded by a heavenly atmosphere. What could he desire more than this?[10]

After resting a few weeks at Littlemore, he visited the centers of Catholicism in England. In the meantime the question came up again and again: What was he to be? Where could he go? It would be almost impossible to remain at Littlemore, in the midst of those whose perplexity he could not possibly relieve, far from Saint Clement's little church where Mass, a support he badly needed, was said only twice a week. There was too the financial sacrifice concerned with moving. He had not only lost the stipend from Saint Mary's but also the income from his fellowship. What was the best thing to do and what was God's will?[11]

It was his bishop, Dr. Wiseman, who found the solution to these problems. The Bishop had followed the Oxford Movement from its beginning with the greatest possible interest. For many years he had prayed and asked for prayers to see Newman's transition to the Catholic Church. It had been a great joy to him when Newman had surrendered. Three weeks after that memorable day, he himself had confirmed him and expressed his conviction that the Church had never received a convert who had joined her in more docility and simplicity of faith.[12] Now he offered him the buildings of Old Oscott College, which had been a major seminary. The several friends who had followed or were to follow Newman into the Church could receive a Catholic education there and be prepared for the priesthood if they so wished. In this way the community of Littlemore might be kept together.[13] After making a novena, Newman and his friends decided to accept Wiseman's offer.[14]

As the day for leaving Littlemore approached, Newman was seized by sorrow and heartbreak. The words "Forget thy people and the house of thy father" kept ringing in his ears. On February 21, 1846, his forty-fifth birthday, he was by himself in the house.[15] God's presence alone comforted him in this great trial. He could not refrain from kissing his bed, the mantelpiece and other parts of the house. In spite of doubt and suspense, anxiety for his friends and relatives, he had been happy at Littlemore. It was perhaps the only place he had ever lived in, he said, which he could look back on without a bad conscience. Here he had been taught his way and had received an answer to his prayers.[16] And now he was to leave it for ever.

But at Old Oscott (from that time onward called Maryvale), he found a treasure which made up for all that he had lost, "the surpassing privilege" of having Christ under the very roof of the house he was to live in. He felt the inexpressible comfort of being with Him Who cured the sick and taught His disciples.

The idea of the Anglican churches without this Divine Presence seemed to him unspeakably cold. Going back would be turning away from heaven itself.[17]

With five young friends he started life at Maryvale according to a rule approved of by Wiseman, which was little different from the way of life at Littlemore. It was not precisely a monastic rule, although several monastic customs were introduced, for example, the confession of faults, the official visit to the Blessed Sacrament, the characteristic prayer before study: "Deliver us, save us, enliven us, O Blessed Trinity", and the equally characteristic one when they began silence: "Holy, holy, holy, Lord God almighty. May the whole earth be silent before His face."[18] The Bishop had sent the converts a priest who said Mass for them and instructed them as children were insructed in the catechism.[19] Now and again the Bishop himself came and brought visitors, and then Newman felt as though he were "some wild incomprehensible beast, caught by the hunter" and now shown to the hunter's friends.[20]

Without any complaint he submitted to everything, even to the strange ways, habits and religious observances that did not appeal to him.[21] He had expressed his wish for a regular Catholic education not only with regard to Catholic theology but concerning the spiritual life as well. In September 1846, on the advice of Bishop Wiseman, he went to Rome for this purpose.

Long before his departure the idea of becoming an Oratorian had crossed his mind. As an Anglican he had known and admired the founder of the Congregation of the Oratory, Saint Philip Neri.[22] Wiseman hoped that he might introduce the Oratorian life into England.[23] But Newman in his prudence considered other possibilities and gave thought to the Lazarists and Jesuits, the Capuchins and the Redemptorists and above all to the Dominicans. For the Dominicans had been the great champions against heresies, and such an order was needed in England. He knew he possessed the necessary qualities, but he decided to wait for Rome's advice.[24]

One of his young friends, Ambrose St. John, was to be his companion in Rome. Newman had always felt a special liking for him, and the arrangement proved a great comfort when the time came for him to leave his community at Maryvale. "It is melancholy work, this leaving", he wrote. "Every one sad and out of spirits—myself included—yet hardly daring to seem otherwise myself, lest I should seem glad at going, and sadden others more."[25]

He never enjoyed travelling, but he endured the discomforts of the journey as cheerfully as possible and felt supported by many consolations. On the continent he rejoiced to see the open churches and the Blessed Sacrament on the altar.[26] Milan especially touched him on account of its numerous associations. He knelt before the relics of Saint Ambrose, of whom he had heard as a boy and whose works he knew more about than about those of any other saint. It was now thirty years since God had made him mindful of religion, and Saint Ambrose was "one of the first objects of his veneration". He thought too of Saint Augustine, who was converted there, and of the great Saint Athanasius, who came there to meet the Emperor, in his exile. Saint Charles Borromeo, too, made a deep impression on him: "My mind has been full of him," he wrote to a convert, "so that I even dreamed of him, and we go most days and kneel at his shrine, not forgetting Maryvale when there."[27]

In Rome the two converts were lodged at the Propaganda building, the major seminary for future missionaries. They attended lectures with young men from all missionary countries of the world. But they were not treated like students; on the contrary, "like wax dolls or mantelpiece ornaments".[28] Rector, professors, students looked up to Newman and his companion with the greatest respect. As he wrote to Henry Wilberforce, he thought it wonderful to find himself there: it was a kind of dream, so quiet, so safe, so happy. It was as though he had always been there, as though there had been no violent rupture in his life. "I was happy at Oriel, happier at

Littlemore, as happy or happier still at Maryvale, and happiest here." He thought it a blessing that he should ever be thinking the state of life in which he happened to be, the happiest of all.[29]

All this he wrote a few days after a singularly unpleasant experience. He had received only minor orders, was not yet a subdeacon, but nevertheless had been practically forced to preach at the funeral of an Englishwoman, and this on a particular subject: the irreverence shown by English Protestants in Italian churches. The English Catholics had brought their Protestant friends to the funeral, and when they listened to his reproaches they were disgusted. The incident caused a great deal of talk, which tried him very much, especially because an English prelate spread abroad the word that the Pope himself had not only spoken unfavorably about the sermon but that it had caused him pain.[30]

This was only one of his trials. He was tried by the climate, the cold, the heavy and insidious atmosphere, the alternation of whirling dust and ankle-deep mud, the water pipes emptying their contents upon his head, and the damp, which caused rheumatic pains down his side.[31] Worse still, he noticed that the Roman theologians suspected him. It was possible that the French translation of his *University Sermons* might be brought before the Index. Dr. Grant of the Scots College spoke against his *Essay on Development* and expected a condemnation of its principles. Newman felt that his talents had not received the justice due to them. He regretted that philosophers and theologians did not take the trouble to deepen their views. But he consoled himself with the thought: "I must leave all this to Him who knows what to do with me. . . . He who gives gifts, is the best judge how to use His own. He has the sole right to do as He will, and He knows what He is doing. . . ."[32] And to Mrs. Bowden he wrote: "If Providence means to use me He will, and if He wills to put me aside, it is with Him." So he was content to let things take their course. He could not believe that he had been brought to where he was for nothing. But God's ways are mysterious. "He uses one man for one purpose, another for another. He breaks His instruments when He will. He may intend to have done with me."[33]

During the first months of his stay in Rome he visited a saintly Russian Abbess, who had suffered by being injured, flogged and burned, in order to ask for her prayers for himself and for his vocation. The Pope had called her a living martyr and many people confided in her, for she had gained wonderful answers to her prayers for them. She advised Newman to be very careful in making up his mind and to be prompt in acting directly he had done so.[34]

He continued his investigations concerning the various congregations and orders, and in January 1847, after some time spent at the Oratory in Rome, he began to think definitely of becoming an Oratorian and introducing the Oratory into England. He was well aware that his own tastes and those of his friends differed greatly, and that the Oratory allowed greater scope for these differences than other institutions. It appeared to him to be especially suited to Oxford and Cambridge men,[35] because it resembled to some extent an Oxford College. In general, every Oratory has a good library and a handsome set of rooms. Each Oratorian keeps his own property and has his own furniture. Now, Newman was very averse to the notion of giving up his own property. He would never be able to do it, he wrote, unless he had a clear call to do so. His originality of mind and his special talents could only be shown to their full advantage in his own surroundings, and he wisely wished to continue to be his former self.[36] So after fervent prayers to find out whether or not he had a vocation to the Oratory and under advice of his confessor he decided in the affirmative.[37]

He then began a thorough study of the Oratorian Rule and observed that there was a permanent part, which could easily be followed in the nineteenth century provided some slight changes were introduced. What remained was but a collection of recommendations, to be printed separately and eventually to be followed or not, at the discretion of the English Oratorians.[38] The Oratory is not a religious order or congregation in the strict sense of the word. There are no vows or severe monastic practices. The rules do not bind under sin. Every house is independent, but there is community life in a union of wills and minds and opinions and conduct. The bond among the Oratorians is love, based on humility and detachment. Humility is to be shown by the subjection of the intellect and the will, that is, in obedience, and detachment is to be acquired through an unworldly life. In this way the Oratorians imitate the religious in perfection. And perfection, according to Newman, is the power or faculty of doing our duty exactly, naturally and completely, whatever it is, in opposition to a performance which is partial, slovenly, awkward, clumsy and with effort. It does not consist in any especially heroic deeds; it does not demand any fervor of devotion, but it implies regularity, precision, facility and perseverance in a given sphere of duties. He is perfect who performs the duties of the day perfectly. Historically, the Fathers of the Oratory were gentlemen and possessed the culture which learning gives, the accomplishments of literature, the fine arts and similar studies. Newman realized, however, that Oratorians could not teach theology, classics or philosophy. Following Saint Philip they would work for souls by laboring for the conversion of great towns, yet with time for literary activities. These were his conclusions from his investigations.

Newman's ideas and plans were duly written down and taken to the Secretary of Propaganda and later on to the Pope, who was delighted and suggested that he summon as many of his friends from Maryvale as possible in order to pass a sort of Oratorian novitiate in Rome.[39]

Before the plans were carried out, Newman and Ambrose St. John were ordained priests on May 30, 1847. Newman seems to have been deeply impressed. But he did not write a great deal about it as he had been accustomed to do concerning other important events of his life. In the foregoing December he had expressed his satisfaction that he had heard nothing of ordination because there was still much to read and to think about. Four weeks later he wrote: "The responsibility of orders grows greater and greater upon me, as I approach them."[40] In one of his retreats he had written: "I am much afraid of the priesthood." He regretted that his devotion was so cool; he could only creep or walk in the spiritual life; he could not fly. He felt oppressed by a certain mediocrity. The old desire for a quiet, carefree life was growing. He liked his own way; he hated change; the least things sometimes troubled him. Of course, he did not long for wealth, influence or fame, but on the other hand he realized that he was averse to poverty, difficulties, anxieties and discomfort. He was afraid of losing his health. He grieved because he had lost the energy, vitality and versatility of youth. Though wishing to lead a stricter life, he was now troubled by the multitude of devotions. The exercises he had loved at Littlemore had become stale. He complained of his loss of trust in God's love, of resignation to God's Providence and of confidence in the power of prayer. True, he referred everything to God's will, but he doubted his own motives. Nevertheless he could say wholeheartedly, "My God and my All", and these words were always on his lips. Neither had he lost his intimate sense of God's presence, nor his good conscience, nor the consequent serenity of soul.[41]

Two years later he himself gave the explanation of all this, though not referring to himself, when he preached: "It is indeed most true that the holier a man is, and the higher in the kingdom of heaven, so much the greater need has he to look carefully to his footing, lest he stumble and be lost; and a deep conviction of this necessity has been the sole preservation of the Saints. Had they not feared, they never would have persevered. Hence, like St. Paul, they are always full of their sin and their peril. You would think them the most polluted of sinners, and the most unstable of penitents."[42]

In this humble mood he received the sacrament of Holy Orders. He had prepared himself by intense prayer. Every morning before the great day he was in chapel as early as three

o'clock, for two hours, alone.[43] The privilege of being allowed to consecrate bread and wine into the Body and Blood
of Christ made a deep impression on him: "To me is nothing
so consoling, so piercing, so thrilling, so overcoming, as the
Mass. . . . It is not a mere form of words, it is a great action,
the greatest action that can be on earth. It is, not the invocation
merely, but, if I dare use the word, the evocation of the
Eternal. He becomes present on the altar in flesh and blood,
before whom angels bow and devils tremble."[44] He seems to
have been in the habit of thinking of Our Lady as present at the
celebration of the Mass while he prayed: "O Holy Mother,
stand by me now at Mass time, when Christ comes to me, as
though didst minister to thy infant Lord—as thou didst hang
upon His words when He grew up, as thou wast found under
His cross. Stand by me, Holy Mother, that I may gain somewhat of thy purity, thy innocence, thy faith, and He may be
the one object of my love and my adoration, as He was of
thine."[45]

He realized that as a priest he had to do his utmost to become
a saint. It was a very difficult task and nothing but humble
confidence in God's grace could bring it about. It seemed to
him that he had to climb a high ladder which swayed to and
fro. He was afraid, but he would not give up because God had
promised the necessary grace.[46]

On the other hand, a deep joy must have possessed him.
When he put on his priestly vestments before Mass and kissed
the cross of the maniple saying: "Let me deserve, o Lord, to
wear the maniple of tears and sorrow", he used to ask himself:
"Where is the sorrow? Where are the tears?" and then he
added: "I suppose it will come."[47] And indeed, it was not long
in coming.

After some weeks Newman and Ambrose St. John left
Propaganda. "The College has lost two most beautiful examples
of virtue", the Rector wrote in the official diary.[48] They went
to Santa Croce, and with five more friends from Maryvale
they began the novitiate under the direction of the Oratorian

Father Rossi. It was a probationary period of only a few months, but it was a dull, gloomy time. "How dreary (after the many happy months, thank God, at Propaganda) how dreary Father Rossi and Santa Croce", he wrote in later years, though without giving any particulars.[49]

When Newman and his friends had been shaped into a homogeneous group and sufficiently trained to establish the Oratorian life in England, the Pope presented them with a carefully prepared brief, describing their tasks, sending them to the larger towns and especially to people of the higher and more educated classes and appointing Newman as the Superior.[50] At the end of 1847 he arrived in England.

The Feast of the Purification had always been a great day for him. It reminded him of Oriel, because on that day, centuries earlier, the College had been established. It was also the day commemorating Our Lady's great sacrifice and surrender. So he rejoiced in inaugurating the English Oratory at Maryvale on February 2, 1848.[51]

And now Frederick William Faber entered Newman's life.

He was a remarkable character: spontaneous, impulsive, sensitive, intensely religious, even, in a manner, heroic. As the Curé d'Ars had done, he had transformed an irreligious village into a deeply pious community. Later he became a Catholic and, with a group of his young converts, had established a certain kind of monastic life. He called himself "Brother Wilfrid" and his followers "Wilfridians". As soon as Newman returned from Rome, Faber asked for the Oratorian habit for himself and his companions. Simply and absolutely, he offered his house, his money, his all.[52]

Although Newman felt grateful to God for such a generous offer, he realized at once that the undertaking might be fraught with difficulties. He wondered whether Faber had fully mastered the Oratorian idea. Faber was a poet. Oratorianism was not poetical. Faber was a man of emotional devotion. Oratorianism had no liking for emotionalism. There was also the question of how his companions would react to the Oratorian life. Faber, however, full of generosity, had written: "You should consider us as giving ourselves over to you in the spirit of surrender. . . . Make what you can of us in the way you think best."[53]

So two weeks after he had started the Oratory at Maryvale, Newman admitted the Wilfridians as novices and after a few weeks appointed Faber as novice master.[54]

While we may admire Faber's magnanimity, we should not overlook the considerable difficulties with which Newman was burdened by the steps he had taken. One problem which took several years to solve was concerned with the fact that the Wilfridians lived at Cheadle in a large house, called Saint Wilfrid's. It seemed advisable that the Maryvale community should join the Wilfridians there, but after nine years of continuous moving, from Oriel to Littlemore, from Littlemore to Maryvale, from Maryvale to Rome, and back again, Newman longed for permanence and peace. The papal brief had ordered him to work in the large towns, but Cheadle was not a town.[55] On the other hand, Lord Shrewsbury, the wealthy benefactor of the Wilfridians, hoped they would remain in the place because of the beneficial influence of the community on the local surroundings. Faber, who converted "almost by touching", had made hundreds of converts. For him to leave would savor of ingratitude to Shrewsbury, who had shown such deep interest and spent a great deal of money on the house and the community. Yet the fact remained that an Oratory proper could thrive only in a town.[56] It was obviously impracticable to retain both houses, and eventually Newman decided to relinquish Maryvale and move to Cheadle until such time as he could see his way to realize the Pope's wishes.

It was far from easy to mold so many different characters into one community. Before the move to Cheadle, the Maryvale group bore one another's burdens in a spirit of fraternal love, freely offering their services at all times. As far as was possible, they endeavored to conceal one another's imperfections and mistakes, dwelling rather on the finer points of character.[57] But at Cheadle things were different. The Wilfridians, following Faber's emotional type of devotion, more reminiscent of Italy and France than of England, caused considerable irritation to the Maryvale community.[58] There were complaints of incompatibility of temperament and differences of opinion as to the time and place of meditation. Some found it impossible to meditate when it was cold, others desired greater privacy. One of Faber's followers wrote a questionable book on plainchant which Newman could not allow to be printed without risking the reputation of the young congregation. The writer was a man of difficult character, and Newman instructed Faber to be severe with him and insist on his implicit obedience, even to the point of forbidding him to say Mass. It would be a comfort if the man left the Oratory, but Newman felt bound to do what he could to keep him.[59]

About this time Bishop Wiseman was moved to London and succeeded by Bishop Ullathorne. Newman, having no precise idea of the relationship between the Bishop and the Oratory, had written to Rome about it. Naturally he desired to be helpful and obedient: "Our most earnest desire is in all things to approve ourselves to your Lordship," he wrote to the new Bishop, "and to co-operate with you according to the duties of our vocation."[60] Bishop Ullathorne, however, did not at first understand Newman as Wiseman had done, and this became the cause of painful disagreement.

Before Faber took the Oratorian habit, he had begun a series of *Lives of the Saints* translated from the Italian and French. Although Newman did not altogether approve of the tone of the translations, he had encouraged Faber to continue with them. He was not alone in his objections. In a Catholic magazine, *The Lives* was attacked by a convert priest who accused Faber of sanctioning "gross, palpable idolatry" in his Life of Saint Rose.[61] Ullathorne too raised objections when Newman asked his advice and support.[62] He considered the translations offensive to Protestants, and he wished them to be rewritten in a more English idiom. He compared them with the *Lives of the Saints* published during the time of the Movement, which were appreciated both by Protestants and Catholics, and he advised the writing of original *Lives* in the manner of the Oxford authors. He not only refused support for the translations but advised stopping them.[63] Newman of course obeyed and told Faber of the Bishop's wishes.

Faber therefore published a circular to the effect that he had stopped the translations, and he included a letter from Newman to himself expressing the reason and containing the words, "No one can assail your name without striking at mine", for Newman considered himself the natural protector of the young English Oratory. Because of this he was pained when he realized that the Bishop had sent only a mild rebuke to the priest who had accused Faber of promoting idolatry. He had presumed that the Bishop would regret such an attack on one of his own priests and would realize that the reputation of the congregation had been injured by it. He acquainted the Bishop with his views frankly.[64]

But Ullathorne misunderstood Newman's meaning. He considered him too sensitive and even pugnacious. By means of a letter written in an anxious state of mind, he tried to explain to Newman his own difficult position, and he revealed his anxiety about what he called the "little of human nature fermenting in his sensitiveness". He found self-love and a delicate shade of intellectual pride in Newman's conduct. Only from faith in Newman's humility did he venture to speak thus.[65]

Newman took no offense. It was clear that he and the Bishop were at cross-purposes, therefore he could afford to smile at his words.[66] Ullathorne misunderstood him as did many of the clergy. They regarded the converts with suspicion even to the extent of considering that they had been made too much of and needed a lesson in humility.[67] Some of the old Catholics even suspected them of heresy.[68] In London, Wiseman, who held totally different opinions, suffered attacks in print, by letter and by word of mouth, so that at times he felt almost heartbroken.[69] Criticism came from all sides. Why did they keep together? Why did they not go to Rome? Why did they not do something? What a short novitiate they had had. When did they study morals? Newman realized how detrimental all this might become, but he did not lose heart and said: "We must go our own way; we must look to the Fount of grace for blessing and for guidance."[70]

Blessing came. With all the publicity it became evident that Faber's *Lives of the Saints* was badly needed, and, as early as January 1849, the Oratorians were able to have a circular printed, announcing that the series was to be continued.[71]

Not long afterward Ullathorne's attitude regarding Newman changed altogether. It was a simple religious, Mother Margaret Hallahan, the Foundress of the Dominican Sisters in England, who cleared away all doubts and mistrust. She was a highly gifted woman, with spiritual discernment and intense Catholic instinct. She knew that the Bishop kept Newman at arms' length, mistrusted his submission to authority and was inclined to hinder his plans for pastoral work. But she realized too the beauty of Newman's generous spiritual life, his heroism and his honest wish to work only for God. She spoke to the Bishop and opened his eyes to these facts. Newman always remained grateful for her intervention. From that time onward the relationship between the two men grew warmer.[72] In later years Ullathorne often spoke about Newman's humility and tenderness of conscience in all that concerned obedience to his Bishop. The slightest intimation of his wishes made Newman comply in such a prompt manner that the Bishop had to be careful in expressing them.[73] On one occasion, when Newman had been slandered, the Bishop published this statement: "I know of no dignitary in the Catholic Church whom I consider more sound in orthodoxy, more solidly formed in ecclesiastical and christian virtues, or more deferential to Church authority than Newman. I love him as one of my dearest friends: I have often consulted his judgment, and admired his prudence: and I have nothing in my mind or my heart that I could have the slightest wish to conceal from his knowledge."[74] An act of humility on the part of Newman once drew from the Bishop's heart the cry: "There is a saint in that man. I felt annihilated in his presence."[75]

In the early difficulties and during all the following years, Newman asked for prayers. "We do indeed need many prayers, for no one ever began a good work without ten thousand oppositions and trials as the Lives of the Saints abundantly show." And it was especially Our Lady and Saint Philip whom he invoked most intensely.[76]

Since his stay in Rome Newman was full of devotion to Saint Philip. He had tried to imbibe his spirit by studying his life, by reading the Oratorian Annals and by visiting the Oratories of Rome and Naples. From that time he continually spoke of Saint Philip, mentioned him in his works and in his letters and said again and again that he trusted in "Our Lady and Saint Philip". Many answers to prayers he ascribed to the Saint's intercession. He had made up his mind to write his life and, with this intention in view, collected many notes. In trials he wished to follow Saint Philip's example. In troubles with his ecclesiastical superiors he consoled himself by considering that Philip, too, had been misunderstood by the authorities. In one of his writings he indulged in affectionate complaints about Saint Philip, who made it impossible for him to practice detachment. He called Saint Philip his father, "the Father of an unworthy son". Every year he celebrated the feast of the Saint with great solemnity: it was preceded by a novena, guests were invited and he made it a point to be at home and to preside.[77] He admired Saint Philip much more than younger saints like Saint Aloysius or Saint Francis Xavier, because he thought it much more difficult to be a saint in one's old age than in youth.[78] And when he saw the restlessness and unfaithfulness of some Oratorians he made up his mind never to be unfaithful to Saint Philip, even though he did not see how the Saint was going to help him.[79] His mistrust of self was encouraged by the example of Saint Philip, who prayed every day: "Lord, beware of me today lest I should betray Thee"; who complained in his last illness that he had promised so many times to change his life and had not kept his word that he despaired of himself; who used to shed many tears and to say: "I have never done any good action"; who, when somebody called him a saint, turned to her with a face full of anger and said: "Begone with you! I am a devil, and not a saint."[80] Saint Philip figures in many of Newman's verses, written on various occasions, and in his meditations and devotions. To him he addresses the humble words: "I have long dedicated myself to thee, but I have done nothing worthy of thee, and I am ashamed to call myself thine, because thou hadst a right to have followers of great innocence, great honesty of purpose, and great resolution, and these virtues I have not."[81]

It was only for a short time that the Oratorians lived at Cheadle. Bishop Ullathorne had expressed his wish that they should establish a house in one of the poorest districts of Birmingham. So in the early days of 1849, most of them left Saint Wilfrid's and started a so-called Mission at Alcester Street, a quarter "destitute of outward recommendations" but "overrun with religious error".[82] The people of these slums were selfish, obstinate, worldly, addicted to drink and self-indulgent. They neglected their children. They were fond of idle amusements.[83] "O my very dear sons", Newman said to them in their poor little church, "O my very dear sons, whom I love and whom I would fain serve—oh! that you could feel that you have souls! oh, that you would have mercy on your souls! oh, that before it is too late, you would betake yourselves to Him who is the Source of all that is truly high and magnificent and beautiful, all that is bright and pleasant, and secure what you ignorantly seek, in Him whom you so wilfully, so awfully despise!"[84]

At one time a friend of his had called him "the refined John Henry Newman". Now he gave himself with all his abilities and learning to the poorest of the poor, uncivilized, rude people of the slums. It was his love for souls that made him forget his natural disgust. He could not endure to see the blood of the Redeemer shed in vain, wasted, as he expressed himself. And he exclaimed: "O mighty God! O God of love! it is too much! it broke the heart of Thy sweet son Jesus to see the misery of man spread out before His eyes. He died by it as well as for it. And we, too, in our measure, our eyes ache, and our hearts sicken, and our heads reel, when we but feebly contemplate it."[85]

This anxiety about souls made it possible for him to leave the delightful house and surroundings of Cheadle and to exchange them for a dark street in a dark town. He would have preferred to work among the better classes, the intellectuals. This had been his line, and the Pope had ordered it. But Alcester Street "was simply the appointment of Providence", so he did not trouble his mind about it, as he wrote to Mrs. Bowden.[86]

At that time the English Catholics had hardly emerged from their catacombs. They were still timid and feared publicity. Their priests' main occupation had been to avoid notice. But the Oratorians, all of them converts, had the courage and the energy to make themselves seen and heard by the world. They threw open their church. They preached and lectured. They gave instructions to prospective converts. They heard confessions at all times. They held services for the children. And they encouraged music and singing in church. "They were as water in the desert to the poor, parched and withered in soul by the grey, unceasing struggle for existence."[87]

But Newman must have suffered from the discomfort he shared with these paupers. House, furniture and food showed the consequences of his poverty. He was deeply in debt. Once when he wished to go to London he could not, as he was literally penniless and there was no one to borrow from. He was not even able to buy necessary shoes and socks. He felt ashamed of how little he had given in charity. He was obliged to learn to play the organ for he could not afford an organist.[88] This poverty must have made his words more acceptable when he told his poor flock that their plight might be a blessing.

His friends, fellow Oratorians, who shared his poor life, lived "in the sunshine of his example", as one of them expressed it. Nevertheless, in spite of his love and gentleness, in spite of his pure motives, in spite of his prayers for light and strength, for wisdom and prudence—he was actually their Superior—he suffered from a difficulty which made contact between himself and some of his young subjects now and again very trying.[89] His habitual shyness and reserve caused him to appear stiff and cold. Thus Philip Gordon complained that Newman did not care for him. His brother, Joseph Gordon, thought Newman repulsed his affection. Anthony Hutchinson imagined him unfair. The community considered that he had an undue preference for Ambrose St. John, though he tried hard to love others as well.[90] Bernard Dalgairns felt as if he were cast away by him.[91] But Bernard himself had caused this breach by his own behavior. He was a man who never asked advice. He was arrogant and impertinent. He took young people into the house, kept them there for hours, allowed them to make a terrible noise and to regard any conduct as permissible. When Newman protested, he laughed and answered that the Oratorians had to sacrifice themselves for these half-converted boys.[92]

The great number of Oratorians and the impossibility of retaining the big house at Cheadle made Newman consider starting a second Oratory. At that time Bishop Wiseman was trying to attract all sorts of priests and religious to the metropolis, where souls were starving for want of spiritual aid. He would have loved to see the whole community come to London, but this would be against the wish of the Pope, who had placed Newman in Birmingham. The best solution was a division.[93] In January 1849 the community began a novena, for there was a major difficulty involved in the question of the division. Faber preferred to remain with Newman in Birmingham, while Newman considered him the providen-

tially intended Superior of the London house. The former
Wilfridians had no wish to leave Faber or Newman. Several
other Oratorians had joined the Oratory to be guided and
supported by Newman's presence; therefore they too disliked
the thought of living far from him.[94] Newman himself was in
a dilemma about his own place. Many things drew him to
London, many other things kept him in Birmingham. If only
he could know God's will![95] He prayed for light and said
Masses for this intention. He asked for the frank opinions of
his fellow Oratorians. And on Low Sunday 1849 he made the
final decision. His main principle had been to divide the
community according to which members were likely to live in
accord with one another. When he sent the adopted plan to
Cheadle he concluded his letter with the characteristic words:
"Give my best love to all and every one—and tell them, that,
as they all have brought the matter before God for so long a
time, with such a desire to know, and resolution to follow His
will, whatever it might be, so they now ought to rejoice and
give thanks for what we may all trust is His decision."[96]

Very touching letters of thanks were sent in answer. Newman, they said, had thought of everybody's wishes and not
consulted his own desires. His sole object had been to establish
a really good Oratory in London.[97] Faber went there on
Newman's behalf to prepare things, and in May 1849 the King
William Street Oratory was opened.

Newman governed the House by means of letters sent from
Birmingham, but very soon he appointed Faber as Rector. In
greater and smaller things Faber asked Newman's advice and
consulted him about the difficulties. Cheerfully Newman let
Faber know what to say and how to act. He wanted him to use
kind words to all, but to go forward and not become involved
unduly through his love of talking. He warned him against his
love of publicity. These things—talking much and love of
publicity—were well meant but might get him into trouble.
Moreover, Protestants might interfere with his extravagant
show of Catholicism.[98] But in spite of all difficulties and

troubles, he could write to a friend: "Almighty God is, I trust, leading us all separately not in our own way, but in His way, to His glory—and it matters not whether we see one another here or not, so that He is with us, and brings us one and all about His Throne in His Kingdom. . . . We have been abundantly blessed since we have been here, and ought to be very grateful to Our Lady and St. Philip."[99]

In September 1849 cholera raged at Bilston, not far from Birmingham. When its two priests were no longer able to assist the sick and dying, Bishop Ullathorne asked Newman for two Fathers. Without any hesitation Newman himself went at once, accompanied by Father Ambrose.[100] When Newman's parishioners heard about it, all of them began to pray for their safe return. Newman visited the sick at the hospital; it was a terrible sight, and it impressed him deeply. But no sooner had he arrived than the danger appeared to be over. The epidemic made no further progress. The Alcester Street Catholics considered this event a most merciful intervention of God's Providence. Newman and his companion returned much sooner than they could have hoped.[101]

At the end of 1849 the London Oratory proved such a success that Newman ordered a joint triduum of thanksgiving. But Alcester Street too was blessed. What first was a spiritual desert had become a flourishing "mission". Newman only doubted if he were thankful enough. And in the background of it all hovered the cheerful, quiet figure of Saint Philip, to whose fatherly care Newman ascribed the abundant success. More than once he recounts remarkable answers to prayers after the application of the Saint's relic. A young Catholic was suddenly cured from dropsy in very striking circumstances. About the same time two young women and a child were raised from near death in the presence of the relics.[102] In his great financial difficulties, too, he prayed for Saint Philip's intervention. In July 1849 he wrote to his London Oratorians, "All we want St. Philip to do for us, is to get us a little money". The house at Cheadle was a heavy burden. He could neither get rid of it nor make it pay. When he considered measures to change it into a school, he received "a knock on the knuckles" from Rome. In these circumstances he saw no light except his trust in Saint Philip. He continually repeated the Saint's words: "Never fear. Don't be afraid."[103] His confidence was not in vain. In a year all difficulties had disappeared. Before the end of February 1850, he had received donations for the Oratory to the amount of 9000 pounds. He could look out for a new site on which he could build a proper Oratory according to the Rule and resign the Alcester Street "mission" into the hands of the Bishop.[104] In the same year he sold the Cheadle house to the Passionists.[105]

Amidst the numerous and difficult tasks of the three past years Newman never lost sight of the church he had left and the Tractarians who hesitated to follow him. His correspondence with converts and future converts was extensive. In order to help those hesitating friends he gave a series of lectures at the London Oratory on the problems connected with Anglicanism. They proved such a success as to bring him from Rome the title of Doctor of Divinity,[106] an honor about which he seldom spoke, no more than about the rumor of his being made a bishop. "No one can seriously wish it, who is loyal to Saint Philip," he wrote to Faber, "and there are no lengths to which I would not go to prevent it."[107]

This was the year when in England the hierarchy was restored, a year of troubles and riots, full of fanaticism directed against the Catholics. Newman could not tell what would be the end of it all. An old friend of his spoke in public about kicking the Catholics out of the country.[108] Newman did not feel sure that the Oratorians would be allowed to stay; so he made plans in case his congregation were banished.[109] He admitted that he did not feel a hero. "I confess I have no love of suffering at all; nor am I at a time of life when a man commonly loves to risk it. To be quiet and to be undisturbed, to be at peace with all, to live in the sight of my Brethren, to meditate on the future, and to die—such is the prospect, which is rather suitable to such as me."[110]

In the meanwhile lands were bought, plans made and a new building erected at Hagley Road, Edgebaston, Birmingham. In February 1852 Newman was able to live in the new house, and by April 15th all the Oratorians had left Alcester Street. Full of gratitude he recorded: "For myself, when I look back eight or nine years, and bring before my memory the changes that then took place in my life, how little could I fancy that in the course of so short a time I should find myself in a house like this, so truly a home in every sense of the word, spiritual and temporal. How little had I reason to expect, except that the word of promise was sure, that by giving up I should so soon receive back, and by losing I should gain!"[111]

From that time he aimed at enforcing the strict observance of the Rule, which had been in some respects impossible owing to the unsettled circumstances. So it was that he could finish his chapter discourse on the new house with its large rooms and spacious corridors thus: "As Philip has given you a good house, do all of you your best to provide it with good tenants, and to adorn it with a visible attractiveness and a moral beauty."[112]

CHAPTER EIGHT

ACCUMULATING TRIALS

1851–1858

> Don't forget to pray for me. We all must have trials in this
> life—they are for our good, or rather they are simply
> necessary for us. I have had accumulating trials for several
> years, and I expect that they will increase rather than diminish.
> But on the other hand, so great and many mercies, that the
> troubles are as nothing by the side of them.[1]

These words, which Newman wrote in 1858 to one of his
spiritual children, may be considered a summary of the seven
years which followed the events described in the foregoing
chapter. They were years full of trials and disappointments but
also of great blessings.

The fanatic outbursts against Catholicism at the restoration
of the English hierarchy in 1850 had subsided a little when an
apostate priest from Italy, Giacinto Achilli, started a course of
lectures on "Rome and her Perversity". He posed as a victim
of the Inquisition and told the most atrocious stories about the
cruelty of the Roman authorities. Wiseman, who had been
made a Cardinal, endeavored to counteract Achilli's harmful
influence by writing an article about him in the *Dublin Review*,
recounting the crimes which had caused him to be exiled from
Italy. He not only gave the sources of his information but also
place names and dates. Because this article was published in an
Irish review, however, it was not read by the English, who
continued to attend the lectures.

At that time Newman himself was lecturing in Birmingham
on the position of Catholics in England, teaching Catholic

laymen how they could best master their situation and perform their duties in a Protestant country.[2] After taking counsel and praying for light to know God's will in this delicate matter,[3] he enumerated Achilli's crimes in one of these lectures, in the hope of putting an end to the pernicious influence of the apostate priest. As Wiseman had done, he gave dates, places and aggravating circumstances.[4]

Contrary to his expectations, Achilli brought an action for libel, and in November 1851 the case came up for hearing. This caused Newman considerable difficulty. He had both spoken and preached about suffering for the truth, and now he himself would have to bear unimaginable troubles and anxieties. He knew beforehand that the cross would be severe. But on the other hand, he did not underrate the spiritual blessings hidden in it. For months he prayed, looking forward to it, in he words of Saint Andrew: *O bona Crux, diu desiderata*. Whatever he had written about coldness in his spiritual life, this prayer shows how intensely his will was determined to make progress. "I am perfectly clear, that, if trouble is to come on me, it is for some greater good in a higher order. May I continue to be prepared for anything."[5] It had occurred to him that he might even go to prison. And he had wished: "May I come out a Saint."[6]

To be acquitted, Newman would have to prove that the accusations he had made in his lecture were true. The proofs were in the possession of Cardinal Wiseman, who could not find the relevant documents. Two Oratorians went to Naples to ask for the proofs, but the police refused to give them.[7] As Achilli had sworn that each fact stated by Newman was false, Newman had to get oaths of refutation, and this on the part of those who knew as much about this case as Achilli did. There was still another way out, namely a compromise. He prayed and asked for prayers. "What is going on is an attempt at a Compromise", he wrote to a religious friend. "The need . . . for a triduum, is that we all may have strength to bear God's blessed will. Tomorrow we begin a novena to the Holy Ghost for that object. Your good Mother may if she will . . . *add* the intention of my deliverance from the snare of the hunter, but let the main intention be, that we,—that I, may have fortitude, patience, peace, to bear His sweet will withal." Thinking of Christ Who "bore the judgment seat and the prison of the unbeliever", he offered himself as a sacrifice to Him.[8]

But the compromise was refused. Therefore, in order to avoid a scandalous conviction, he was forced to find witnesses in Italy, Achilli's victims, mostly young women, and persuade them to come to England. An almost superhuman task in those times! He held a novena to Saint Anthony for the discovery of evidence; another to Saints Peter and Paul that the Church might gain advantage by the trial; a third one to Saint Philip that the Congregation might gain by the matter. And he prayed, thinking again of the possibility that he might be imprisoned: "May it be accepted for my sins."[9] To the London Oratorians he wrote: "A load of prayers are discharged daily and if they don't do something, it is strange. It is strange if our Lady and Saint Philip do nothing—but, I am most thankful to say . . . I have not had any interruption to the simple feeling, that I am in God's hands, who knows what He is about, and that everything will be well, and that I shall be borne thro' everything—I cannot at all divine the event, but that it will be good in some way or other, I am *sure*."[10] On the last day of the novena to Saint Anthony, he could gratefully write to the Sisters: "Your prayers and those of other good friends are telling. It is but a beginning, still it gives hope. We have prevailed on one woman to come—unless she changes her mind. How necessary then is prayer! Prayer alone can do anything— it is like the uplifting of Moses' hands in the battle."[11]

Among the good friends who were willing to go to Italy for witnesses was Maria Giberne. She had been a friend of the Newman family since Mary's sudden death and had become an admirer of John Henry, a follower of the Oxford Movement, and after him a Catholic. She took the many witnesses, some with their husbands and children, safely from Italy to

Paris. They had to wait there because the anti-Catholic judges had heard of Newman's enadeavors and postponed the trial in order to tire him. He was obliged to provide for the Italians, who were impatient to return home, for six months, which was costly and caused heartbreaking troubles for Miss Giberne. The financial aspect of the affair became appalling. The witnesses needed at least forty pounds a week. One of his lawyers sent him an account for seven months amounting to 2300 pounds. Later he wondered that it had not turned his brain. It was the immense mercy of Providence, he said, which brought him through it, though these were months of continual suspense and anxiety. He kept repeating: "I cannot think that with so many prayers I shall fail."[12]

The burden became even heavier because of a promise he had made to an Irish bishop, Dr. Cullen. In April 1851, this prelate had asked him to give lectures in connection with a Catholic University, to be founded in Dublin. In July he had offered Newman the rectorship, which would entail much preparatory work. After his characteristic deliberations, consultations and prayers, Newman accepted the proposals. But because of the impending trial he could do nothing except study for the ten lectures he was to give.[13] "I have had anxiety and work beyond belief in writing them, expectations none. At least, my good Lord has never left me, nor failed me in my whole life—nor has He now", he wrote afterward to Manning.[14] It had been extremely difficult work. Again and again he had stopped, utterly unable to go on with his subject. "Nothing but the intercession of the Blessed Virgin kept me up to my work", he wrote. Once he sat at his desk for three days from morning to night and each night put aside as worthless the work he had done that day.[15] He had not had a holiday for two years, and he needed rest badly.[16] How remarkable that in these lectures we cannot find any trace of his anxiety and the painful trouble they gave him.

It was a relief when at long last the trial took place and the worst was known. Newman was kept in court for four days.

In spite of the lucid and orderly evidence given by the witnesses, in spite of Achilli's immoral life, continued even during his stay in England, on June 24, 1852, the verdict was given against Newman. The jury agreed that all Newman's charges except one were not proven or at least not proven to their satisfaction. He had lost his cause.

No wonder that after trials like these he could pray: "Remember me, O God, for the bitter things Thou bringest on me."[17]

All England had followed the proceedings in the papers. But while judges and jury apparently succeeded in putting Newman and the Catholics down, he gained a moral victory in the eyes of all Englishmen, and "Achilli's teeth had been drawn."[18]

Newman felt exceedingly grateful. He saw how wonderfully all prayers had been answered. It was a defeat but at the same time a triumph. He let Faber know: "You must none of you be doleful. . . . Of course, we are floored . . . in a worldly standard, but we must steadily recollect that we are above the world, above human law, above the feelings of society—and therefore must cultivate a lightness of heart and elasticity of feelings, which, while deeply based on faith, looks at first sight to others as mere good spirits. . . . We must have no indignation against Judge and Jury. . . ."[19]

It is understandable that in July 1852 Newman felt extremely worn out. The troublesome journeys to Dublin, the immense stress of the lectures, the anxieties about the trial, the installment of Dr. Cullen as Archbishop of Dublin and a stormy meeting of the University Committee had had their effect. Nevertheless, in that month he was needed at Oscott for the first Synod of Westminster, where the bishops gave him twenty-four hours' leave to prepare what would be one of his masterpieces, a most beautiful sermon entitled "The Second Spring". On the day the Synod ended, July 17, 1852, his sister Harriett, whom he had not seen for nine years, suddenly died.[20]

He had suffered deeply on account of her and his other relatives. "Do you think", he had written to Jemima, "that I have not a portion of the Apostle's great 'heaviness and continual sorrow' for his 'brethren and kinsmen according to the flesh'?" And he grieved especially for Harriett's husband, "who turns his back on his true home and refuses to listen to the voice that calls him there". That God might touch their hearts, was his constant prayer.[21]

But his relatives suffered as well. Once Harriett had expressed her intense sorrow to a friend who had been talking to her of the talents of the Newman family. "Alas, alas," Harriett had added after relating her words to her husband, "if persons were malignant they could not find a better means of piercing me thro' and thro'." And she had remembered with a heavy heart what her brother John Henry had been and what he was now.[22] At another time she had solemnly assured someone else that her brother would return to the Anglican church. She said she knew him well, better than anyone else, and she became agitated when the woman did not at once agree. Newman thought this incomprehensible.[23] Now that Harriett had died, he communicated his grief to Mrs. Bowden: "You may think how tried I am at this moment with my sister's death. . . . My lectures at Dublin require, at my age, all the steam I can put on—and this affliction, coming upon the Achilli affair, pulls me down so much, that nothing but God's grace can keep me up."[24] A few weeks later his aunt Elizabeth, who had had a great influence on his piety when he was a little boy, died too. One of his sermons had been written with the thought of her. He could not help feeling that the Achilli verdict in June was one of the immediate causes of the sudden deaths of his sister and his aunt.[25]

Greater than all these sufferings, however, was the thought of his own imperfection, the fact that he did not grow in sanctity. "I am sure so many prayers ought to make me better, and I am sensible they do not—and this is pain—but it is not the trial and its consequences that pain me."[26]

Meanwhile, Ireland and its future University required a "reconnoitring visit". It proved a great penance. The exuberant affection shown by the Irish embarrassed and tired the reserved Englishman. The feather beds they provided for him caused him sleepless nights. The food did not agree with him at all. He could not take pleasure "in large legs of coarse veal, boiled mutton, as red as in the shambles, and blood-shot kidneys". But while his physical strength failed, his mind and soul, he said, through God's grace, were strong.[27]

At the end of 1852, the year of trial, Newman accepted the offer of his friend James Hope Scott to stay for a few weeks at his mansion "Abbotsford", the house built by Sir Walter Scott as a medieval castle. Newman's medical adviser had told him to leave home and to take rest, on pain of premature old age and death.[28] He obeyed, but it cost him a great deal. Though everyone at Abbotsford was kind and considerate, he suffered terribly from homesickness. When a friend who had stayed there since Christmas Eve left, Newman was horrified that he might have called out in the presence of hosts and other guests: "O that I were going with you." He succeeded, however, in being "merry and cheerful to everyone but with an aching heart".[29] He thought of Saint Philip, who also submitted to medical advice when it did him no good. Philip was burned with irons as a medical treatment, whereas nothing worse had happened to Newman than to be sent to kind friends.[30]

From one letter it appears how shy he was and how conscientious. He wondered whether he did not argue too much, laugh too much. He doubted whether it was good for a man such as he to be in such a house with other guests. In three weeks' time, however, he was able to go to confession four times. And the chapel with the Blessed Sacrament was "the great consolation of his banishment".[31]

For the Oratorians at home he wrote a Chapter Discourse on the value of trials. He considered it, he wrote, to be characteristic of the very constitution of the Kingdom of Grace that its children must all suffer. If we have no trouble here, either we shall have a long purgatory, or, what is infinitely worse, we are not the children of grace at all and are going to a worse place. It was only a few months since the great Duke of Wellington had died. Newman looked with especial fear on the fact that this hero had been so singularly fortunate from first to last. He had had a long life, overwhelming glory and almost a sovereign sway over the hearts and wills of his countrymen. Now, at Abbotsford, Newman thought in contrast of another great man, as famous in his way as Wellington, namely, Sir Walter Scott. Scott's temporal aspirations and ambitious hopes had been frustrated. He attempted to gain his reward here and was disappointed. His days became more and more troubled as life advanced. His years were shortened by toil of brain and anxiety of heart. Newman looked tenderly and hopefully on his life compared with the life of the great Duke. "It seems as if his Maker, Redeemer and Judge had not abandoned him to the god of this world and to the glory thereof but had been training him by disappointment for a future which is better." Therefore Newman loved trials. They were his own portion here. They were a double proof of God's love if he bore them well.[32]

In January 1853, just before the final scene of the Achilli affair was to take place, he prepared another discourse. He wanted it to be read to the Oratorians on February 2, if he should be in prison or going to prison. He could imagine the sadness of his brethren. He wished to encourage them and make them consecrate the pain in a supernatural consolation. He even tried to bring them to a mood of joy and thankfulness. In his characteristic style he gave them a summary of what had happened:

> You recollect how strangely and suddenly we seemed from the beginning given over (as it were) to some strong and furious wind, which took us off our legs, and hurried us here and there at its pleasure, and landed us, we did not know where—how, day by day, our best stays and confidences broke down, how an impenetrable darkness came over the scene, and we found ourselves, week after week, worse off and worse still, without being able to predict what was to be the worst; and then, how that, after the prospect cleared, it got thick again, and promised and threatened by turns, promised and threatened without result, raising hopes merely to mock them; and how we were tossed to

and fro, without or against our will, like nothing else than a ship in a storm, and how, when we were close to the shore, we were carried off back into deep waters, till we gradually and irresistibly were drawn on into that settlement of our long conflict, which of all others had from the first seemed the most intolerable and the least likely, and I find myself in jail.

But this extraordinary disposition of Providence must have a special meaning, he said. Something good must come of it.[33]

This touching discourse was never read to the Oratorians. On January 31, 1853, after a humiliating lecture by Mr. Justice Coleridge, the sentence was pronounced, and a fine was imposed of one hundred pounds, with imprisonment till it was paid—which, of course, meant no imprisonment at all. Coleridge had implied that after his conversion to the Catholic Church, Newman no longer aimed at holiness of life, had lost the spirit of charity and humility and had acted in a way unworthy of his great abilities and ardent piety. But this "horrible jobation" left Newman unconcerned. Not only supernatural motives but mere habit kept him from being annoyed. "I have not been the butt of slander and scorn for twenty years for nothing."[34]

Then followed that tremendous outburst of gratitude toward the many benefactors, all over the world, who had helped him with their prayers and now gave him their money. The immense sum—above 100,000 pounds—was paid by generous contributions from all parts of the world, from large countries such as the United States and France, from small countries such as Holland and Belgium and from poor countries such as Poland and Ireland. For a full year he said two Masses a week for his benefactors. And touching is the Dedication of his University Lectures to those many friends who had alleviated the stress of that great anxiety.[35]

In the spring of 1853 the news reached him that Cardinal Wiseman wished to make him a bishop. Liverpool or Nottingham was named as his future see. Naturally, he felt this to be a great compliment, but nevertheless the very thought of it made him ill, and he was anxious for his health should the plan become reality. On the other hand he knew that his fears were insufficient reason for refusal. "If it were the will of the Holy See to shorten my life, it may do so—it has a right to do so—and I take it as God's will." But he had other objections. He felt most deeply that the office of a bishop was not suited to him. He was not a fully trained theologian and knew nothing of Canon Law. He did not possess the power of ruling; he knew that he would get so oppressed with a sense of his responsibilities and shortcomings that it would break his spirit. Removed from the University where he could do something, he would be in a situation where he could do little or nothing. He hoped that Dr. Cullen would do something to prevent all this, and he wrote to Father Stanton in Rome, asking him to do everything he could to hinder it. Fortunately, the plan came to nothing.[36]

It tried him exceedingly, however, that no news reached him about the future University nor any official summons to start the preliminary work. He had his plans ready. For many weeks, thinking he might get a letter, he did not leave the Oratory for even one night.[37] The time seemed wasted.

About this time Father Joseph Gordon died. He had been one of the three good preachers of the Oratory. "His loss to us is inexpressible", Newman wrote, "St. Philip must make it up for we cannot. God's will is our sole, though an all-sufficient consolation."[38] As Father Bernard Dalgairns of the London Oratory was a very good preacher and longed to leave London for Birmingham,[39] Newman ventured to ask the London Oratorians by letter to spare him Father Bernard. In the same letter, however, he showed some annoyance at the fact that Faber did not object to taking a certain novice from the Birmingham Oratory provided Newman gave his assent. The young man had been charitably received by Newman with the idea of joining the Birmingham Fathers, and now he was going to Faber without any referral to Newman.[40]

This letter hurt and wounded Faber. He rebuked Newman for assuming facts. He considered him unjust and cruel. What had he done to deserve such treatment? Newman judged before he had heard the defense.[41]

Newman, however, had not acted from anger. He believed it true that Faber was taking the novice from Birmingham, letting him know nothing of the affair. He again looked into the letter from which he had drawn his conclusions and considered for the second time what he thought it meant. But as he had learned that he had misunderstood the Londoners, he withdrew his words at once in a letter to Father Antony and begged his pardon for having said them.[42] Faber was simply "heartbroken" that Newman had not answered his letter personally but had written to Father Antony.[43] When Newman became aware of this, he too felt greatly distressed, so much so that he dared not open the subsequent letters sent by Faber till a message came from London by word of mouth that Father Bernard Dalgairns was transferred to Birmingham.[44]

Such generosity overwhelmed Newman. Not once, but several times he asked Faber's forgiveness: "I will only ask your pardon, my dear F. Wilfrid", he wrote in his first letter, "for every unkindness and want of consideration I may have shown you in the business—and beg you to suggest to me anything I can do to show you the perfect love and gratitude which I feel to you and all of you."[45] The next day he wrote again to complement this letter, telling Faber how much he himself suffered from his own rudeness and lack of consideration. His pain was intense and continued. He admired Faber for his noble and heroic conduct.[46] Regarding Father Bernard, the Birmingham Oratory welcomed him most cordially and gave him two of their most important offices, those of confessor and of novice master.[47]

At the end of 1853 Newman's feelings regarding the apparent apathy of the Irish bishops and Dr. Cullen's inactivity came to a head. He was wasting precious years, doing nothing as far as his future task was concerned. He wrote to the Archbishop and asked for a public act so that he could begin his operation.[48] The answer was unsatisfactory and occasioned a dilemma. If the University were to be opened in the autumn of 1854, he had to be recognized publicly as rector at once; otherwise he did not see how he was to be ready by then. If the bishops wanted to start the University in 1855, he would be obliged to wait nearly two more years. This would make four years lost, which he could not afford by any means. Hence either recognition or resignation. But Newman seldom acted rashly, so he consulted three friends and they advised patience. Newman was patient.[49]

This patience was effectual. In January 1854 he received an intimation from Dr. Cullen, recognizing the justice of his demands and involving the first step toward their realization.[50]

Another favorable fact helped him to be bold. Cardinal Wiseman, aware of Newman's difficult position, wished to make things easier for him by consecrating him bishop *in partibus infidelium*. This would give him the right to sit with the bishops of Ireland in all consultations. When Wiseman broached the subject with the Pope, he at once consented. Newman was pleased: "I really did think that the Cardinal . . . had effected what would be a real remedy against the difficulties which lay in my way." In a grateful letter he wrote to him: "I accept it most humbly as the will and the determination of Him, whose I am, and who may do with me as He will." Within a few days Bishop Ullathorne published the news and in a letter to Newman he called himself "Your devoted Brother". Congratulations poured in from high and low, and friends presented him with suitable gifts.[51] Now that the highest authorities had in a sense publicly recognized Newman as rector of the future University, he could rightly take the next step and visit the bishops in Ireland, sound other influential people, engage lecturers and prepare the University House. Early in February he embarked. He met with extreme kindness in Ireland but at the same time with great pessimism. He noticed the awful dissensions among the Irish. It seemed that he would have to raise the dead, he said. The weather was shocking, the winter being the worst in forty years. He wrote to his Oratorians: "I have nothing to rely on but God, the Pope and myself." He did not gain any encouragement. Nevertheless he could still say: "As yet I have not any sort of misgiving."[52] He did not lose heart. He wrote cheerfully about his experiences. He could see the trials of his troublesome journeys in a humorous light, and his report at one time resembled Dickens' *Pickwick Papers*.[53] After visiting six bishops he was forced to return to Dublin. He had caught a severe cold and felt extremely weak.[54]

From this time on he travelled to and fro from Birmingham to Dublin. In Dublin he frequently wrote to the Oratory. "Husbands and wives write to each other daily when separated", he said, "I trust it will be taken as my penance, and be of eternal good to me—but it has been my lot through life, to make friends and to be sent away from them."[55] In one of those letters he asked Father Bernard, the community confessor, for dispensation in fasting and abstinence.[56] In another he complained about his own weaknesses. He observed that he should pray more and live more in the next world.[57] He asked Father Caswall forgiveness for rude behavior.[58] It was on his conscience that he was not doing his duty to Saint Philip by not compelling his subjects to keep the Rule strictly enough. He wished to remind them of many points. But he doubted if he could succeed and wondered if another would govern them better than he himself from a distance.[59] These anxieties continued as long as he stayed in Dublin. When he came home sometimes he would be received negligently and would find that things he had asked to be done had been neglected. "It is hard", he wrote to Brother Frederico, "that, when I desire as some momentary refuge, to come home, I should be treated as if I were unwelcome."[60] He felt anxious for the future because his subjects showed a tendency to act each for himself, as though they were impatient of authority.[61] Such was his concern for the Oratory, his love for what he had founded.

This love also made him unobtrusively give considerable donations from his own property to the Congregation.[62]

Not long after the great winter journey, the Irish bishops received from Rome the brief establishing the University. But nothing was said about Newman's consecration as a bishop. Dr. Cullen showed him the document and seemed embarrassed when he pointed to a few words of praise, inserted by the Pope. This was all. Never after was any word spoken about the subject, either by him or by Cardinal Wiseman. Never did a definite and official intimation about a bishopric reach the patient Rector. And never was he consecrated. He did not feel troubled about this, nor did he do anything to find out the cause of what at first he considered a delay. On June 3, 1854, he was to be installed as Rector. Another man might have refused to submit to this ceremony until he had been consecrated. Not so Newman. He kept silence, and that was the end of the whole affair.[63]

One reads again and again about the immense difficulties he had to overcome in Ireland. But it is characteristic that in his letters only few traces can be discovered of these difficulties. Seldom does he complain about the Irish bishops. There is little sign of sadness or weariness. He appears to be in very good spirits.[64] He likes to tease Father Ambrose, his substitute in Birmingham, and calls him "my Rabbi".[65] He sometimes shows great confidence and thinks that things are going remarkably well.[66] On his fifty-fourth birthday he writes: "I am not over worked now and have so many blessings. I don't know how to enumerate them. You know I have a Chapel with the Blessed Sacrament here."[67] People who lived with him in Dublin tell us in their own simple way how beloved he was; "ever so nice, and full of fun . . . quite charming, so very simple and so fond of his old Oxford recollections. . . ." This is a summary by one of his professors about his amiability and cheerfulness.[68] He understood the Archbishop's difficult position among a divided episcopate, in a country suppressed by the English and suffering still from the consequences of the great famine. Misery caused rebellion even among some of the clergy. Many could not keep away from politics. There was much disagreement concerning the methods used against the oppressors. Which were permissible, which were the right ones? Dr. Cullen had his own ideas about this, differing from those of other bishops. He had been too long in Rome to know the precise historical details or the political developments. He had adopted the Italian attitude to new tendencies, an attitude of resistance to scientific and political developments, afraid that they might damage the Faith. In addition, there was the question of differing temperaments, originating from the divergence of race. The Irish character is as different from the English as the Celtic is from the Germanic. Newman saw and acknowledged the good qualities of the Archbishop and bore with the disagreeable things resulting from these circumstances. He did not complain to his Oratorians about Dr. Cullen's habit of not answering his letters, of delaying necessary decisions, of ignoring urgent requests. To all intents and purposes the University was governed by the Archbishop. The other bishops lost interest in the project and refused to support him. Newman bore the consequences of it all. But in spite of this treatment he continued conducting the University affairs in a masterly way, making himself all things to all men[69] instead of leaving Dublin in anger.[70]

Though founder and rector of a university, he still remained a minister of Christ. With great care he looked after the spiritual welfare of his students and asked prayers for them. Some lived in his own house. They were gentle and modest; they could not be more religious or more innocent; they set an example to the whole body of students.[71]

While everybody considered him the right man in the right place, he himself had another opinion: "The same clearness which makes me see others' failings, makes me see my own", he wrote to Father Ambrose.[72] He felt that he should be "a more showing, bustling man"; that he should dine out every day, mix in literary society, be twenty years younger. But he consoled himself by thinking of Saint Gregory of Nazianzus, whom he resembled in his deficiencies.[73]

When Newman had been rector for about a year, he realized how badly the Birmingham Oratory needed his presence. There was trouble with the London Oratory. Five or six times Newman alludes to this fact in the *Autobiographical Writings* while complaining bitterly about Faber. From other writings, too, it appears how much till the end of his life this event grieved him and how much it influenced his behavior toward his London brethren.

This conflict was only expressed in writing. Not a single discussion by word of mouth took place. Newman kept the correspondence in its entirety, and it is published in full in the *Letters and Diaries*. A first reading creates a strange impression and feeling. It may seem difficult to understand how these great personalities, Newman and Faber—great in different ways—could disagree to such an extent. It makes us think of the conflict between Paul and Barnabas, between Augustine and Jerome. But for a true comprehension we need a description of the circumstances and the background.

The facts are these. Newman had been a Catholic for ten years while the English Oratory was not yet seven years old. The young foundation needed all his care and solicitude. He had to be on the alert against circumstances that might injure or destroy his work. He felt intensely responsible for the realization of Saint Philip's ideal. The disagreement between himself and the London Oratory caused him grave anxiety.

It is not likely that Newman changed when the discussion started. He cannot have become tactless, selfish or cruel, for he had always been discreet, brotherly and gentle. We have seen how since his boyhood conversion he had tried to know God's will and to fulfill it; he cannot have been deliberately and consciously arbitrary or self-willed, stubborn in this one instance. In the preceding years there was never any trace of pettiness, small-mindedness, lack of generosity. How could he suddenly show these qualities when he was a man of fifty-five?

True, Newman was very sensitive. When pained, he could withdraw into himself. When betrayed by a friend, he could withhold further friendly association. When confidence was broken, he could not reestablish it. But is this not natural? Of course, he might sometimes have been mistaken; he might have explained facts, acts and words in the wrong way; he might have seen a breach of confidence in other people's conduct that was not there. And thus there may have followed misunderstandings. Indeed, if one studies the correspondence concerning the complicated matter, one is inclined to think of mysterious misunderstandings, especially as there is evident honesty and sincerity on both sides.

As to Faber, whoever knows him from his books and poems must be aware of his piety. Newman himself appreciated and praised his works even after the estrangement. The influence Faber exercised by his writings was great. It can be compared with the influence of Newman's sermons. Those writings may be more devotional than philosophical, more oratorical than theological; they may sometimes contradict one another; yet thousands of people have drawn spiritual wisdom and comfort from them and have been brought to a deeper inner life. These writings led the readers to living, real piety, even in the most humdrum circumstances. Faber's idealistic disposition and his imaginative nature knew how to throw light on the doctrines of the Faith in an attractive, poetical manner. Both his sermons and his written words carried people away from their worldly life. His kindness and persuasiveness fascinated his hearers and led them to God. With his excessive activity, however, went an annoying psychological complaint which influenced his moods in a conspicuous manner.

These circumstances make the discussion a tragic one. Newman's extreme sensitivity caused him to be silent and introverted, whereas Faber's extreme sensitivity caused him to be talkative and extroverted. Newman would speak to nobody

about it, Faber to everybody. Thus it happened that Newman
suffered from Faber's speaking out, and Faber suffered from
Newman's silence.

There is another factor which explains in part the disagreement. Every Oratory is autonomous. There is no higher
authority than the local superior. The superior of each house
depends only on the pope. At first the London Fathers regretted this. They would have preferred that Newman should
retain some authority over them. But he wished to follow
Saint Philip's Rule conscientiously, and in 1853 he made them
entirely independent of Birmingham.[74] He only hoped that
the tie of friendship between the London and Birmingham
Oratories would be stronger than among the Oratories on the
Continent, who had as little contact as if they had been
different Orders.[75]

The occasion of the disagreement was this. According to
their Rule, the Oratorians were not allowed to hear nuns'
confessions because it would take them away from their home
and their proper work.[76] But Cardinal Wiseman had so few
priests who could fulfill this task that he tried to, and did,
persuade Faber to ask for an interpretation of the rule in favor
of his request or at least for permission to put the rule aside,[77]
but Faber did not inform or consult Newman on the matter.

In October 1855, Bishop Ullathorne called on Newman and
told him that a rescript from Rome was on its way to the effect
that the Rule in this particular point was to be put aside for
both the London and Birmingham houses.[78] This news took
Newman by surprise, and he became alarmed. He was convinced that the Oratorian vocation and life depended entirely
and solely on the Rule. It was the only bond between Oratorians
of the same house. Gifted with an extraordinary talent for
foreseeing important and lasting consequences arising from
such measures, he guessed what might happen in the future. If
vital points of the Rule could be swept away, what would
remain of the real Oratorian life? The institution would lose its

raison d'être and its appeal as well, and there would then be no vocations.[79] There was also the danger—and he felt it to be a realized fact now that Bishop Ullathorne had informed him—that the Birmingham Oratory was to be subjected to a measure against their will, which might occur again and again.[80] Father Dalgairns made matters worse by maintaining that the Birmingham Fathers would be bound in conscience to accept the rescript and to put the Rule aside.[81] Newman reflected further that the Rule was expressly committed to his keeping.[82] He remembered that Saint Philip had appeared after his death and had said that the Oratorian Rule must not be altered.[83]

Thinking of all these things, Newman felt the need of an immediate protest. He first informed Cardinal Wiseman[84] and then wrote to Father Faber. One might think that it would have been better had he gone to London and discussed everything in person. But this would have been difficult if not impossible owing to his work in Dublin. Once the correspondence had started, Newman did not wish to finish in an informal way what had begun formally. Therefore he asked Faber in writing and very categorically, not to refuse a dispensation or relaxation of the Rule, but to draw up a formal petition to the authorities in Rome to recognize the fundamental principle of the Oratory of Saint Philip by which its houses are independent of each other, and he gave three strong reasons for this.[85]

Faber and his Oratorians, however, did not see the importance of this request. They were offended by the formal tone of the letter and refused to comply with Newman's wish until they had received an answer from Rome. They believed Newman to be angry.[86]

Newman felt deeply pained, not only because they answered in a formal way (he did not realize that his own formality had been the cause) but much more because of their refusal. What could he do but reply officially and ask them again and more urgently to safeguard the Birmingham Oratory against measures which he believed to be a considerable danger to the

Oratorian life? He ended his letter with the words: "I repeat my request, distinctly, formally, more earnestly. Rather, since justice comes in, I make it a demand."[87]

But still the London Fathers could not comply. They felt obliged to send a second refusal, adding the reasons why they thought a letter to Rome impossible. These reasons can be summarized in one sentence: "It would be disrespectful to send such a petition", which sounded futile and worthless to Newman. They suggested, too, that the Birmingham Fathers had better write to Rome themselves if they felt strongly on the point.[88]

Newman was struck dumb. He felt driven into a corner by the young London Oratorians. They unanimously refused to do what he demanded. They did not enter into his strong feelings. They did nothing to remove the danger. They did not give one valid reason why they made no move in the matter.[89]

Here is the deepest cause of the misunderstandings. The London Fathers thought they had very good reasons for not complying with Newman's wish until the rescript had come. Newman was convinced that their reasons were worthless, and he ignored them.

Although he could not believe that the London Fathers thwarted him intentionally,[90] he felt distressed and humiliated. He wanted to express his feelings, to show a forgiving mind. He longed to be cheerful, according to Saint Philip's example, but at the same time he gave up all hope of receiving help from London and thought it best to put a stop to the correspondence. In a short note, he wrote that he still loved them all, in spite of the fact that they had so painfully wounded him, but they would oblige him by not answering his letter.[91]

This troubled Faber and his Oratorians. They thought it very harsh. They had been acting with a sincere wish of doing what was pleasing to God and Saint Philip. And now Newman appeared to forbid correspondence.[92]

In December 1855 the official rescript arrived. It was a temporary suspension of the Rule relating to nuns' confessions but applied only to the London Oratory. However, since the Londoners did not do anything regarding Newman's wish, he thought it necessary to go to Rome himself, in spite of the difficulties of a journey in winter, the work he had in hand at Dublin and the great expense.[93] He did not inform them of his plan, but they heard about the journey and imagined all sorts of dangers for themselves, including loss of independence. They thought that he wanted to be their General.[94] They talked freely about the matter,[95] while Newman placed his Fathers under obedience not to mention it to anyone.[96] He would not say one uncharitable word about the London Fathers when visiting the Oratories on his way to Rome.[97]

As soon as Newman arrived, he walked barefoot to Saint Peter's, convinced that without prayers and penance he could not overcome the difficulties. In a short time he became aware that the Oratories he had visited on the way, Cardinal Barnabò of Propaganda and the Pope himself had all been influenced against him by the London Fathers. The Cardinal as much as said to him: "What have you come for? You needed not to have come."[98] The Pope thought he had come to make himself head of the London Oratory. He showed the letter sent by the London House and asked: "Is there not some quarrel?" Then Father Ambrose, Newman's companion, explained matters sufficiently for the Pope to say: "Now I understand everything."[99] By the end of his stay in Rome, Newman was able to write that everything was turning out well. He had achieved as much as he wished for—even more.[100]

He had asked the Pope's blessing for both the Birmingham and the London Oratory, and when at home again he at once notified the London Fathers.[101] This fact and a gift for their Poor Schools gave the Londoners heart to begin writing private letters, composed in a touching filial tone, explaining things again and again. They supposed Newman's displeasure to be against Father Faber personally.[102] And at last Faber himself tearfully asked Newman to forgive them, although he did not know what he had done wrong.[103]

But Newman answered each in a few words to the same effect. He even refused to read one of their long letters. He did not want private, informal letters intended to retract what had been done formally.[104] From long experience he knew the mischief caused by such proceedings.[105]

So at length, on May 22, 1856, the London Oratory wrote to him formally as a body. They asked his blessing and forgiveness for the pain they had unintentionally caused him. But they suggested nothing to remove the difficulty and their present danger regarding the Rule and the Oratorian life. By his appeal to Rome, Newman made his own house secure, but he feared that after his death either London or Birmingham might lose independence or that a common superior might be elected. It pained him,[106] and it was a mystery to him that their answer to his reply should again evade the heart of the matter.[107]

Now he concluded that Saint Philip had wanted to teach him a lesson, namely, to remind him that the Oratories should see little of each other, a lesson that had been practiced always on the Continent, and he decided: Let us be kind to the London Fathers individually; let us pray for the welfare of their Congregation; but let us keep clear of them.[108] From this time onward he would do so. He notified the Londoners about his decision, and they promised to follow the same line of conduct.[109]

Both parties kept to their resolution. They visited each other very seldom. There were friendly messages when joyful or sad events took place in either Oratory. There was a desire to help each other if help were needed. Faber felt glad when he received proofs of kindness from Newman, and he replied thankfully and affectionately. Newman visited Faber when he was dying, and he was present at his funeral. But the old cordiality and intimate fraternal intercourse were never restored. And Newman himself had entirely lost his former trust and love of Faber. London continued to suspect that Newman wished to be the General of the English Oratories, and Newman suspected the Londoners of feeling a certain contempt for the spirit of the Birmingham house. London was of the opinion that Newman was led by his hypersensitivity; Birmingham supposed that London had not acted sincerely. Faber and his subjects continued to complain about Newman and freely talked about "the quarrel" or "the row", whereas Newman forbade his subjects to discuss with them the internal matters of his house.[110]

Whenever, in later life, Newman mentioned his grief—always confidentially and never willingly—he showed at the same time that he had forgiven the London Fathers. And after Faber's death, when Newman needed help from heaven in order to be successful in his fight against slander, he invoked Faber's intercession, and he ascribed the success of his self-defense, expressed in the *Apologia*, to Father Faber's prayers.[111]

During all these disappointments and anxieties from October 1855 to July 1856, the University labors and difficulties continued. Back in Dublin after his Roman journey, he felt as though he were at sea in a little boat, alone, out of sight of land, or as though he had a mountain to move. He felt relieved, however, that there was no more chance of his being made a bishop. To be a bishop would have been a great help in his work, but he would never have been able to resign his rectorship,[112] though resignation seemed imperative. Moreover, the Holy See had given him leave of absence for three years only.[113] So he informed the Archbishop of Dublin that he wished to retire in July 1857.[114]

There was yet another reason for resigning. It seemed to him that Dr. Cullen had no confidence in him. He had the greatest difficulty in putting up with the Archbishop's treatment. He once gave a graphic description of it to a friend. If he were to ask Dr. Cullen a question in June, he would call on him again and again for an answer. Then in July he would put the question in writing but would still get no answer. In August he would write to an intimate friend for an answer, without success. In September he would give up all hope and leave things alone. Then in January he would find out accidentally that Dr. Cullen had solved the problem but in a manner in which Newman had asked him in July not to solve it. And even in February he himself would have received no answer, either directly or indirectly. And this happened not once or twice but regularly.[115]

Dr. Cullen's ways, however, were not the main reason why Newman eventually left. "I had rather show gratitude to the Professors by remaining than mark my want of gratitude to the Archbishops by resigning", he wrote to a friend.[116] Nor did other disappointments as, for example, the small number of students, make him want to leave. When in 1855 the University of Oxford was opened to Dissenters and Catholics, and the Catholic aristocracy of England could send their sons to this time-honored English university, it was a blow to Dublin because it would draw students to Oxford who otherwise would have been at Dublin, but it did not discourage Newman. He only regarded the wishes of the Pope, and therefore he considered it his duty to do all he could to advance the Irish University.[117] Many letters of that time show his happiness, his cheerfulness, his eager expectations. He called his work a risk, a venture, but a venture made in faith, conducted under the Holy See and a Catholic hierarchy, and therefore he need have no fear.[118] He felt physically and mentally well and wrote: "My only fear is that I shall be too happy and too fond of life, to be willing to leave it."[119]

These words must not be understood too literally. Besides the difficulties just mentioned there were several more unpleasant things to be endured at the time. Father Dalgairns, a restless, inconsistent character, went back to the London Oratory.[120] George Ryder, whose spiritual director Newman had once been, wrote him a furious letter and accused him of something akin to lying. Archbishop Cullen disappointed him, as he would not fulfill his promise to help him in clearing the debt taken to build the University Church. He feared he had secret enemies. "I was never surrounded with troubles as I am now",[121] he wrote to Henry Wilberforce, hardly a month after his cheerful letter mentioned above. This friend, however, pained him by talking of his "sensitiveness, which is the penalty of great ability".[122] He felt oppressed by the burdens in Dublin; too many things to do; no leisure at all, while the Oratory needed his presence.[123] There were whisperings against his Oratory, and no novices came.[124] He wrote to Father Ambrose, saying: "I have a load of care on me, and no one to take pity on me. Well, I hope it will make me rely more on the source of comfort."[125] In February 1857 Robert Wilberforce, one of the tutors who had worked with him at Oriel, died. "Alas! Alas!" Newman wrote to Robert's brother, "I never found it so difficult to say God's will be done. But I say it—only, we are superexceedingly blind, we know nothing. . . . We have not the key to Divine Providence, and we are ever blundering when we try to enter into the All wise Mind of our most loving God. . . ."[126]

In these circumstances he officially announced to each of the Irish bishops that he actually intended to resign his rectorship on November 14th of the current year. He gave several reasons, but they were all connected with one problem: the University requires such residence as was incompatible with his duties in Birmingham.[127] Of course, he did not conceal his other motives: the ways of the Archbishop, the indifference of the English Catholics, the conviction of his own imperfection and deficiencies; he felt, he said, "an ass in a lion's skin".[128] But the Oratory was evidently the decisive reason. Thus he wrote to a friend that he had never doubted success; that he was quite satisfied with the progress; that the feeling of disappointment, even the very shade of despondency, had not come upon him, but that his strength and his Congregation would not let him go on:[129] "I am wanted in Birmingham more than I can express",[130] and a month later: "It will go near to be ruined, if I am much longer absent."[131]

The Irish bishops reacted to his letters in such a way that he feared an appeal to Rome. Alarmed by the prospect, the Birmingham Oratory sent him a formal order recalling him. This upset the Archbishop, who had a nervous interview with him. Outwardly unmoved, Newman melted interiorly, but thinking of his Congregation he could not and would not withdraw his decision. He only left open the possibility of a middle plan.[132] The Archbishops officially begged the Birmingham Fathers to retract their command. But the answer, respectfully worded, was clear and contained their reason: "We can consent to a non-resident Superior even less than you perhaps can contemplate a non-resident Rector."[133]

While Newman continued to insist on a new Rector, he suggested a compromise if the Archbishop could not comply with his wish. This suggestion, however, was ignored.[134] They wanted him to reside in Dublin unconditionally.[135] Therefore he acted on his own middle plan from November 1857 onward, and in October 1858 he wound up matters, left Dublin on November 4 and never saw the city again.[136]

The personnel of the University considered his departure a disaster. They had admired his plans, his unsparing efforts, his perseverance. They remembered how he drew up statutes, gave lectures, wrote essays, preached sermons, built a church. They had witnessed the provoking treatment of Dr. Cullen, and the world of business and vexation he had had to live in. They wondered that he had not broken down under it long before.[137] But he never really broke down: "Do ask for me that I may do God's work faithfully and well, whatever he puts upon me. I know he puts nothing on me, which I ought not to be able to do. . . . But at my time of life, when I look back and see how little I have done, I sometimes get out of heart."[138] He continued, however, praying for the University. He gave much help by his advice, his articles, his extensive correspondence. And his ideals remained a source of inspiration.[139]

When we consider this episode of Newman's life in its entirety, several things strike us. First of all, he could have resigned the honor and the burden of the rectorship as soon as he realized the numerous and frightening difficulties. "Perhaps any other man in your position would have thrown it off long ago", a professor told him.[140] He could have made complaints and threatened the Archbishop without intermission. He could have neglected his duties in order to force the Archbishops into compliance with his ideas. But none of these things ever entered his mind. He did not make scenes, he did not quarrel, he worked with unflagging zeal, he remained patient and respectful. He wrote his letters in a courteous tone and was grateful for every service done to him. "You are the tenderest and gentlest of men", one of his Oratorians once observed.[141]

Newman had learned from history that over and above the gift of infallibility of the popes, a gift of sagacity had always characterized them, so that what the Pope determined was the very measure expedient for the time. Years afterward he saw, without denying the general principle, that in his own case regarding the Irish University there had been an exception, and the explanation lay in the fact that the Pope had not been properly informed concerning Irish affairs any more than he himself had been.[142] But on the very day that he began his last journal he wrote an optimistic and prophetic review of his work in Dublin: "It does not prove that what I have written and planned will not take effect some time and somewhere, because it does not at once. . . . And since I hope I did what I did, not for the sake of men, not for the sake of the Irish hierarchy, not even for the Pope's praise, but for the sake of God's Church and God's glory, I have nothing to regret and nothing to desire different from what it is."[143]

The early months of 1858 showed again how difficult it was for him to stay away from Birmingham. In January, Father Stanislaus Flanagan fell seriously ill. In February, Father Henry Bittleston received the last sacraments. At the same time Father Robert Tillotson was far from well. After Father Stanislaus had recovered a little, Father Robert went with him to France for convalescence. In April, Father Ambrose was ill.[144] And Newman wrote: "We are much tried. I feel like Abraham, but I ought to feel his consolation too." He remembered God's words: Have no fear, Abram, I am here to protect thee;

thy reward shall be great indeed.[145] He tried to comfort his
Oratorians by recounting his personal experiences. It had been
his destiny to appear to fail at first but in the end to succeed.
Misfortunes befell his family when he was young. Later, he
missed honors at the final examinations. When a tutor, he lost
his office. Then there was the misery concerning Tract 90.
Later still, the Achilli lawsuit. All failures! Well, the Oratorians
were joined to him, so they had to share his trials.[146] Nevertheless, they were not without their rewards. He admired and
was thankful for the great charity his Oratorians showed by
their assiduous nursing and their willingness to take over the
tasks of the sick. He was edified by their total trust in God.
Father Henry was a vital member of the Oratory, and twice
death had been very near. But the prayers said by the Oratorians
gained the benefit of his recovery. "It was the victory of hope
. . . and we had nothing left to do, but to be grateful, and to
feel what a good thing it is to trust in Him. . . ."[147]

From the time he became an Oratorian, there was no saint to
whom Newman referred more than to Saint Philip. In numerous
letters he mentions him. He continually confided in "Our
Lady and Saint Philip". He was always entrusting matters to
Saint Philip. And during the distressing days when the Oratory
was threatened with loss of its members, when the pressure of
work was a heavy burden for the few Fathers in good health,
he began to fear that he was "out of favour with St. Philip".
The Saint appeared to have cast him off. He was inclined to
regard this as cruelty, but he realized that he could not see
behind the scenes and that Saint Philip must have his salutary
purposes in acting as he did. Newman did not wish to complain,
but sometimes he felt tempted to exclaim with Julius Caesar,
attacked by his great friend: "Et tu, Brute!": Do you, too, join
the conspirators? or rather: "Can a woman forget her child?
She has forgotten him."[148] But all his sighs and complaints
were only the expression of "inarticulate feelings which are
too deep for words". And the end was always: "Please God,
and I hope not from pride, I will be faithful to Saint Philip."[149]

CHAPTER NINE

GOD WILL PROVIDE

1858–1864

> God will provide. He knows what is best. Is He less careful
> for the Church, less able to defend it than I am? Why need I
> fash myself about it? What am I?[1]

When Newman was still an Anglican, his interests and activities
were continually directed to the promotion of the Kingdom of
God on earth. After he had entered "the one true Fold", there
was no change in this respect. His life as a priest and an
Oratorian, his sermons and discourses, his labors for the
University at Dublin, were all inspired by the wishes of the
Church and aimed at her well-being, because he knew that
God wanted him to use his talents on her behalf. In the years
that followed he continued his work. But what had happened
in his Anglican period repeated itself and made him again
suffer disappointments: the various authorities in the Church
who gave him many tasks did not appreciate the way he
performed them.

Long before he had left Dublin for good, he had cherished
the plan to write a thorough study of the relation between faith
and reason. The problem had intrigued him for many years. It
would seem that this study was necessary for clarifying the
connections between the Church and modern science. The
task attracted him. He alone could write such a work, his
friend Ward said.[2]

He had not yet begun the execution of this plan, his "magnum
opus",[3] or great work as he called it, when Cardinal Wiseman

entrusted him with "the most onerous though most honourable task" of revising the English version of Holy Scripture.[4] It meant giving up his own plan, a real sacrifice.[5] But he considered the wishes of his ecclesiastical superiors as the will of God, and therefore he did not make any objection. He thought of combining the two tasks by prefixing this study as a long introduction to the new translation.[6]

At once he started finding competent translators and asking advice. But more than a year after he had accepted the undertaking, when he was making progress and after he had already spent a considerable sum of money on it, difficulties arose in connection with American plans. He needed instructions from the Cardinal. But Wiseman, old and ailing, did not answer his letters, seemed to be at a loss or to have forgotten all about it. Newman was forced to make his cooperators stop for the time being, and he never heard a word about it again.[7] When later he enumerated his many failures in an intimate journal, written "in God's sight", he added: "I do not wonder at trials; trials are our lot here; but what saddens me, is that, as far as one can see, I have *done* so little, *amid* all my trials. My course has been dreary, because, to look back on it, it is so much of a failure."[8]

While still working on his translation he felt compelled to undertake another work for the Catholic Church in England. The new converts, often aristocrats and intellectuals, complained that their children could not have an education comparable to that which Anglicans received in their public schools, since the Catholic schools were much inferior to them.[9] They contacted Newman, thinking that he would be the right man to change the situation and to afford Catholic boys the advantages of the great public schools, while sparing them the evils. He saw how necessary this work was; he knew he had special talents for it; but he also realized it would "increase anxieties, responsibilities, and enemies", as he wrote to James Hope Scott.[10]

In the Oratory he gave a discourse on this subject. He wanted to know God's will and asked his Oratorians to begin a novena to Saint Philip, in which the "burden of their supplications" should be: "O St. Philip, give us no new mortification, but either prevent the School, or prosper it." They need not pray, he said, that humiliation, contempt, slanders should be their lot. Indeed, he did not consider these things as mortification, unless they went so far as to hurt the Oratory. But they should pray that their labor, thought and anxiety in erecting a school should not bring disappointment and prove a failure. He felt a little sad and discouraged, he said, because he found it so difficult to be sure about Saint Philip's will and wish. "For my own personal comfort I would much rather give up the plan altogether—I very much want to be at peace—but then comes the question, is that St. Philip's wish too?"[11]

After the novena he felt convinced that he had to found the school. Two people were to form its strength: Mrs. Wootten, an Oxford convert, "more like a Saint than most people you come across",[12] was to be the boys' matron, and Father Nicholas Darnell, as Newman's representative, was to give them a truly liberal education.[13] On May 1, 1859, the school was opened. It was destined to be a success and a great benefit for aristocratic Catholics but at the same time "a hair shirt" which Newman could never take off, and this on account of the never-ceasing "responsibility, the chances of day and hour, the prospect of accidents, the caprice of parents, the imperative need of unflagging vigilance". He therefore prayed that he should "be able to offer it up to God worthily, and gain merit from it".[14]

At this time, too, circumstances laid a third task on his shoulders. For several years he had followed with great interest the studies of a group of young, energetic Catholic thinkers, mostly converts, who were highly interested in the problem of the relation between reason and faith, between new views and old dogmas, between the scientific discoveries of the times and the doctrines of the Church. He hoped that they might preserve Catholicism from intellectual isolation and on the other hand show non-Catholic thinkers the absence of all real contradiction between the truths of science and those of religion. But those young men badly needed a leader. Their tone and their extravagant methods created suspicion and irritation among Catholics. Newman felt called to do what he could in order to prevent disastrous consequences. He had seen this as another reason for leaving Dublin. After having read what he called a frightening article in their review, *The Rambler*, he wrote to Father Ambrose: "Do pray for me that I may find out what use God wishes to put me to, and may pursue it with great obedience."[15]

In the year 1858 the tendency of the *Rambler* to criticize and offend had become so alarming that public disapproval was threatening, and in February 1859 Bishop Ullathorne gave Newman private notice of unavoidable censure unless the *Rambler* were to have another editor. Therefore Newman persuaded the editor, Richard Simpson, to resign so that the censure was withheld.[16] But who was to be his successor? Who could satisfy the ecclesiastical authorities and at the same time preserve the intellectual reputation of the review? Unless Newman wished the *Rambler* to die, he could but comply with the wish of Cardinal Wiseman and Dr. Ullathorne and take the editorship himself.[17] "Most bitterly against my will, I am for the present, Editor of the *Rambler*", he wrote to a friend. He had promised himself "a fallow year", but now this proved a dream.[18] All his plans had to be cancelled or changed. He felt like "a vessel without rudder or compass". But he found consolation in thinking that God willed it so.[19] "Pray for me, please—for I expect the *Rambler* will get me into a great deal of trouble."[20]

Richard Simpson, however, could not see the Bishop's conduct as Newman saw it, and asked bitterly: "Is this kind of thing always to be acquiesced in? or is it at one time or another to be resisted? if so when?" Newman answered, thinking of Cardinal Wiseman's ways:

> It seems hardly kind when you have so much to try you, to preach, yet I know you will excuse what comes from one who has had on various occasions already, had [sic] to practise what he preaches. I assure you that the principal person who has unfairly used you . . . has been personally unkind to me, by

word and deed. I consider myself much aggrieved, and, had not the experience of long years made me tire of indignation and complaint, I could indulge myself in both the one and the other. But, depend upon it, no advice is better than that of the Holy Apostle: "If our enemy hungers, to feed him"—and to leave our cause simply in the Hands of the good God. He will plead our cause for us in His own way, and, even though it be not His high Will to redress us openly, He can make compensation to us by inward blessings. . . . To fret, and to be troubled, does not pay—it is like scratching a wound, instead of letting it heal. . . ."[21]

Newman wisely wanted to effect the necessary changes, not at once, but gradually. Only in this way could he preserve the fair name of men whom he believed were sincere Catholics. He thought it "unfair, ungenerous, impertinent, and cowardly to make on their behalf acts of confession and contrition". But the bishops could not follow him and had no patience. The very first number which Newman edited aroused sharp criticism. They noticed little improvement in tone and were aware of the scandal it created. They wanted rest and peace in Catholic England, no stirring up of doubts which never had entered the heads of most Catholics. In their solicitude for the present time, they did not see the intellectual dangers of the future. In a personal interview, Bishop Ullathorne expressed the hope that Newman would resign the editorship after the July number. Newman could not agree with the Bishop's views and stated his opinions in a strong manner. He saw a side of things which the bishops did not see. He felt a call to fight against future dangers. On the other hand, he could not resist the voice of a lawful superior speaking in his own province. He never could, not even in his Anglican period. He knew that God had appointed the right time for everything, and if he attempted to do a good work at the wrong time, he might become a heretic or schismatic. Therefore he gave up the *Rambler* after July. But he compared the consequence of this interference with the shock caused by "the pat of a lion".[22]

At that moment he did not yet know that an article of his in the July *Rambler* had been formally accused before the Roman authorities as heretical. Only in January of the following year, 1860, when Dr. Ullathorne had returned from Rome, was Newman informed about the fact and told how he had given pain to the Pope. It was disturbing news, and he wished to express his great sorrow as soon as possible. He wrote to Cardinal Wiseman, asked him for particulars about the supposed heretical views, promised a full internal and external assent to the dogmatic propositions which his article seemed to attack, and expressed his wish to explain his ideas in strict accordance with these propositions.[23] In this way he practiced what in September 1852 he had written to the editor of the *Tablet*: "This I trust I may say, that if there be a man in the whole Church, whom from faith, obedience, and love towards her would rejoice and exult in sacrificing any opinion of his own at the bidding of his Ecclesiastical superiors (if I dare speak of myself), I am the man."[24]

The Cardinal, however, never answered this letter, and Newman never came to know that it was but one single sentence that was denounced. At the end of six months, Manning, now a convert and Wiseman's right hand, said to Newman that the question was settled.[25] It was not clear what he meant, and Newman did not inquire, but for more than seven years he would be suspected in Rome on account of this announcement.[26]

Under these circumstances and in this state of mind Newman commenced a new and special journal in which he revealed his deepest thoughts about himself and about those who had wronged or benefited him.[27] It is a very touching book, written in God's presence. In December 1859 he began it as a prayer and on his knees. With long intervals between them, he wrote new entries, finishing it twenty years later as a Cardinal.

He starts by complaining about the consequences of old age: He is dissatisfied with himself. He lives too much in the past. He cannot pray as he used to when he was young. He lacks the generosity, the cheerfulness, the unselfishness of youth. He thinks himself a coward with little faith and love.[28]

As regards his intellectual labors, he has been exerting himself, toiling, ever since he became a Catholic. He has tried to supply the wants of Catholics, especially regarding education. Better than a born Catholic, he is aware of the needs. He has worked for God but still with a great desire to please the bishops and the Pope. But in various ways he has been treated only with slights and unkindness. He has no friend in Rome. He is misrepresented and scorned in England. He has labored in Ireland, with a door ever shut in his face.[29] And all this, connected with the sympathy of the Protestants, causes the temptation of looking out for their praise.[30]

In still stronger terms he repeats his complaints three years later and mentions the many failures and disappointments he has suffered.[31]

These sad accounts find their explanation in a thought which unites the sporadic entries into a whole. It is his longing to open his heart to God, to express his sadness to the Almighty, because he is an old man now and still far from the ideal that he had cherished as a young man.[32] "I am tempted to look back", he wrote. "Not so, O Lord, with Thy Grace, not so! . . . It has been my *lifelong* prayer, and Thou hast granted it, that I should be set aside in this world. Now then let me make it once again. O Lord, bless what I write and prosper it—let it do much good, let it have much success; but let no praise come to me on that account in my lifetime. Let me go on living, let me die, as I have hitherto lived. . . ." And he added: "Teach me how to employ myself most profitably, most to Thy glory, in such years as remain to me; for my apparent ill-success discourages me much. O my God, I seem to have wasted these years that I have been a Catholic."[33]

These last words suggest the following observations. He knows God has given him special talents. He is sure he sees special dangers threatening Catholicism and religion in general. And when he tries to use his talents according to his duty in order to avert these dangers, he is stopped as soon as he starts. He realizes that the condition of the English Catholics should be improved by a careful survey of their argumentative basis, of their relation to the philosophy and the character of the day, by giving them juster views, by enlarging and refining their minds, in one word, by education. And they feel insulted, so that he is discouraged and regarded suspiciously by the authorities.[34] What is worse, he has a feeling that it is his own fault. He had done so little amid all his trials.[35]

All this was so saddening because he deeply sensed his own vocation. "Every one who breathes," he wrote in the sermon on God's will as the aim of life, "high and low, educated and ignorant, young and old, man and woman, has a mission, has a work. We are not sent into this world for nothing. . . . As Christ has His work, we too have ours; as He rejoiced to do His work, we must rejoice in ours also. . . . Alas! alas! for those who die without fulfilling their mission!"[36] The same thought often occurs in his letters: "I pray that God may not take me away till I have done all the work that He has meant that I should do—but I do nothing and this teases me."[37]

One must not lose sight of this when reading the journal lest it should be misunderstood. Newman knew what he was doing when writing it, and why he was complaining. In certain circumstances, complaining is a good thing. Did not Christ complain sometimes? Did not Job complain to his friends, and did not the Psalmist, and Jeremiah? "To let out one's sorrow is a great relief," he wrote to Father Ambrose "and I don't think an unlawful one. . . . What is so common in the Psalms and in Jeremias, as the sentiment 'Just art Thou, o Lord, yet will I plead with Thee.'?"[38]

But the most moving justification of his complaints is to be found in one of his Anglican sermons, in which unconsciously he pictures himself while speaking about the Patriarch Jacob: "Jacob seems to have had a gentle, tender, affectionate, timid mind—easily frightened, easily agitated, loving God so much that he feared to lose Him. . . . Such men are easily downcast, and must be treated kindly; they soon despond, they shrink from the world, for they feel its rudeness, which bolder natures do not. . . . You recollect his touching complaints. . . ."[39]

In all his trials, faith in God's Providence and wisdom gave him strength to be patient: "When we get to heaven, if we are worthy, we shall enjoy the sight of how all our failures and disappointments, if borne well, have been for God's glory and our own salvation."[40]

One of his trials was the loss of his Anglican friends, especially of Frederic Rogers, who had been very close to him: "My severance from him and others", he wrote to William Froude, "is a wound which will never heal. This is no inconsistency to say so, though I feel myself in possession of supernatural truth and consolation. The natural heart has wounds as well as the body."[41]

In the Oratory itself there were difficulties. Too few Fathers for too many tasks: the jail, the workhouse, the school, the confessional and other parochial duties. So very often Newman was forced to take over other Fathers' work. "It is God's will", he let his friend Ornsby know, "that we have hardly any preachers . . . and we have no one for the music—and I have literally been copying out music from morning to night. . . ."[42] While the church was being enlarged and decorated, he was incessantly called to see to everything.[43] One of the Fathers, Robert Tillotson, had gone to his relatives in America, and when there he informed Newman that for very good reasons he had offered himself to the Paulist Fathers. Newman felt "distressed beyond measure" by that "great, unexpected, undeserved blow".[44] Then he had difficulties with the laybrothers, who made no vows and so had very little relationship with the Oratory. Father Ambrose hoped that no more would come. "They are all trouble and no profit. They require immense labour and training."[45] Last but not least, there was Father Nicholas Darnell, the headmaster of the school, who excluded Newman from any knowledge whatever of school matters and made the school exclusively his own.[46] Is it a wonder that under these circumstances a kind of breakdown, a sort of crisis in health should have come about?

In June 1861 he suddenly became ill. He suffered from pain and restlessness. His nights were uncomfortable from distress and sleeplessness. Three times he went to London to consult an eminent doctor. The doctor, however, assured him that it was only a complaint of the nerves and told him to eat and drink, to amuse himself and to travel. He needed "good air, good scenery, good food, good everything".[47]

So for several weeks he went from place to place. He visited the homes of his infancy and his schooldays and went to Cambridge, Brighton and the Isle of Wight. He spent four weeks at a friend's house in London.[48] But travelling and being away from home were a new trouble: "the mere points of saying or hearing Mass, going to Communion, going to confession" were a real vexation for him. Only by moving about did he manage to keep off the depression of homesickness.[49] The worst of all was that he was not to say Mass.[50] Nevertheless, his indisposition went away, and he received positive good.[51] At the end of 1861 he wrote in the diary full of entries of the seven foregoing years: "Shall I get through a book of another seven years? Anyhow, what unknown unconjectured events, what trials, will in that next seven years be recorded! Guide us safely through them, good God!"[52]

This was exactly at the moment when his young Oratory school went through a dangerous crisis. In the summer of 1861 Newman had given the headmaster, Father Darnell, a list of points he wished to be changed. Darnell, however, had ignored them altogether. Now without consulting Newman he had drawn up new rules which made it impossible for Mrs. Wootten, the matron, to do for the boys what she had promised their parents. He had taken from her the command of the houses where the boys received board and lodging, and the boys had no longer free access to her. So Mrs. Wootten wanted to leave, which would have meant disaster for the school. Her presence was one of the main reasons why parents sent their sons.[53]

When Father Darnell noticed that Newman preferred her to

himself, he became very angry: Newman had better appoint that "insolent, perverse, and blindly frantic woman" headmistress! But Newman remained self-possessed and tried to find a way to keep both Father Darnell and Mrs. Wootten. He made a proposal: he was to draw up rules so that they each could act in their own spheres without collision. But Father Darnell would not for a moment contemplate such an arrangement. The matron and her assistants were his subordinates and had no right of appeal to Newman. And he expressed his firm resolution to resign the headship without a day's delay if Mrs. Wootten did not go from the school at once. He had, moreover, persuaded four of the masters to tender their resignations as well.

It was a characteristic act of humility for Newman to appeal to his Oratorians. He explained to the Fathers that he considered the school as his own because he had founded it. He believed the parents had entrusted their boys first to himself, then to Father Darnell. But, he realized, the Oratorians might side with the latter and would say so if left to themselves. So he proposed that they should give leave of absence to Father Darnell and himself and then investigate whose school it was. He knew they might give the decision against him, but if so he would "cheerfully submit" to it. As a matter of fact, it would be a relief, because differences like this were enormous trials to him. After the vote, however, they should consider how they could hinder scandal, mischief to the school and a slur on Father Darnell's and his own character. He imposed, by virtue of obedience, an absolute silence on every Father, and he wished them to say three Masses for light from above.

Before the Fathers met, however, it came out accidentally that Father Darnell had made known his unconditional resignation as a fact both in Birmingham and in London. He had shown a document signed by the four masters in which they resigned their places if he resigned his: Moreover, he formally expressed his request to be released from the Congregation.

This changed matters altogether. The Congregation could not but accept these resignations, and thus in one moment the school was deprived of its head and its masters. Immediately Newman went to London for advice. It is remarkable that in four weeks he should have succeeded in providing the school again with the necessary staff, he himself becoming the headmaster.

The whole affair was a most severe trial to Newman. "I really think no one has so many troubles as I, and I hope they are a proof of God's love for me." But "never did things begin so soon to mend".[54]

A few years later, Father Darnell wrote to Father Edward Caswell: "My conduct was unsufferably insolent, ungrateful and ungracious."[55]

But like a thunderbolt in a clear sky the Oratory suddenly received a new cross when Father Stanislaus Flanagan, the novice master, and the best theologian of the house, declared that he must leave the Congregation. He was no longer able to do the community duties and to bear the responsibilities he had without fearing serious injury both to his mind and his body. In August 1862 he obtained the necessary permission. "It is the most tragical event which has befallen the Oratory, since it had been set up", Newman wrote. Apart from himself there was only one confessor left.[56] After the holidays several boys did not return. Was it on account of his departure? At any rate tongues began to wag, intimidating people with the idea that the Oratorians were secret heretics. Perhaps they thought that Father Flanagan went because he mistrusted Newman's orthodoxy.[57] Under these circumstances the nervous symptoms of the last year returned. As never before, Newman needed a complete change.

He began to look like an old man. His face showed lines of intense grief, disappointment and sorrow, caused by mistrust and slander regarding his orthodoxy. When he spoke, the expression softened, but when at rest there was a look of terrible weariness. His conversation was often broken by spells of absentmindedness. All this is easy to understand.[58] His strong efforts to raise the Catholic Church of England from the depths of her backwardness, narrow-mindedness, fear of new ideas, anxiety about the development of science and lack of aristocratic manners and liberal education seemed to be in vain. He remembered that when he was twenty he was cut off from the rising talent of the University by his failure at the examinations; when he was thirty he was cut off from distinction by being deprived of the tutorship; when he was forty he was virtually cast out of the Church of England by the affair of Tract 90; when he was fifty he was cast out of society by the disgrace of the Achilli sentence; and now that he was sixty he would be cast out of the good opinions of Catholics and especially of ecclesiastical authorities! What would happen to him if he lived to be seventy? he complained to Father Ambrose. But after enumerating these disappointments he concluded: "Don't be angry with me for mentioning them. . . . I suppose it is all intended to keep me from being too happy. How happy should I be if let alone—how fond of living. On the other hand certainly, I have been carried marvellously through all those troubles. . . . Now be kind enough to say a Hail Mary for me instead of quarrelling with me for saying all this."[59] So, no bitterness, no rebellion.

In 1862 the *Rambler* was turned into *The Home and Foreign Review*. Newman read the first numbers with great interest and gave advice as to how the editors might win all candid intellectuals. But when the old offensive tone of the *Rambler* was again heard in it the bishops very soon censured the review in their pastorals. Moreover, Bishop Ullathorne sent a circular to his clergy, containing a detailed censure of some articles.

Immediately Newman wrote to him: "I hope I need not assure your Lordship that I concur with all my heart in your condemnation of the doctrines which you find in those publications." And Dr. Ullathorne replied: "Amongst the letters I have received on the subject of my Letter to the Clergy, none, nor all together, have given me so much gratification as the one you have so kindly written to me."[60] Newman, however, thought that the Bishop had read the censured articles carefully and that the condemned doctrines were really to be found in them. But in a short time it became clear to him that Ullathorne had misunderstood part of what had been written and consequently had condemned innocent people. He wondered whether he had become involved "in the sin of calumny". So after much deliberation he wrote another letter to the effect that he had not intended to give judgment but only his submission.[61] In the summer of 1861 he had declared: "It seems to me that a man who opposes legitimate authority is in a false position",[62] and in December of the same year: "I do not at all follow Dr. Ullathorne in what he says; but no good ever comes of disobedience, and I submit as a duty."[63] When shortly after the Pope himself censured the methods pursued by the review, Newman then concluded that God wanted him to be patient and wished him to be silent on controversies in connection with scientific investigation, interpretation of Scripture and other religious problems. "And I am not sure", he added "that it will not prove the best way."[64]

At that time there was still one tie with Dublin. Newman had built the University Church and paid 5600 pounds for it, received from three sources: the remainder of the gifts after the Achilli process; the special sums he had been given for that church; and a large loan, borrowed at high interest. In 1857 the Irish bishops had promised to buy the building from him, but in 1862 they had not yet fulfilled this promise, so he could not repay the loan. Certainly he knew that Ireland was extremely poor and the University highly expensive. The bishops had immense financial difficulties. Nevertheless, he was of the opinion that the delay was an injustice. So he wrote a strong letter in which he expressed his anxiety for the settlement of the affair. After some correspondence he proposed magnanimously that the bishops should pay 2400 pounds and that the rest, 3200 pounds, should become the property of the University on condition that a weekly Mass should be said for himself and the benefactors at some University Church altar as long as the building should be used as a church. "Their Lordships were highly pleased", one of the bishops wrote to him, "and, not only pleased, but edified by (let me call it) the high-souled disinterestedness, and, much more, by the pious munificence you have displayed." In January 1864 Newman received the last installment and made a note which shows some remorse: "Thus this anxious matter is ended. At first sight, on revising the correspondence, I seem to myself to have been hard on the Archbishops and not to have entered into their difficulties— but 5600 pounds is a large sum to lose, and unless I had followed up my rights sharply and perseveringly, those difficulties should have caused me to lose my money."[65]

This period, 1859–1864, is above all a period of slanders. It was said that Newman tried to found another Oratory in London in opposition to Faber and his subjects.[66] It was reported that he had quarrelled with the Pope.[67] It was stated as a fact that the Oratorians allowed their boys to go about Birmingham at their will; that they went to public houses and dance halls; even the word "brothel" was used.[68] Rumors were floating about that he was "unpracticable" and difficult to work with.[69] In July 1862 it was openly asserted in a newspaper that he had left the Oratory and was going to return to the Church of England.[70] In Rome it was suspected that he had wrong views about the temporal power of the pope and might leave the Church.[71] It was even rumored that he had preached in favor of Garibaldi.

The origin of this last slander was one word, spoken in a sermon. In that sermon Newman had asked prayers for the unfortunate people "whose homes were then perhaps made desolate in a land then being overrun by an able general". The "able general" stood for Garibaldi! That was all. And it ended in a rumor that Newman had sent him a large sum of money.[72]

Newman was accustomed to slanders of this kind, though he suffered especially from Roman displeasure and from slanders regarding the Oratory and the school. Not only were the latter believed in Rome, but several candidates were thus put off from joining the Oratory life. "I take all this," he wrote, "and can only take it, as the will of God."[73] That was his way of reacting against slander. But for once in his lifetime he replied and tried to put an end to the slanders, and with success. The story of the *Apologia*, which is here summarized, was the outcome.

In December 1863, a friend made an attack on his truthfulness which was printed in a magazine. The author of a review accused Newman and the whole Catholic clergy of not loving truth for truth's sake, implying that there was no harm in lying. Newman could not possibly leave this unnoticed. He started a correspondence with the editor and with the author, the Anglican clergyman and man of letters, Charles Kingsley. The latter, however, did not satisfactorily defend himself. With the silent permission of Kingsley, Newman published the entire correspondence and added a page of "Reflections", so brilliant and so devastating that before he had it printed Newman wondered whether it were unfair to his opponent. But a good, wise friend advised him not to change it by "concocting ditchwater instead of champagne".[74]

Newman considered it a great trial, however, to be called to such a public protest. At his age and with his occupations, he said, controversy was a hard thing. For a while he had tried to be satisfied with his private remonstrance and with the lame apologies Kingsley had made. But his deliberate judgment revolted from it. He felt it would be cowardice. After all, his severity in the "Reflections" was far less than the severity of Kingsley's unprovoked attack.[75]

When Kingsley saw the correspondence in print and the brilliant satire as a summary, he became angry and wrote a long pamphlet in which he heaped slanders upon misunderstandings, sarcasms upon generalizations, blunders upon downright falsehoods. He accused his adversary of not believing what he said, of being a dishonest man, a crafty deceiver, sapping the very foundation of historic truth. Newman had "worked his mind into that morbid state in which nonsense is the only food for which it hungers". Kingsley claimed Newman indulged in subtle paradoxes, in rhetorical exaggerations and took a perverse pleasure in saying anything to shock plain English notions. Catholic priests did not honor truth for its own sake. "There are, doubtless, pure and noble souls among them, superior, through the grace of God, to the official morality of their class: but in their official writings, and in too much of their official conduct, the great majority seem never, for centuries past, to have perceived that truth is the capital virtue, the virtue of all virtues."[76] Here again the strong attack on the Catholic clergy. The whole of the pamphlet was an appeal to the anti-Papist, anti-Catholic attitude of the great masses. And Newman felt obliged to do something against it. But what?

After considering the situation he recognized in half an hour what he had to do. The whole strength of the pamphlet lay in Kingsley's prejudice that he had been a Catholic while he was an Anglican. The only way in which he could destroy this idea was to give the history of his mind.[77] Never had he had such an opening to defend himself against slanders, especially against the slander of untruthfulness.[78]

It was an anxious undertaking, he wrote. Who could know himself and the multitude of subtle influences which acted upon him? Who could recollect, from the distance of twenty-five years, all that he once knew about his thoughts and deeds, during a time when perplexity and dismay weighed upon him? Who could well perform such self-analysis without full and calm leisure to look through everything he had written? It was a cruel operation: the tearing up of old griefs, he called it. Only an imperious call of duty made him attempt to do so. But it was to head and heart an extreme trial. This was the boldest undertaking he had ever attempted in his life. Were he not sure he should after all succeed in his object, it would be madness to set about it.[79] He was going to write because he thought it necessary, for his own sake and for the sake of the Catholic priesthood.[80] He knew that in the long run truth would prevail. He was confident that his readers would believe him in what he should say: they were his own countrymen who would be the judges. True, when excited, Englishmen might be un-

reasonable and unjust, but when calm they were generous and
fair. He did not like to be called a liar and a knave to his face.[81]

So he began to write. Indeed, he repeatedly heard the words
ringing in his ears: *Secretum meum mihi*, my secret belongs to
myself, I must not betray it. But then he thought: I am
drawing to my end, and therefore why should I care about
disclosures?[82] He continued writing for two whole months.
He had to leave his letters unanswered, send away visitors,
refuse invitations. Sometimes he worked for sixteen hours
running, once for twenty-two hours,[83] as the publisher wanted
him to hand in one chapter a week. On several occasions he
worked straight through the night, and he was found with his
head in his hands crying like a child over the painful task,
almost impossible to him, of public confession[84] and of revealing
the intimate relationship between himself and his Maker.[85]

It was like fighting under the lash. He could not read the
numerous letters he had kept. He could hardly remember what
he had written in his printed works. But he had made up his
mind to set down nothing as certain for which he had not a
clear memory, some written memorial or the corraboration of
some friend. There were witnesses enough up and down the
country to verify, correct or complete it.[86]

While writing with all his heart against Kingsley, he did not
feel any resentment toward him. How could he? He had never
seen him. Nevertheless, as he knew from experience, it was
necessary to show deep indignation in order to be taken
seriously. Therefore there are sharp and indignant remonstrances in the *Apologia*, and justly so. He called Kingsley's
methods of controversy most base and cruel. "What I insist
upon . . . is this unmanly attempt of his . . . to cut the ground
from under my feet; to poison by anticipation the public mind
against me . . . and to infuse into the imaginations of my
readers, suspicion and mistrust of everything that I may say in
reply to him. *This I call poisoning the wells.*"[87] And then he
adopted Saint Paul's conduct when challenged: he forgot for a
moment the humble thoughts he used to cherish about his

own achievements and pointed to his own good qualities. Had he not always been fair to the doctrines and arguments of his opponents? Had he ever slurred over facts and reasonings that told against himself? Had he ever given his name or authority to proofs which he thought unsound or to testimony which he did not think at least plausible? Had he ever shrunk from confessing a fault when he felt he had committed one? Had he not always consulted for others more than for himself? Had he not given up much that he loved and prized and could have retained but that he loved honesty better than name and truth better than dear friends? So he was confident that the English public would not be ungenerous or harsh and would believe him.[88]

Thus in a few weeks grew the *Apologia*, the largest book written by him thus far; the most beautiful of all English autobiographies; a book only to be compared with Saint Augustine's *Confessions*. It does not contain the story of Newman's spiritual life in its completeness but only as regards the development of his religious opinions. After a few words about his childhood, it starts with the great change that took place in him when he was fifteen. From that time he entertained a definite creed. Then he describes how books and facts gave rise to new religious ideas; how they developed through study and reading, discussions and experiences; how at long last they became a system. At first he thought it possible for him to adhere to this system without being disloyal to the Anglican church and his ministry in her. But at long last it collapsed, while the Catholic religion began to light up as the truth, and the Catholic Church as the one true fold, of which Christ had spoken. When he had become certain, he surrendered. The dramatic exposition of this story finished with Saint Philip's name upon Saint Philip's feast, May 26, 1864. He added a moving dedication to his brothers, the priests of the Birmingham Oratory, who, as he wrote, had been so faithful to him; who had been so sensitive to his needs; who had been so indulgent to his failings; who had carried him through so many trials; who had grudged no sacrifice if he asked for it; who had been so cheerful under discouragements of his causing; who had done so many good works and let him have the credit of them; with whom he had lived so long, with whom he hoped to die.[89] And thinking of his old friends, still Anglicans, he ended his story with the words: "I earnestly pray for this whole company, with a hope against hope, that all of us, who once were so united, and so happy in our union, may even now be brought at length, by the Power of the Divine Will, into One Fold and under One Shepherd."[90]

He had still to write the last part, which was to contain an answer in detail to Kingsley's accusations. And after its appearance the almost universal cry of approval burst forth which took even his warmest friends by surprise. From one end of the kingdom to the other, people expressed their assent, their gratitude, their admiration. The great Oxford watchword *Credo in Newmannum* became full of life again.[91] He was publicly praised by his bishop, by the clergy of his own diocese and of many other dioceses and also by the laity.[92] For the Anglicans he was no longer the lost and forgotten leader: he had regained their respect and their faith in his honesty. From this time onward they would listen to him and take all his words seriously. The Catholics, among whom he had not been appreciated for a long time, influenced as they were by rumors and slanders, became proud of him and would consider him henceforth with affectionate reverence. It was as if he had risen from the dead.

Kingsley felt humiliated, crushed. He said in great stubbornness: "I have nothing to retract, apologize for, explain. Deliberately, after twenty years of thought, I struck as hard as I could. Deliberately I shall strike again, if it so pleases me, though not one literary man in England approved."[93]

How differently Newman acted. When he had achieved his purpose, he cancelled in subsequent editions all violent passages against his adversary and even his name. Eleven years later, at Kingsley's death, he said Mass for him at once. He remembered that he had never felt any anger against him. He was grateful that, "in the good Providence of God", Kingsley had given him an opportunity of vindicating his character and conduct. His passionate attack had made him one of his best friends. He had always hoped that through some happy chance he might meet him. He felt sure that there would have been no embarrassment on his part, and he would have heartily shaken hands with him. He never did meet him but always cherished his memory.[94]

CHAPTER TEN

STILL UNDER A CLOUD

1864–1870

O how light a Cross—think what the Crosses of others are!
And think of the compensation, compensation even in this
world. . . . I have had, it is true, no recognition in high
quarters—but what warm kind letters in private have I had!
and how many! and what public acknowledgments![1]

If we open Newman's last journal to discover his interior state
after the success of the *Apologia*, we find him entirely changed.
He observed that he had become hardened against all opposition
and had lost all sadness at the ill-treatment on the part of
influential Catholics. He thought himself marvellously blessed
because he had gained the favor of the Protestants and the ap-
probation of a good part of the English Catholic priests. Former
Anglican friends such as Keble and Rogers wished to come into
contact with him again. And he wrote: "My temptation at this
moment is, to value the praise of men too highly, especially of
Protestants—and to lose some portion of the sensitiveness
towards God's praise, which is so elementary a duty."[2]

The opposition in influential quarters, however, was to
continue. Though Bishop Ullathorne remained his staunch
defender and even wrote to Rome to beg the authorities for
caution in believing what was said against Newman, the
Archbishop at Westminster did not lose his suspicions. They
were made known to the representative of the English bishops
in Rome, Monsignor Talbot, who had the task of informing
the Pope about the English situation and English problems.
He was the man who blackened Newman's reputation with
the authorities.[3]

In England it was first and foremost Cardinal Wiseman's adviser, Henry Edward Manning, who was concerned about Newman's influence. Before the latter entered the Church there was for a time a certain friendly contact between the two men, in particular when they corresponded with each other after Mrs. Manning's death. The relationship was neither reserved nor difficult before 1862. True, there is the story of Newman's rudeness in refusing to receive Manning after his Fifth of November Sermon, preached in Newman's pulpit against the Church of Rome, two years before Newman's conversion.[4] But this is a legend. Not any allusion to this story in either Newman's or Manning's letters proves its truth.[5] When the latter, a few weeks after the alleged slight, wrote to Newman, he made no reference to the incident. On the contrary, Newman's answer is a piece of humble, magnanimous self-accusation in connection with his farewell sermon at Littlemore without any allusion to what is alleged to have happened.[6] And in Manning's summary of the later disagreement between Newman and himself, written in 1887,[7] it is not mentioned at all, though Manning would no doubt have remembered and included it had it been true. In 1851 Manning had become a Catholic and, in less than three months, a priest. In October of the same year, Newman had tried to obtain him as his vice-rector at the Catholic University in Dublin, but without success.[8] Six years later Newman dedicated his *Occasional Sermons* to Manning, which gave him much pleasure.[9] In 1862 Manning, in Rome, had written one of his tender, delicately worded letters to comfort Newman in his trials: "It seems to me that Our Lord must have a special love for you, and a special design over you: for you have had many trials; and after many years of great favour and help from Him Our Lord has begun to purify you for a higher world by crosses. . . . If I can be in any way of use to you here let me know."[10]

But it was in the same year that Newman lost his confidence in Manning. What happened? Manning called at the Oratory, and Newman thought he had come to console him, chiefly over the school troubles. He had opened his heart to him and said confidentially that he had lately compared the Church with the land of Canaan, flowing with milk and honey, but this was only if he considered her supernaturally; from an earthly point of view he lived in a dreary desert.[11] After Manning's visit, Bishop Ullathorne warned him: Manning never goes anywhere but in order to find something out.[12] Not long afterward Newman saw a formal list of Catholic schools in England. The Oratory school was not mentioned. This could not have been an oversight.[13] After the appearance of the *Apologia*, Manning wrote a pamphlet in which he more or less accused Newman of three heretical statements.[14] True, he called the *Apologia* the greatest of Newman's works, but he thought the first chapters unworthy of him.[15] Newman was aware of this. No wonder that when in 1865 Manning became Archbishop of Westminster Newman should exclaim: "Manning is so mysterious, that I don't know how one can ever have confidence in him."[16]

Nevertheless, from his letters, diaries and memoranda it appears that Manning was actuated by noble principles; that he showed great patience and magnanimity in trials; that he developed immense zeal for God's glory and the salvation of souls; that he cherished an enthusiastic love for the Church and her visible Head; and above all that he constantly tried to do God's will. Surely, his biographer has given us a dark picture of the man, but his charity covers all his deficiencies. It was a heroic charity, long-suffering in its persistence, wonderfully supernatural in all its activities. To the very end of his life Manning loved to spend and to be spent in the service of all who were the victims of injustice, poverty and crime, in order to bring them all to their heavenly destination. At the same time his great detachment from the things of the world is very conspicuous.[17]

In spite of all this Newman was more congenial in his relationship with others than with Manning. The latter was applauded and courted but not loved. The difference of character and talents proved extremely great. Manning was by nature an active man who loved to work and accomplish; Newman naturally desired to be quiet and keep himself in the background. Manning acted from natural impulses, strengthened by supernatural motives; Newman often acted from supernatural motives only, finding little encouragement in natural inclinations. Manning enjoyed a fight for a good cause; Newman longed for peace, a quiet life, study, meditation. As soon as Manning believed a contest to be desirable, he attacked his adversary; Newman shrank from the difficulties of a just cause and was continually hampered by the fact that he saw in every idea numerous facets which he could not at once reconcile.

Apart from inner factors, Manning was often stimulated by friends, especially by William George Ward, an Oxford man and a convert, the leading spirit of English Catholics, intolerant of all those who did not share his opinions. In spite of his great admiration and love for Newman, his old master, he encouraged Manning in his opposition to him. He was convinced that Newman was unwittingly disloyal to the Pope and entertained worldly ideas. He suggested to Manning that he should not "magnify the Christian duty of forgiveness while not adequately pondering on the Christian duty of protest".[18]

It would be unjust to blame Manning for ambition, double-dealing or disloyalty, as has been done, especially with regard to Newman. Indeed, Manning possessed an extraordinary administrative ability. He knew it and was anxious to exercise it. If this is ambition, Manning was ambitious. He was not so, however, in the sense of being overmastered by this talent and tendency. His natural gifts were regulated and ennobled by his profound spiritual life. It is as though Providence had a special object in making him the head of the English hierarchy. The Catholic Church in England needed a leader who could rid her of her inferiority complex and her insularity.

As for double-dealing, it is true that Manning could speak very differently on the same subject to different people so that he was accused of insincerity. Various utterances of his are indeed hard to reconcile. He possessed a talent for "the improvisation of lifelong convictions". He was far too busy and far too engaged with all sorts of problems to be able to remember everything he had formerly said or written. His mind worked energetically and reacted quickly, but this gift enabled him to change his opinions without much difficulty, sometimes even unconsciously. The new opinion became as strong a conviction as the old one. He even forgot that he had held any other. As to Newman, on several occasions Manning also expressed his reluctance to hurt his old friend, and this feeling might have made him appear close, mysterious and insincere when one considers his actions.

Neither was Manning disloyal to friends. In great generosity he had given his love to God's Church and especially to the Catholic Church in England. Everything else was made subservient to her welfare. He determined to promote discipline and ecclesiastical unity. Everybody had to work to this end. When he saw that Newman stood in his way because of his differing ideas about aims and means, he began to consider him an adversary not only of himself but of the Pope, the Church, the Holy Spirit. Consequently, although he maintained a genuine admiration for Newman's genius and a tender recollection of the old relationship, Manning felt obliged to watch him, to oppose him and, if necessary, to overrule him. It is understandable that Manning should be accused of disloyalty.

His enthusiasm for everything connected with the Holy See led him to inform Rome and the Pope about all English ecclesiastical affairs, either by means of letters or by visits to Monsignor Talbot. Newman's words and acts were being reported at headquarters in an unfavorable light because Manning could not approve of his spirit. In the end he went so far as to consider him "the most dangerous man in England".[19]

In the course of the years the differences of opinion came to a head. There were three important matters about which Manning and Newman strongly disagreed. The first of these was the problem of Catholic students at Oxford. Here are the facts:

A few weeks after the publication of the *Apologia*, Newman was offered a large tract of land within the city of Oxford. He decided that such an opportunity for Catholics must not be lost, although he had to borrow nearly 9000 pounds at a high rate of interest to meet the costs. Sooner or later the Catholics might want to use the ground.[20] To his surprise, Bishop Ullathorne, who had heard about the transactions, called at the Oratory and asked him to start a Mission there, that is, a Catholic parish. After deliberation and consultation Newman decided that he would accept the offer not only with the few Catholic inhabitants of Oxford in mind but also for the young Catholics at the University. And this he considered "the chief and most important missionary work".[21]

In 1855 the prohibition against admitting non-Anglican students to the University was withdrawn, and Cardinal Wiseman had given tacit consent to parents who wanted to enter their sons. He knew how grievous the disadvantages had been for the Catholic aristocracy on account of the impossibility of university education. He expressed the warmest sympathy for the idea of founding a Hall or College under Catholic management. But after he had come under Manning's influence his views began to change. Manning was vehemently opposed to the idea. He was convinced that the only way to preserve the faith of the Catholic aristocracy was a prohibition. Newman, however, entertained quite different ideas. A Catholic University in England would be impossible. A Catholic College at Oxford would be ideal. Unless it were established on an equal basis with any Protestant College, parents would not send their sons. But to make it so, much money would be required. If it were successful, it would, however, excite the jealousy of the Protestants.[22] The only solution appeared to be, not to forbid young men to go to Oxford, but to protect them by the presence of a well-run Mission. A community of capable priests should preserve the young students from the dangers of Oxford free thought. Moreover, a prohibition would create a strong temptation to disobey.[23] But however deeply he disagreed with Manning, he desired to act according to the Pope's wishes.

In the beginning of his pontificate, Pope Pius IX had honestly attempted to remain open to modern ideas. His efforts, however, had been in vain and bore bitter fruit. Since that time he had become opposed to all compromises and all contact with unbelief, liberalism and rationalism. Newman understood that the Pope would be unlikely to encourage Catholics to study in Protestant universities. But he knew also that England differed immensely from Italy with regard to circumstances, tendencies, currents of thought. He could not concede that a strong line must be adopted. He believed that there were young men who might study at Oxford without risk, provided they received Catholic guidance. But the will of the Pope was for him the will of God.

This does not mean that he had no objections to the Oratorians going to Oxford. There was a scarcity of priests at the Oratory,[24] besides the fact that he himself would be obliged to go. "I must leave my home where I have everything I want about me. I had enough of that in going to Dublin", he said to his Oratorians.[25] He wondered too whether his health would stand the strain of the anxieties, both pecuniary and ecclesiastical, connected with the move. He had so often been abandoned, not only over the Achilli affair and the Dublin rectorship but also in his Dublin church and in the project for the translation of Scripture. Would he not be abandoned again?[26]

In spite of all this he accepted the offer. "Our only hope is that we are doing God's Will in thus portentously involving ourselves both in money matters and in work."[27]

He therefore drew up a circular in order to acquaint people with his plans and to collect the necessary finances. But before the publication of the circular, Dr. Ullathorne showed his concern, fearing the idea would be regarded as encouraging Catholic parents to send their sons to Oxford. With the utmost readiness, Newman complied with the Bishop's wish to withhold publication and spontaneously offered a copy to be read at the coming meeting of bishops.[28] Ullathorne was gratified. He knew how great the opposition was going to be. Especially when William George Ward acted against the scheme "with the zeal of a Crusader".[29] This lay theologian wanted to preserve the unity of a Catholic atmosphere for the Catholic aristocratic youth at whatever cost. He had strong allies in Dr. Grant, the Bishop of Southwark, the future Cardinal Herbert Vaughan and Manning, who had the ear of Cardinal Wiseman. Even Henry Wilberforce, a great friend of Newman's, sided against him and averred that he would rather see his son dead at his feet than send him to Oxford. They were all of the opinion that Newman's presence at Oxford would mean the triumph of what was called mixed education.[30] He would attract young men there as a magnet does steel.

Before the bishops met, a list of questions on university education was sent by Wiseman to many leading Oxford converts. But to Newman's surprise and distress, neither he himself nor his sympathizers received copies. When a friend procured him one he remarked that all those questions might be summed up in this way: "Are you or are you not, one of those wicked men who advocate Oxford education?"[31] It was Manning who had drawn up the list.[32]

At their meeting, only two bishops—one of them Wiseman himself—wished to forbid Catholics to study at Oxford. The rest were vehemently against a prohibition. But all of them agreed to the impossibility of founding a College or Hall and the inadvisability of sending Catholic students to Oxford.[33] When Newman became acquainted with the proceedings he felt that the bishops on the whole did not trust him and that he would be secretly thwarted. He realized that the very fact of his going to Oxford would encourage parents to send their sons to the University.[34] He decided that it would be better to lay his plans aside, for to continue with them would be both unbecoming and inconsistent.[35]

A few weeks later, early in 1865, an official letter from Rome concerning this matter was received. This letter was the result of the advice of the bishops, and a strong directive was sent to all their clergy telling them to dissuade parents from sending their sons to Oxford. This was not, however, a total prohibition.[36] Newman regarded the action with deep regret, especially since the bishops did not put forth any positive measure to meet the need or offer any compensation for their negative approach. "Are Catholics to be worse educated than all other gentlemen in the country?" he asked.[37]

He was well aware that the December meeting must have been strongly influenced by Manning, the great adversary in this affair. Manning had imbibed the spirit of Pius IX and wished to avoid all contact with the enemy. He desired only to realize the Pope's views and was convinced that Newman's presence at Oxford would be fatal. Newman came to the conclusion that this was in fact an act of the Pope himself, who uncompromisingly opposed all "mixed education", and he reconciled himself to it. There was the possibility that another pope might conceivably reverse the decision.[38] "It is still the Blessed Will of God to send me baulks. On the whole, I suppose, looking through my life as a course, He is using me, but really viewed in its separate parts it is but a life of failures."[39]

He sold the land and wrote to his bishop that he considered the Oxford Mission plan at an end.[40]

In September 1865, Pusey published a book to promote the reunion of Christians. He called it an *Eirenicon*, that is, a way to peace. But it caused indignation among Catholics because Pusey attacked the Catholic doctrine regarding both Our Lady and papal infallibility without precise knowledge of what these doctrines contained. He had consulted the writings of Faber and Ward, both of whom had extreme views on these subjects. He quoted statements of Faber's such as: "That the mercy of Mary is infinite; that God has resigned into her hands His omnipotence; that it is safer to seek her than to seek her Son; that Our Lord is subject to her command; that Mary alone can obtain a Protestant's conversion"; and many other exaggerated expressions.[41] Of course, such statements can be explained according to orthodox doctrine, but out of context they appeared blasphemous. Moreover, Faber was certainly not a representative exponent of Catholic teaching on this subject; neither was Ward on infallibility. He was under the impression that the Pope frequently made infallible pronouncements.[42]

Many people wanted Newman to reply to Pusey. But Newman was wary. By his *Apologia* he had obtained the ear of the Anglicans and the sympathy of Catholics. He had no wish to lose what he had gained by so much effort. On the other hand, was not Pusey's book a chance to disclaim Faber's exaggerated views on Our Lady and to utter a protest against Ward? Newman decided that God wanted him to write.[43] Thus the *Letter to Pusey* was composed.

In this document two things strike the reader: Newman's deep devotion to Our Lady and his tenderness toward friends.

One of the greatest difficulties in his Anglican years had been the Catholic devotional manifestations in honor of Mary.[44] This is not to infer that he had not always entertained a great reverence and love for the Blessed Virgin. At Oxford he had taken a pride in living in her College and serving her altar. One of his earliest sermons dealt with Mary's immaculate purity.[45] As early as 1839 he showed his dislike of opposition to the devotion of the Immaculate Conception.[46] When he became a Catholic he took Mary as his Confirmation name.[47] When in 1849 he learned about the near possibility of a papal decree on the Immaculate Conception he observed: "Certainly it is a joyful thing, and in a queer way, I have not been able to think of Our Lady since I heard of it, without a feeling like 'I know something good has happened to you, but I can't recollect what it is.' And then I have brought it to mind, and also reminded myself that it was only her accidental glory which it affected. However, it's very joyful and pleasant, anyhow."[48] In December 1854, the month of the definition of the dogma of the Immaculate Conception, he received a sum of money which relieved him from considerable financial difficulties, and he called it "a bounty of the Great Queen upon her festal day".[49] When Henry Bowden's children lost their mother he wrote in a touching letter of sympathy: "And now while you bid adieu for a while, only for a while, to dearest mama, offer yourselves, my dear children, to your great and tender mother in heaven, the Blessed Mother of God, who will not refuse to have you, and to watch over you, and to give you all that gentle and true guidance which you need so much, and which you hoped to have from her whom God has taken from you."[50] A very great part of his *Meditations and Devotions* is devoted to our Lady, "the humble-hearted Mother of God, whom the world despises",[51] and there he speaks of her in a most tender way. He often preached about her.[52] These proofs of Newman's love for Our Lady could be multiplied, and they were crowned by this beautiful *Letter to Pusey*.

He sings her praises in his own manner. He shows how she was venerated in the primitive Church and how this veneration grew in a natural way. His arguments strike us by their cogency and their devotional character. For Newman's love of Our Lady is simple and childlike but at the same time real and solid. A serene harmony pervades his doctrine. There is no pious exaggeration in strong statements, while on the other hand his praises are like panegyrics unsurpassed for their reality and beauty.

He finished his work on the eve of the Immaculate Conception with one of his wonderful paragraphs:

> The Feast of the Immaculate Conception is upon us; and close upon its Octave . . . come the great Antiphons, the heralds of Christmas. That joyful season, joyful for all of us, while it centres in Him who then came on earth, also brings before us in peculiar prominence that Virgin Mother, who bore and nursed Him. There she is not in the background, as at Easter-tide, but she brings Him to us in her arms. . . . May the sacred influences of this tide bring us all together in unity! May it destroy all bitterness on your side and ours! May it quench all jealous, sour, proud, fierce antagonism on our side; and dissipate all captious, carping, fastidious refinements of reasoning on yours! May that bright and gentle Lady, the Blessed Virgin Mary, overcome you with her sweetness, and revenge herself on her foes by interceding effectually for their conversion![53]

The other striking quality of the *Letter* is his tenderness for his Anglican friend Pusey. From the very beginning Newman had been anxious lest he should pain him. He had written several letters to him before publishing his thoughts.[54] The introductory remarks were tender and fair, full of true friendship, and at the same time honest in the clear remonstrances against Pusey's one-sided views, his violence toward Rome, his "olive branch discharged as if from a catapult".[55] "Have you not been touching us on a very tender point in a very rude way?" he asked. "Is it not the effect of what you have said to expose her to scorn and obloquy, who is dearer to us than any other creature? Have you ever hinted that our love for her is anything else than an abuse? Have you thrown her one kind word yourself all through your book? I trust so, but I have not lighted upon one. And yet I know you love her well."[56]

With the same delicacy he writes about Faber. He refers to the fact that the Fathers of the Eastern church use strong expressions when they address Our Lady, and he concludes: "Such a phenomenon . . . ought to make the Anglicans merciful towards those writers amongst ourselves, who have been excessive in singing the praises of the Deipara."[57] He admits that it would be wrong, through false devotion to Mary, to forget Christ. But he would like the fact of any such forgetfulness to be proved first. And in this he refers to Faber's books: "Did the author write nothing else? Had he written on the Blessed Sacrament? Had he given up 'all for Jesus'?"[58]

The refutation of Ward's statements on papal infallibility was entrusted by Newman to the able pen of the youngest Oratorian in the house, Father Ignatius Ryder. He wrote two pamphlets on the subject according to Newman's ideas and views. And Newman gratefully observed: "This seems to me wonderful and shows that we are in God's hands, and must be content to do our work day by day, as He puts it before us, without attempting to understand or to anticipate His purposes."[59]

It was at this time that he received what he considered incontrovertible proof of Our Lady's gratitude. While he was preparing his work for the press he suffered acute attacks of pain. They came on so suddenly and without warning that he dreaded to leave home in case he should suffer an attack while travelling or at the house of a friend. The doctor attributed the illness to the strain caused by his work on the *Letter to Pusey*. During a night of January 1866, when the work was finished, the attacks ceased. When the doctor came in the morning, he was astonished. Although as an unbeliever he was loathe to attribute Newman's recovery to a miracle, his surprise and the way he spoke of the healing, both at the time and later, expressed his inner conviction. Newman always attributed this great favor to the Blessed Virgin Mary, whose honor he had defended, and he would never permit any other explanation.[60]

Newman's answer to Pusey's *Eirenicon* and Father Ryder's pamphlets were followed by many expressions of approval. Manning, for instance, wrote flattering letters to him. Nevertheless, there were points to which he objected, and he wrote an article, intended for the *Dublin Review*, severely criticizing certain passages. This article he sent to Bishop Ullathorne for approval, but the Bishop dissuaded him from publication. This came to Newman's ears, and he sighed: "I think that as a matter of prudence, I never shall trust him till he has gone through purgatory and has no infirmities upon him."[61]

There were further reasons for suspicion when Cardinal Reisach came to England to familiarize himself with the Oxford University question. Manning took care that the Cardinal did not meet Newman. Reisach spent a few days with Ward, inspected the ground Newman had purchased in Oxford and even visited Oscott near Birmingham but did not seek Newman's opinion. In fact, Newman was not even aware that he was in the neighborhood.[62] This was hardly the way to achieve understanding. When Manning had been consecrated bishop he had expressed delight at seeing Newman, and he had embraced and kissed him. But Newman could no longer appreciate this cordiality because he desired only "fairness, frankness and a determination never to do things behind one's back".[63] He explained the deepest ground of this mystery and his own distrust of Manning when he wrote: "When you ask an explanation of all this, I don't impute to him any animosity to me—but I think he is of a nature to be determined to *crush* or to *melt* every person who stands in his way. He has his views and is determined to carry them out—and I must either go with him or be annihilated."[64]

The doctrine on the temporal power of the pope was a second point about which Newman had disagreed. In the sixties, when a revolutionary movement swept through Italy and endangered the Papal States, it became a much discussed subject. Both indignation and loyalty were expressed among Catholics all over the world. Manning maintained that the temporal power was necessary for the liberty of the Church and the spiritual independence of the papacy and could not be dissolved except in the times of the Antichrist. He declared that this theory could be made a dogma.[65]

In October 1866 the English bishops devoted a day to prayer for the Pope, and Newman preached a sermon on the Pope and the revolution.[66] From it we learn what he thought about the privileges of the Vicar of Christ: "In his administration of Christ's kingdom, in his religious acts, we must never oppose his will, or dispute his word, or criticise his policy, or shrink from his side. . . . In obeying Him, we are obeying his Lord. . . . He is guided by an intelligence more than human. . . . Even in secular matters it is ever safe to be on his side, dangerous to be on the side of his enemies. Our duty is—not indeed to mix up Christ's Vicar with this or that party of men because he . . . is above all parties—but to look at his formal deeds, and . . . to defend him at all hazards."[67] In this sermon, too, Newman refutes the accusations of the Pope's own people, the Romans. He exhorts his hearers to pray "that the territory still his should not be taken from him". The result would depend on these prayers. He thought it highly probable that the Pope would retain his power in a certain sense. But if it were God's intention to take it from him, He would give another in its place.[68] As he wrote in 1866, Newman could not understand why the Irish bishops lamented as if there were no hope because there was no earthly power to aid the Holy See.[69] He could not concede that the Holy Father should be protected against his own people by foreign bayonets. Anything, he believed, would be better than that. "What he is persecuted he is in his proper place—not when he persecutes—but I don't say this to everyone, for it would annoy most people."[70]

These ideas, however, were considered disloyal. The sermon was submitted to the Index, but it was returned with the remark that it contained nothing with which to find fault.[71] Was it Manning who had submitted the sermon to the Index? Newman believed so. Till the end of his life, Manning would maintain that Newman cherished wrong ideas about the temporal power. And though Manning was obliged to change his views, he could not refrain from writing in his 1887 account of the disagreement that in this point he sided with the Holy See, which he said Newman did not.[72]

Strange to say, after the *Letter to Pusey*, and in spite of the disappointment of the foregoing year, Bishop Ullathorne again offered Newman the Oxford Mission.[73] Because of the increase of Catholics there, he did so with such urgency that Newman did not feel he could refuse.[74] He submitted the wish of the Bishop to the judgment of the Oratorians, and in June he accepted the offer, although under certain conditions.[75] To a religious friend he had written a few weeks before: "St. Philip has been very good to us, but we want him to be better still—for there is again a chance of the Oratory making its appearance in Oxford, and the prospect is a load which requires a great deal of faith and love to bear without wincing. I am so old, have so little strength, and so little heart for anything."[76] It would cause him considerable pain to live in Oxford as "a stranger in his dearest home". Only an imperative call of duty could force him to contemplate the move. "But I trust God will strengthen me, when the time comes, if it is to come."[77] He was afraid "of getting into hot water", afraid of publicity, "but it seems the will of God, and I do not know how to draw back."[78]

This turn of events caused surprise in Rome. Had it not been judged that Newman's presence in Oxford would attract students? How had this situation come about? Bishop Ullathorne gave as explanation the fact that Newman himself would not be residing there.[79] But Newman became suspicious. Was it worthwhile to force himself into a position which he did not want and which others did not desire for him? Nevertheless, in July 1866 he let the Bishop know that he wished "to acquiesce in the Holy Father's decision", whether in favor of the Oxford Mission or against it.[80] He reminded the Bishop also that he felt no call whatever to go to Oxford except to care for Catholic undergraduates and to convert graduates. He feared that Rome did not fully realize this and that it might lead to trouble.[81]

By the end of the year, Rome sent a message giving permission for a Mission in Oxford but only "for the time being and conditionally". Newman was alarmed by these words. His alarm would have been far greater had he known the condition which Bishop Ullathorne concealed from him. It was a secret instruction to the effect that the Bishop should gently recall him should he take up residence. This situation was the direct result of Manning's letters, and the Bishop was distressed and anxious about it. He hoped to persuade Rome to cancel the condition when he went there six months later.[82]

Newman, full of misgivings, definitely wanted to postpone the whole matter for six months. But both the Oratorians and his own friends insisted on his not delaying the decision. So a start was made on collecting the necessary funds, and he determined to open the Mission the second week after Easter.[83] "I only go because I fear to be deaf to a divine call, but, if anything happened in the six months to prevent it, that would be to me a sign that there never had been a Divine call."[84]

His fear increased when in March he received a rebuke from Cardinal Barnabò in Rome accusing him of preparing boys to enter Oxford and of disobedience to the declarations of the Pope and the Holy See. But Newman could honestly state that he had never heard a word of such declarations.[85] "As I now for the first time learn from your Eminence that the Sacred Congregation wants me to abstain from anything that seems to favour directly or indirectly an Oxford education for our youths, I promptly and diligently promise you to obey. I am surprised, however, how little confidence your Eminence has in me regarding this matter after twenty years of a most faithful service. But God will see to it."[86] These last words roused the Cardinal's anger.[87] He considered them impertinent,[88] tantamount to a threat.[89] They were, however, the same words used by Saint Philip Neri in similar circumstances.[90] They did not imply disappointment at not having received a promotion. He had never had any motive of secular or ecclesiastical ambition in writing. But he felt a sense of injustice when he considered that after his anxious and not unsuccessful attempts to promote the Catholic cause, his first mistake in the *Rambler*—presuming it was a mistake—should have caused him to be suspected and rebuked. The words "God will see to it", however, would for many years have their sad consequences for him.[91]

The whole affair affected him to such a degree that he sent Fathers Ambrose and Henry to Rome to speak on behalf of the school. He prepared a lengthy statement on the calumnies which had been circulated and the false assumption that its system of education had been formally and intentionally directed to the preparation of youths for Oxford. At the end of his statement he expressed his hopes that Rome would either openly vindicate him or recommend him to bring the school to an end. "As we began it to the greater glory of God, and the benefit of Holy Church, so, if the Sacred Congregation will it, we will cheerfully put a close to it."[92]

In Rome, however, the atmosphere was all against Newman. Monsignor Talbot had influenced the Pope and Cardinal

Barnabò against him. Again and again the article in the *Rambler* and the sermon supposedly in favor of Garibaldi were brought up. Thus it happened that a Roman correspondent, who made his meager living by retailing every piece of Roman gossip he could scrape up, revealed in a Catholic weekly that the Pope had forbidden Newman to go to Oxford. "This distinguished man has no longer, in Roman opinion, the high place he once held. It could hardly be otherwise, after the sermon on the Temporal Power, certain passages of the *Apologia*, and the having allowed his great name to be linked with that of one of the bitterest haters of Rome."[93]

Bishop Ullathorne saw the article on April 6 and felt very much upset. It even affected his health.[94] Not long before, he had spoken with Father Ambrose about the soundness of Newman's faith, and he had said: "My dear Sir, his faith is the faith of a Saint."[95] As soon as he had read the article, he decided that he wanted Newman to learn the facts from himself. So he sent a message at once and told him about the secret instruction: if Newman wished to reside at Oxford personally, the Bishop should recall him "in a gentle and sweet way". Ullathorne further informed him that he had hoped to have this secret instruction cancelled during his visit to Rome the next summer.[96] At the same time he besought Newman not to say that he would not accept the Mission.[97]

Newman's first thought was: "How can I possibly go to Oxford under such circumstances?" A stay of only a few days might easily be construed as "residence" by Rome.[98] He realized that the difficulties over the school were solely a consequence of the great mistrust Rome entertained for him. He felt inclined to say: "Gentlemen, settle it among yourselves. I do nothing till you make the Letter writer . . . eat his words." But first he asked the advice of the Oratorians. He refused to be influenced by indignation. He desired to ascertain what was the best course of action and how scandal could be avoided.[99] Agreeing with the advice of his Brothers, he asked permission to suspend the move to Oxford for the time being.[100]

In the meantime Fathers Ambrose and Henry had arrived in Rome and had approached the authorities in order to defend Newman's cause. Both Cardinal Barnabò and Monsignor Talbot clarified their various complaints against him. The Oratorians had two meetings with the Pope. It was not difficult to trace the influence of Newman's English adversaries. Father Ambrose discovered that the only substantial charge against Newman was the *Rambler* article of 1859, and he produced a copy of the letter which Newman had sent to Wiseman in January 1860, in which he expressed unconditional submission. But either the original letter had not been brought before the authorities or else Barnabò had entirely forgotten its existence. This move was a complete success. The Cardinal was thunderstruck. The letter absolved Newman from all guilt. The authorities realized his innocence, and the Pope declared him to be "wholly obedient". Barnabò even declared that he loved Newman: he was a saint, and saints had always been persecuted. He declared further than an Oratory in Oxford was not forbidden; the sole condition was that Newman was not to change his residence. A stay of a month or so would not be considered as "residing". It seemed as if the disposition to speak well of Newman was universal.[101]

But he himself foresaw that the dispersal of the cloud would be of short duration. He was afraid of further secret instructions. He understood that under these circumstances he would not be able to discharge the duties of a Mission with greatest effectiveness, so he formally asked permission to withdraw. Bishop Ullathorne was not surprised. He would have done the same had he been in the same position. He complied, although "with a sense of pain both acute and deep".[102] Newman hoped that one day another religious body would do what he was unable to do, and with this in mind he kept the money he had collected.[103] In the private circular, sent to the benefactors after the affair, he did not show the slightest sign of indignation.[104] He could rightly testify: "I . . . see but one thing, that I, from first to last, have acted simply in the presence of God."[105]

When later he pondered on these events he called them "the lightest of trials" compared with ill-health, loss of friends or poverty. "Therefore I have nothing to complain of, nothing to wish otherwise, everything to rejoice at", he wrote to a lady who had pitied him.[106] One of the Oratorians said explicitly that Newman took the disappointment "in the quiet way in which he always took the interference of authority", and he remarked that his fellow Oratorians felt it perhaps more than Newman himself did.[107]

When in October of the same year Bishop Ullathorne issued a personal letter discouraging Catholic parents from sending their sons to Oxford, Newman showed his obedience and inserted a notice in the Oratory School Prospectus: "There is no preparation provided for the examinations at Oxford and Cambridge."[108] When in special cases parents asked his advice about Oxford, he answered with the words of the Apostle: "Obey them that have the rule over you . . . and submit yourselves, for they watch for your souls as those who must give account."[109]

After this second failure Newman himself described his inner state. He was aware that the authorities would remain suspicious and that all his efforts would displease them. Nevertheless he could truly state: "These external matters have all wonderfully promoted my inward happiness. I never was in such simply happy circumstances. . . . I enjoy life only too well. The weight of years falls on me as snow . . . but I do not feel it yet. . . . What can I want but greater gratitude and love towards the Giver of all these good things? There is no state of life I prefer to my own. . . . There is nothing I desire. . . . I am as covered with blessings and as full of God's gifts, as is conceivable. And I have nothing to ask for but pardon and grace, and a happy death."[110]

By that time the antagonism between Newman and Manning had become known to both Catholics and Protestants, and Manning was accused by the Catholics of thwarting Newman, especially over the Oxford affair.[111] Manning greatly regretted this division, and in the summer of 1867 he attempted to effect a restoration of intimacy with the help of a mutual friend who made the first step. "The only and serious cause of any distance between the Archbishop and myself", Newman wrote to him, "is the difficulty I have in implicitly confiding in him."[112]

After a few letters, Manning himself began to write, without any reserve. Newman repeated what he had told the mutual friend: "I say frankly, and as a duty of friendship, that it is a distressing mistrust, which now for four years past I have been unable in prudence to dismiss from my mind, and which is but my own share of a general feeling . . . that you are difficult to understand."[113] Manning answered that he thought the same of Newman: "I cannot put my meaning into more precise and delicate words than by using your own. I have felt you difficult to understand, and that your words have not prepared me for your acts."[114] Manning then proceeded to reveal the acts which had disappointed him deeply.[115] But after this Newman decisively proved from documents that Manning had obtained these points from gossip and that they were entirely false.[116]

Strange to say, Manning then stopped writing and did not add anything to the list of his grievances. He did not say that he considered Newman the most dangerous Catholic in England; that he suspected him of heretical opinions; that he thought him worldly and disloyal to the Holy See; that he wished to get some of Newman's works on the Index; or lastly that he could not understand why Newman did not follow him blindly in his line of ecclesiastical government. Nor did Manning in his turn press Newman for a list of his complaints and an explanation of his mistrust. Newman might have told him that he hated his habit of extorting secrets; that he was pained by his action against the school and by his belief that Newman had secretly carried on the *Rambler* after 1859; that he regretted his underground action against the Oxford plans; that he was disappointed when he heard about Cardinal Reisach's visit because he had not seen him; and so on and so on.

Nevertheless, it is the opinion of this author that the two were equally sincere when Newman wrote to Manning: "That God may bless you and guide you in all things, as my own sun goes down, is, my dear Archbishop, the constant prayer of yours affectionately, John H. Newman", and when Manning wrote to him: "That God may bless you, and make the evening of your life happier and more useful even than its beginning, is my sincere prayer."[117]

Still, in subsequent letters Manning managed to evade the main point at issue, so that Newman ended the correspondence appealing to posterity and promising to say seven Masses for Manning's intention. Manning thought it the best way to solve the difficulties and promised him twelve Masses.[118] From all these letters it becomes clear that Manning simply failed to understand Newman. Manning was inclined to forget facts. He saw only one side of the question. He concealed. But he never lied.

Two years after this unsuccessful attempt at reconciliation, Manning again made overtures. He wanted to know who, specifically, had come between Newman and himself, because the estrangement had become a public danger to peace and to the fair name of the Catholic religion. Newman was puzzled. How could Manning ask such a question! He sent Manning a note to the effect that he really never knew what to think when they were in active correspondence; in spite of friendly feelings this was the judgment of his intellect.[119] Manning did not write him again for years.

It was at this time that the extension of papal infallibility was hotly discussed. It became the third issue on which the two great men differed. As early as 1864 when Pius IX condemned the errors of the time in two sensational documents, this point was a cause of dissension. Ward and his friends called these documents infallible and considered them an absolute condemnation of modern civilization. Newman had always held and taught that Catholics "are bound to receive what the Pope says and not to speak about it,"[120] but he could not see that the propositions and statements in the two documents should be pronounced infallible. He feared that such ideas might drive many Catholics to anti-religious free thought. He even called these documents "a heavy blow and great discouragement to Catholics in England".[121] He agreed entirely with their contents, but he thought the circumstances connected with them painful for many Catholics and non-Catholics.[122]

Although Manning did not openly support Ward's extreme views, published in the *Dublin Review*, neither did he rebuke them.[123] He had such an elevated idea of papal infallibility that he once wrote: "The one truth which has saved me is the infallibility of the Vicar of Jesus Christ."[124] Therefore he hoped that this doctrine would be made a dogma at the next council.

From the writings of the Fathers and the history of the councils, it was clear to Newman that Ward went too far in his ideas. Although Newman believed in the infallibility of the pope, he was of the opinion that a definition would have many bad consequences. He foresaw "the increase of scoffers" and "the throwing back of inquirers".[125] Again, he feared that a definition might make the Pope act alone, without consulting the bishops, although he was sure that even in that case Christ would direct His Vicars. He said, however, that he would not find fault with the definition after it had been passed.[126] He did see the advantages, but he had more reasons for wishing infallibility to remain undefined.[127]

In these circumstances he was visited by a convert who was anxious on account of the rumors about a coming definition of infallibility. She opened her heart to him, described her problems and showed her great concern and distress regarding the consequences, especially for converts like herself. She could not understand and deplored Ward's statement: "I should like a fresh dogma announced every day."

"God cannot leave His Church", Newman said.

"No," she answered, "but I may cease to believe in it as His Church. I may leave it."

"You will not", he replied calmly. "We all must go through

the gate of obedience, simply as obedience, and mind, if the dogma *is* declared, you will find that it will not make the slightest difference to you."

These simple words seemed to draw away a veil, and light shone in her soul. She remembered the apostles in the boat. When Christ stepped into it, they were at once in the safe port. Her doubts had vanished for good.[128]

When in the autumn of 1869 the bishops assembled in Rome and the discussions began, it was Manning who with great diplomatic skill and indomitable energy persuaded the Fathers of the Council that the pope's infallibility should be included among the doctrines to be defined. Newman was not present. The Pope had asked the Bishop of Birmingham whether Newman would be disposed to accept an invitation. Newman had been pleasantly surprised by this compliment, but he had many reasons not to go: his age, his health, his difficulty in speaking foreign languages, his shyness regarding ecclesiastical superiors, his embarrassment at being a member of boards and committees, and lastly the consequent necessity of interrupting his "magnum opus", the *Grammar of Assent*, on which he was working at the time.[129] Nevertheless, though absent, he exercised a strong influence on the Council, especially through his *Essay on the Development of Christian Doctrine*.[130]

While the Fathers were continuing their discussions in Rome, Newman was afraid. If the strong wording which Ward and Manning advocated were used in the definition, it would make the defense of its contents extremely difficult. The resulting situation might play into the hands of the enemies of the Church. It might check the gradual spread of the Catholic Faith. Moreover, the pro-Catholic feelings of the English Ministry might change into disfavor and anger.[131]

Newman's fear continued to grow. Although the outcome of the Council would be the work of the Holy Spirit, many human factors were involved. He followed every movement of the parties and asked himself what he could do. There seemed to be no call for him to express his views publicly, but on the other hand he could now keep them to himself. So during the Council he wrote confidential letters to his own Bishop in Rome. In one of these letters he expressed his fears very strongly and vehemently. In it he observed how a council ought to inspire the faithful with hope when a great heresy or other evil is threatening. But now the reverse was happening. "An aggressive and insolent faction" made several souls suffer, he thought. They were told "to prepare for something, they knew not what, to try their faith, they knew not how". He mentioned the names of various papers and reviews in Italy, France and England, and "a clique of Jesuits, Redemptorists and Converts". All he could do was to pray to the great early Doctors of the Church, Saint Augustine and the rest, to avert the calamities he foresaw.[132]

A journalist got hold of this letter and published it. Manning must have been irritated by its fierce tone and the unkind names Newman gave to some of the advocates of a definition. Had Newman thought of him? In the correspondence following the publication, Newman's extreme honesty was revealed; he made clear to whom he had referred. It was not the body of bishops who were in favor of the definition nor any ecclesiastical order or society but only a collection of people drawn from various ranks and conditions of the Church.[133]

From all that Newman wrote during the Council it appears that he strongly confided in God's Providence. Whatever the causes, whatever the mistakes made or the faults admitted, whatever the consequences, God would take care that the pope would never abuse his powers. As early as 1867, referring to the Council, he had written: "Its proceedings will be directed from above, and no mistake, and whatever it enacts will be true and holy."[134]

On July 18, 1870, the definition of papal infallibility was solemnly declared, but not in the strong exaggerated form for which Manning and Ward had hoped. Infallibility did not mean a direct revelation to the pope. It did not give him such absolute power to judge of matters of faith without counsel, deliberation and the use of scientific means.[135] When Newman read the formula he was pleased at its moderation.[136] He had no difficulty in admitting it. He was grateful that God had kept his faith unaffected by all these troubles, and he prayed that He might still keep him faithful, because he foresaw a rough time ahead.[137]

It is painful to read what Manning wrote seventeen years later about Newman's behavior in this matter. He did not consider that he had been defeated in his own hopes for a stronger dogmatic wording of the doctrine.[138] He only remembered that through his exertions a definition had been passed. And he wrote in his *Reminiscences*: "Some who ought to have led the right side went wrong. The world worshipped them, and every word they spoke or wrote. They were the 'greatest theologians of the day', the 'leaders of Catholic thought', the 'independent and manly characters who redeem the Catholic Church from servility and meanness'. But the Church decided against them; one was censured and submitted, another would not submit and is excommunicated, a third has happily passed without note, and is in full peace with the Truth and the Holy See."[139] Manning spoke here about Hefele, Döllinger and Newman. So, according to Manning, Newman had gone wrong and the Church had opposed his ideas. But he was left alone and remained a member of the Church. These words show the greatness of the gulf between these illustrious men.

Notwithstanding this antagonism, it seems evident that both Manning and Newman meant well and that there was no sin of willful uncharitableness in the conduct of either. Newman saw the great issues of the time in a clear light: the higher education problem, the question of the temporal power of the papacy, the extent of papal infallibility. He did not think it the right time to make infallibility dogma. Manning, on the other hand, cherished false ideas about these problems, as was proved afterward. But he had no shade of doubt about the correctness of his views. He always thought it a duty to promote them and to act according to them, even if it would thwart Newman. However, he considered it a great danger to the Church should his opposition to the great Oratorian become known to the world. Therefore he had to conceal it. This made Newman mistrust him and feel as if he were always under a cloud.

This antagonism was not one of morals but of psychology. It appears to have been a matter of temperament and of character. Newman, always aware of the manifold aspects of a problem because he was a thinker, a speculative intellect, could not but be slow in making up his mind, in deciding, in acting. Manning, always aware of his ultimate object and a man of action, a practical intellect, did not like hesitation but wanted to be achieving and determining the course of events. Newman's passivity and slowness appeared to him to be a sign of weakness, and this irritated him. To Newman, on the other hand, Manning's activities and methods often appeared hasty, impulsive and inopportune. But both wished to serve the Church and actually did serve her, each in his own way, with his own means and according to his own views. Was there not at one time a similar relationship between Saint Peter and Saint Paul, between Saint Jerome and Saint Augustine, between Fénélon and Bossuet? The contrast was not a contrast between right and wrong but between different aspects of the right.

CHAPTER ELEVEN

THE HAPPY END

1870–1890

What am I? My time is out. . . . It is enough for me to
prepare for death. . . . And He Who has been with me so
marvellously all through my life, will not fail me now, I
know, though I have no claim upon Him. . . .[1]

When we read Newman's letters and intimate writings of the
years 1860–1880 we often come across references to what he
calls his indolence. Again and again he complains that he is not
using his special gifts to the full. Of course he knows that since
his conversion he has been led by his superiors and has always
accepted the tasks imposed upon him by the bishops. But
he observes that nothing he attempted reached a successful
conclusion because the attempt always had to be laid aside
before an end had been reached. He sees, too, that although he
has not wasted his time, others could have fulfilled these tasks
as well as he had. Very often we hear reproaches such as: "If I
could get out of my mind the notion, that I *could* do something
and am not doing it, nothing could be happier, more peaceful,
or more to my taste, than the life I lead."[2] Sometimes he found
comfort in Saint Philip's words: "God has no need of men."
And he added: "He uses them little when He might use them
much, to show that He does *but* use them, and that the real
Opifex of all that goes on is He Himself."[3]

His feelings of distress were sometimes intensified by the
remarks of English Catholics. They regretted that his influence
was not greater. Why had he hidden his talents for so many

years? Why did he waste his unparalleled eloquence on the poor, uneducated workmen of Birmingham? Why should he stand idle while the fields were ripe for the harvest? He could have effected so much more than he actually had done with "his matchless talents, his profound learning, his single-mindedness, unselfishness, and the fragrance of a life of unblemished sanctity".[4]

They were not aware, however, that at that time he was working on a great book. It was a study he alone could write, for only he had the necessary qualifications. He considered it a duty of conscience to finish it before he died. The book was to be a profound study of the human way to certitude, not only in general, but especially concerning natural and revealed religion. He wished, as he told a friend, "to lay some stepping-stones as aids to faith".[5] To show that we can accept the natural foundations of the Faith—the existence of God, the trustworthiness of the Gospels, the liberty of the will, and so forth—with certitude, even if it be impossible to prove these certainties in a strictly logical way. It was his own love of souls that had led him to contemplate such a work. There were intellectuals who tried to apply the rigid rules of logic to the doctrines of the faith, which is impossible, and they had therefore drifted into religious scepticism. There were also believers who could not well explain how it was that simple Catholics accepted the truths of religion without any adequate knowledge of the arguments. He wanted to show that their belief was genuine and justified. To all intents and purposes, he wished to describe the relation between reason and faith.[6]

As can be seen from his *University Sermons*, Newman had been fascinated by the problem even in his Anglican period. He had in fact started the work almost as soon as he had become a Catholic. He had attempted many beginnings but again and again he had been obliged to lay the work aside because he could not see his way clear. But in 1866, while staying in Switzerland, his thought crystallized and he at last achieved a satisfactory beginning.[7] For four full years he worked on the book in fear and anxiety: "Every word I publish will be malevolently scrutinized, and every expression which can possibly be perverted sent straight to Rome."[8] Sometimes he spoke about his unpleasant anticipation that the book would be "a mare's nest".[9] He asked himself despondently: For whom am I working?[10] He felt sick when he thought of "the errors of fact and the imputing of motives. . . , not to say the simple lies" of the past.[11] In his great humility he was afraid of a false originality of thought which might lead him away from God: "I need the mind of the Spirit, which is the mind of the Holy Fathers, and of the Church by which I may not only say what they say on definite points, but think what they think."[12]

When the book approached completion, two difficulties occurred which concerned him greatly. These were caused by Dr. Meynell, a professor of the Major Seminary at Oscott, whom Newman had chosen as his revisor. Dr. Meynell had found fault with what he called Newman's idealism. Not that there was anything in the proofs that could be censured, but Meynell considered that should another author go further in this direction, the work might possibly be brought into disrepute and even into censure. Meynell also took exception to Newman's teaching on instinct.[13] In these difficulties, Newman wrote to a friend: "I am made very sad just now, more than I ought to be by a considerable hitch in the revision of my book. One point of my philosophy is objected to—and I don't see at the moment how I can go on. . . . I have spent so much time and thought upon it that it comes upon me as another of these great failures which have befallen me for many years, whenever I have attempted anything for the Catholic cause."[14]

A few days later, Dr. Meynell, who was a very modest man, imagining that the main work had been done and that his help was no longer required, spoke of "retiring again into his native littleness".[15] Newman was deeply shocked: "What am I to do. . . . I am in a most forlorn condition. . . . Whom am I to ask to do the work which you have so kindly begun? I shall not get anyone so patient as you, and, alas, alas, what is to come is, for what I know, more ticklish even than what you have seen. . . ."[16]

But, fortunately, Meynell realized his mistake and was willing to go through with the revision as he had promised.[17]

To Newman's great relief the book was completed in February 1870. In self-depreciation he entitled it: "An Essay in Aid of a Grammar of Assent", that is, a contribution to a handbook on certitude. In his diffidence he later wrote about his work: "If anyone is obliged to say 'I speak under correction' it is I—for I am no theologian and am too old, and ever have been to become one. All I can say is I have no suspicion, and do not anticipate that I shall be found in substance to disagree with St. Thomas."[18] He had only five hundred copies printed. To his great surprise, the entire edition was sold out within twelve hours.[19]

The book is the most difficult of his many works. But once understood, it appears as no less than a grace. For after dry, theoretical and general observations, it soon becomes more and more lively and concrete, describing in a fascinating way the road to certitude, first in everyday life, then as regards religion, the Christian faith and Catholicism. And it finishes on the sublime heights of God's merciful condescension, culminating in the dazzling image of Christ: "Here, then, is One who is *not* a mere name, who is not a mere fiction, who is a reality. He is dead and gone, but still He lives—lives as a living energetic thought of successive generations, as the awful motive-power of a thousand great events. He has done without effort what others with life-long struggles have not done. Can He be less than Divine? Who is He but the Creator Himself; who is sovereign over His own works, towards whom our eyes and hearts turn instinctively, because He is our Father and our God?"[20]

He was now in his seventieth year. Apart from many other writings he had produced five entirely "constructive works", as he called them. Each had taken him a great deal of time and tried him very much, the last one being the greatest trial of all.[21] But its success was far beyond all expectation.[22] The book proved to be to "many minds a comfort and a help".[23] It has not lost its value in the course of years. On the contrary, it has never been studied more intensely and profoundly than at the present.

But after this achievement he became anxious about the fate of his Anglican books, considering the possibility of their being used against the Catholic Church after his death. He thought it his duty to republish them but in such a way that the change of his views and the correction of his errors should be expressed without alterations in the original text.[24] With this in mind, he engaged the help of an Anglican friend, who, at his request, broke the ice with a republication of his Anglican parochial sermons, so that he himself could continue the work.[25] After careful revision, and with numerous corrective introductions and notes, he had more than ten volumes of his Anglican writings reprinted.[26]

During these years he also devoted much time to arranging his letters and other documents. A formidable task. For his great friend, Father Ambrose, he wrote a long biographical memoir concerning the period from his birth up to the time of the Oxford Movement.[27]

Newman has often been criticized for writing and preserving such a vast amount of autobiographical matter, letters, diaries and memoranda. Does this not show a certain lack of humility and simplicity, a secret desire to live on after death, an abnormal interest in his own inner life, or even hidden resentment? No, for he had good, solid reasons for doing what he did. Introspective people are naturally inclined to write down their thoughts and emotions, their inner and outer experiences, in order to pronounce an objective judgment upon them. Very often Newman's autobiographical writings are of the nature of confession or prayer in God's sight. The sifting, arranging and preserving of such matter were more or less a necessity. In the nineteenth century, even more than in our own time, the custom of publishing biographies and memoirs of public figures prevailed. He could be certain that his turn would come, too. He remembered how he had been slandered and misunderstood, how these slanders and misunderstandings had appeared in print and still lived in the memory of his contemporaries. After his death anybody might make use of those untruths in a biography, a memoir or an article. Such action could damage the good influence of his books and also the good name of his Oratorians and even of the Church. It was essential to provide sufficient material to destroy both lies and falsehoods. He burned many of his papers, but what he kept, he kept for that purpose. "I don't want a panegyric written of me, which would be sickening," he warned, "but a real fair downright account of me." He directed that other people in any way connected with him should not be mentioned in an unfavorable light unless it were strictly necessary. He realized only too clearly that even writers sympathetic to him had been and might in the future be influenced by the opinions, whether written or spoken, of others. High ecclesiastics had thwarted him, and many false rumors about him still circulated. Future biographers might even conclude that something must have been wrong with him, though they might express their views in a kind way: "Great geniuses commonly had infirmities of temper" or "Original minds are hard to get on with." Should such circumstances arise, he asked that the Oratorians request both proof and fact, reminding anyone concerned that their knowledge of him was of necessity fragmentary and that they therefore must avoid giving rash judgments. Then, and then only, his Brothers might make use of his papers, which would reveal the truth.[28]

It was not long before his anticipation proved to be right. Even before his death biographies appeared, of which he complained: "I am as if my skin was torn off . . . by the number of Memoirs written of me (written in kindness). Within this week I hear that one of my Catholic life is coming out—I do feel gratitude—and so I should to a surgeon who performed an operation upon me."[29]

Although past seventy, Newman still preached in the Oratorian Church. People loved to listen to "the old silvery sweetness of his voice", although his tones were not so full and rich as they once had been. His bell-like voice could be clearly heard even at the back of the church. No rhetorical tricks, no attempt at a beautiful style. Everything was natural, easy, spontaneous. "If there was any art, it was that of the highest kind which conceals art." He did not use arguments from logic, but his sermons were "strong, forcible, convincing by persuasion, and above all, clothed with an air of personal conviction so intense that it passed into the calmness of absolute confidence".[30] What he had taught in his last book, he practiced himself: he made religion real. Several people took his sermons down in shorthand. He himself made notes either before or after the sermons, which have been preserved till this day.

It is remarkable how little he had changed. There are the same subjects, often dealt with in the old way; there are the same ideas, sometimes even expressed in the same words. He was still the earnest and somewhat severe preacher who insisted on human sinfulness, on the necessity of perseverance, on gratitude toward God, on Providence. He warned against the world, against the danger of sin, against the unhappiness caused by sin. Again and again he pointed to the Day of Judgment, for there were great tendencies in his times, as he said, to make the world a God.

The temptation is to think that the individual is nothing and the state is everything; that the great and noble thing is the collection of men itself with its inventions and discoveries, and that the time will come when in the enthusiastic sanguineness of some about the future, the science of medicine will be so perfect that all diseases will be cured. All these wonderful elements of power which we have seen in the last fifty years, I mean like steam and the power of electricity, and so on, lead men to think that other discoveries may be made which will make the world a sort of heaven, that in this way we should destroy evil, and we should be a happy land. As for ourselves, these men say, let us enjoy what we have, and they make a Divinity of the world and worship it.[31]

Was he not right?

But he often spoke about heaven as well, emphasizing how extremely difficult it is to explain the joy of seeing God. He loved to speak of Our Lady. His sermons were full of Gospel texts, and they all return to his ever-recurring exhortations to do God's will, fulfill His commandments, live a new life, keep the Day of Judgment before one's eyes.

Apart from these simple Sunday sermons, he now and again preached officially, on a feast, at a funeral or at other special occasions. Then he would prepare his sermon with the greatest care and write down every word of it. These sermons are different from his Anglican sermons. There is something majestic and triumphant about them. They are written with a marvelous rhythm which carries even the reader away. Yet nothing superfluous or ostentatious, nothing affected, can be found in them. They are the summer richness of his rare, highly developed talents.

In November 1874 there appeared a pamphlet written by "the grand old man", Gladstone, on the Vatican Decrees in relation to the civic duties of a true Englishman. This pamphlet was a protest against the so-called usurpations of Catholicism. Gladstone set out to prove that the Catholics were "moral and mental slaves" and that they placed their "civil loyalty and duty at the mercy of anything", in other words, that they could not be good Catholics and good Englishmen at the same time.[32] He quoted Newman, "the first theologian now within the Roman communion", and referred to the letter to Bishop Ullathorne concerning the "aggressive and insolent faction". He mentioned Manning, who was supposed to be in the closest contact with Rome and who had written very strong statements about the temporal power of the popes and the extent of their jurisdiction. Not comprehending that theological language is scientific language, Gladstone misinterpreted the words of the Vatican Council in the same way as the man in the street would misinterpret the legal language of the civil code.[33] The pamphlet was in fact a great and pernicious blunder.

Many friends pressed Newman to write an answer. But he was afraid. "You are so good as to speak of prayers for me", he wrote to a lady. "If I may ask for some, my intention would be this, that I might write, if it was my duty, but not write if I was to fail in it."[34] So he did what he had been doing for so many years; he waited for God's own good time.

After a few weeks he thought that the call to write had come,[35] and he began, but he did not know yet whether there was also a call to publish what he was writing. "It would not be pleasant to make things worse instead of making them better", he observed.[36] He had decided that his reply should take the form of a public letter to the Duke of Norfolk, the representative of the Catholic laity of England. For five or six weeks he worked hard on it, but the results seemed to him unsatisfactory. One morning he said to himself: "I have not said Mass for my attempt." His next Mass was therefore offered for a blessing on his work. From that time on, he was able to continue without hindrance.[37] And in January 1875 the "Letter to the Duke of Norfolk" appeared.

It was received with great approval. "The impeachment of our loyalty fell to the ground, and we stood acquitted and satisfied", the Catholics gratefully told him.[38] Many complimentary letters were sent to him, not only by private people but by bishops.[39] He realized that the work had achieved good results. Even Ward agreed with him, and from that time onward all antagonism between them ceased.[40] "I have cause for great thankfulness," he wrote to an Anglican friend, "and I trust that now I may be allowed to die in peace."[41] Manning, too, appeared to be impressed and softened his manner toward him. He wrote in favor of him to Cardinal Franchi, who probably had seen a bad translation of Newman's *Letter* and desired that some expressions be corrected: "I warmly implore you to take no public steps as regards Father Newman's pamphlet: The heart of Father Newman is as straight and Catholic as it ever was. . . . The aforesaid Father has never, up to the present, so openly defended the prerogatives and infallible authority of the Roman Pontiff, though he always believed and preached that truth."[42]

To die in peace!

From the time of his first conversion up to his last days Newman constantly recalled that he was to die. Life seemed to him a dream, death an awakening. All through his life, one hears the echo of the last words of his *Essay on Development*: Life is short, eternity is long. And for his epitaph, he wished the triumphant exclamation: *Ex umbris et imaginibus in veritatem!* From shadows and images into the truth!

When he was only fifteen years of age he wrote: "A fourth part of my life is now gone."[43] On his eighteenth birthday he sighed in a poem: "Is not the silence of the grave too near?"[44] Afterward, he often expressed the belief that his life was "quickly nearing its decline"[45] and that he might die suddenly like so many literary men. "In the midst of life we are in death. It is as if one were standing in a fight, and any one might be shot down."[46] When he was fifty he felt that he was getting old and therefore prayed that God would not leave him: "Remain with me till death in this dark valley, when the darkness will end. Remain, O Light of my soul, *jam advesperascit* [it is toward evening]! The gloom which is not Thine, falls over me. I am nothing. I have little command of myself. I cannot do what I would. I am disconsolate and sad. I want something, I know not what. It is Thou that I want, though I so little understand this. . . . Stay, sweet Jesus, stay for ever. In this decay of nature, give more grace."[47] This sadness, however, is full of confidence: "I cannot tell what has been Thy everlasting purpose about myself, but, if I go by all the signs which Thou hast lavished upon me, I may hope that I am one of those whose names are written in Thy book."[48]

On a morning in March 1864, the thought that he might die at any moment came vividly to him. Was it his old fear of possible paralysis, returning with force? He was in perfect health. Whatever the cause, the thought came to him as a special grace, urging him to an act of total resignation to God's will and a complete detachment from the things of earth. He took paper and wrote:

I write in the direct view of death as in prospect. No one in the house, I suppose, suspects anything of the kind. Nor anyone anywhere, unless it be the medical men. I write . . . because I do not know how long this perfect possession of my sensible and available health and strength may last. I die in the faith of the One Holy Catholic Apostolic Church. I trust I shall die prepared and protected by her Sacraments, which Our Lord Jesus Christ has committed to her, and in that communion of Saints which He inaugurated when He ascended on High, and which will have no end. I hope to die in that Church which Our Lord founded on Peter, and which will continue till His second coming. I commit my soul and body to the Most Holy Trinity, and to the merits and grace of Our Lord Jesus, God Incarnate, to the intercession and compassion of our dear Mother Mary; to St. Joseph; St. Philip Neri, my father, the father of an unworthy son; to St. John the Evangelist; St. John the Baptist; St. Henry; St. Athanasius, and St. Gregory Nazianzen; to St. Chrysostom, and St. Ambrose. Also to St. Peter, St. Gregory I and St. Leo. Also to the great Apostle, St. Paul. Also to my tender Guardian Angel, and to all Angels, and to all Saints. And I pray to God to bring us all together again in heaven, under the feet of the Saints. And, after the pattern of Him, who seeks so diligently for those who are astray, I would ask Him especially to have mercy on those who are external to the True Fold, and to bring them into it before they die.[49]

The most beautiful expression of his thoughts on death is contained in his poem "The Dream of Gerontius", which has been described as "the happiest effort to represent the unseen world since the time of Dante".[50] Many people, both Protestant and Catholic, have found it a supreme consolation in their last hour,[51] because it describes not only the loneliness and anxiety of death but especially the joy of being freed from visible, material things, the exultation in meeting God, and the resignation to purgatory.

These reflections on death, which urged him to prepare himself ever more intensely, were occasioned by the deaths of many of his friends. In March 1868 Badeley, the lawyer who had been his great support during the Achilli trial, died: "What a heavy, sudden, unexpected blow", he exclaimed sadly. "How dense is our ignorance of the future! A darkness which can be felt, and the keenest consequence and token of the Fall."[52] In 1873 he visited Henry Wilberforce, one of his earliest Oxford pupils and friends, even dearer to him than Pusey. He found him a very old man who knew that eternity was near and who spent his last days in prayer and meditation. He spoke calmly to Newman of the unimaginable wonders he was soon to see. A few weeks later he died in peace, and Newman wrote: "Now he sees them. Each of us in his own turn will see them soon. May we be as prepared to see them as he was." When he went to the funeral, he was unexpectedly asked to preach. In the pulpit, however, he felt unable to speak. After two or three attempts he managed to steady his voice and gave a short survey of his friend's life, "of the position of comfort, and all that this world calls good, in which he found himself, and of the prospect of advancement, if he had been an ambitious man, when the word of the Lord came to him, as it did to Abraham of old, to go forth from that pleasant home, and from his friends, and all that he held dear, and to become"—and here Newman broke down, but at last could finish his sentence—"a fool for Christ's sake". Newman's grief, his simple, unstudied language and his gentle voice were inexpressibly touching.[53]

On his return from the funeral he found a telegram telling him that another great friend had died. This was James Hope

Scott, whom he had visited at Abbotsford the summer before. He was "one of the sweetest-tempered, gentlest, most religious-minded men" Newman ever knew. So great was his grief that he was unable to see anyone or leave the house. "I am too sad to go anywhere", he wrote, "I don't know when I have been so oppressed. I am fit for nothing but to remain silent at home."[54] With a heavy heart he went to the funeral in London and preached his sermon "In the World but Not of the World", with its tender conclusion:

> O happy soul, who hast loved neither the world nor the things of the world apart from God! . . . Happy soul, who, being the counsellor and guide, the stay, the light and joy, the benefactor of so many, yet hast ever depended simply, as a little child, on the grace of thy God and the merits and strength of Thy Redeemer! . . . Happy soul, who, by thy assidúous preparation for death, and the long penance of sickness, weariness, and delay, hast, as we trust, discharged the debt that lay against thee, and art already passing from penal purification to the light and liberty of heaven above! And so farewell, but not farewell for ever, dear James Hope Scott. . . .[55]

When Newman reached the age of seventy-four, he lost "his dearest son and friend", Father Ambrose St. John, a loss which always remained a fierce grief till his own death. In order to fulfill a wish of Newman's, Father Ambrose had started on the translation of a German book concerning "True and False Infallibility". The work proved too much for him. He suffered a mental breakdown and became deranged. Newman feared that he might even suffer "a living death, the destiny of dying without faith or prayer, the death of a dog". But after a few days, hope returned; the derangement subsided, and then, almost immediately the priest died. Newman was not present, but as soon as he received the sad news he hastened in great grief to the house where Father Ambrose lay. It was night. What else could he do but pray? Beside the body he said the Office of the Dead and then went down into the room below to write telegrams and letters. An hour later he said Mass for his friend at the altar in the house.[56] Though outwardly calm, he suffered terribly. For thirty-two years Father Ambrose had lived with him under the same roof. Newman had been "his first and last as far as this world was concerned".[57] He had given himself entirely to Newman. He not only let him dispose of his money, his health, his time, his work, he had even wanted to make a vow of obedience to him. Although Newman had forbidden this, he always behaved as though the vow had been made.[58] He called himself Newman's "alter ego".[59] After Father Darnell's departure, he had generously helped Newman out of the school difficulties by taking on the headship. His lovable character had made him popular with the boys. They compared him to Saint Philip Neri in his cheerfulness and thought him the most unselfish of men.[60]

Newman was confused and stunned by this bereavement. More than once he described it as the severest affliction he ever had in his life.[61] Even more than six months after the event he wrote: "A day does not pass without my having violent bursts of crying; they weaken me and I dread them."[62] But he was always resigned: "I thank God for having given him to me for so long. I thank Him for taking him away when there was a chance for him of a living death. I thank Him for having given me this warning to make haste myself and prepare for His coming."[63] And Father Neville wondered how Newman could appear so calm and cheerful while feeling the loss so acutely.[64]

But one outcome brought him joy in the midst of sorrow. In life, Father Ambrose had been distressed at the lack of novices, yet less than two years after his death four novices, with the prospect of three others, had joined the Congregation. Father Ambrose appeared to be helping the Oratorians in a marked way.[65]

These various bereavements gave Newman a presentiment —quite different from his anticipations when he was younger— that he would live to a great age. "Sometimes", he said, "I have thought that, like my patron saint St. John, I am destined to survive all my friends."[66] He did not, however, cease to prepare himself for death. He wrote several private notes informing his Oratorians what to do during his last illness and after his death. He gave an explicit command that he was to be buried by Father Ambrose's grave. At his funeral there should be no sermon. He made decisions about the disposal of his books, his papers and letters, his money and his funds. He enjoined the Oratorians to refrain from any step which entailed "posthumous laudations or panegyrics".[67]

But his spiritual preparations were by far the most intense. He tried to live more than ever in God's presence and for God's honor. He made up his mind to fix his thoughts and love more steadily "on Him who is the true Lover of souls, recollecting the great danger we lie under of making an idol of the creature, instead of cherishing the intimate conviction that God alone can be our peace, joy and blessedness".[68] Everywhere he saw symbols of death, even in spring: "Now especially as life is waning and friends dropping away, the extreme beauty of the ever-recurring, triumphant spring seems to have something of young mockery in it, till one recollects that that beauty is an image, a promise of something more sweet and more lasting than itself."[69] And again and again he asked for prayers, "because", he said, "I am an old man."

When he had reached his seventy-eighth birthday something happened to him so unexpected and so glorious that he described the event as a great marvel. In 1878 a new pope, Leo XIII, succeeded Pius IX. This occurrence made some of Newman's friends consider an attempt to remove the cloud which still overshadowed both himself and his works. The Duke of Norfolk, accompanied by the Marquis of Ripon, had an interview with Cardinal Manning to discover his opinion of a request to the new Pope to create Newman a Cardinal. On hearing this suggestion Manning lowered his head and remained silent for some moments. Was it a blow to him that the Catholic laity apparently put the old Oratorian on a level with himself and disagreed with his own view of him? Did all the grievances he held against Newman come into his mind?

Did he foresee unwelcome consequences if Newman were given the sacred purple? In any event, he recovered his self-possession and generously proposed that the two should give their reasons for the request in writing and that he himself should use them in a personal letter to Rome. Early in August 1878 he fulfilled his promise and wrote the document as an expression of the desire of the Catholic laity. It was a magnanimous letter but also a diplomatic one, describing honestly Newman's real and great merits within the Catholic Church and avoiding any allusion to Manning's own objections,[70] which he would be able to state privately at another time.

In December 1878 the Duke of Norfolk had an audience with Leo XIII and broached the subject. He told the Pope frankly that there were those who would not be in sympathy with the suggestion because they regarded much of Newman's writings with doubt and suspicion. When four or five months later the Pope received Manning's letter, the matter was soon settled, and in January 1879 Manning received a message from Rome that the Pope wished to make Newman a Cardinal.[71]

Newman was profoundly impressed and overjoyed when Bishop Ullathorne communicated the great news to him. While it meant the lifting of the cloud that had overshadowed him for so long, at the same time he realized that acceptance of the honor would mean leaving his beloved Oratory, his little nest as he called it, in order to live in Rome. It would be a great trial. He wrote a letter to Rome, ending with the words: "By the love and reverence with which a long succession of Popes have regarded and trusted St. Philip, I pray and entreat His Holiness in compassion of my diffidence of mind, in consideration of my feeble health, my nearly eighty years, the retired course of my life from my youth, my ignorance of foreign languages, and my lack of experience in business, to let me die where I have so long lived. Since I know now and henceforth that His Holiness thinks kindly of me, what more can I desire?"[72]

These simple words read like a refusal. Bishop Ullathorne,

however, knew for certain that Newman would gladly accept the dignity if only he were allowed to stay at the Oratory. He knew that he was too sensitive even to appear to bargain with the Pope or to make conditions. In very clear words, which admit no doubts, Ullathorne wrote Manning two letters to this effect.[73]

After a short time Ullathorne began to suspect that Manning had not forwarded his explanation of the real situation. The Cardinal had given notice that he had sent Newman's letter to Rome, but he had not said a word about the Bishop's letter.[74] It is clear that Manning could not believe what the Bishop had written to him and retained his own view, namely, that Newman had declined the cardinal's hat.[75] There was also a rumor in London that Newman had refused the dignity.[76] Therefore Ullathorne felt obliged to inform the Roman authorities himself.[77]

While all this was going on more or less secretly, the *Times* published in large type the following news: "We are informed that Pope Leo XIII has intimated his desire to raise Dr. Newman to the rank of Cardinal, but with expressions of deep respect for the Holy See Dr. Newman has excused himself from accepting the purple."[78] How could the *Times* have come to know this? Only Manning and Ullathorne had seen Newman's so-called refusal. A few weeks afterward, Manning admitted that he had misunderstood Newman's letter,[79] and a few years later Ullathorne unequivocally blamed Manning for trying to prevent Newman from becoming a Cardinal. "You distrust him while there is no honester man on earth", Ullathorne said. He added that Newman's only aim had been to advance the cause of religion and that he hated all duplicity and intrigue.[80]

These facts reinforce the view that in his heart of hearts Manning disliked the idea of Newman being created a Cardinal. The wish was father to the thought, and this to such an extent that he interpreted plain words in a totally erroneous manner. But the Duke of Norfolk opened Manning's eyes and made him see his mistake. Immediately and magnanimously, Manning explained the state of affairs to the Holy Father, who at once gave permission for Newman to stay at the Oratory. Without delay, Manning sent the happy message both by telegram and by letter to Bishop Ullathorne.[81] Now Newman could accept the high dignity with deep gratitude: "So great a kindness, made with so personal a feeling towards me by the Pope, I could not resist, and I shall accept it. It puts an end to all those reports that my teaching is not Catholic or my books trustworthy which has been so great a trial to me so long."[82] When the formal permission for nonresidence in Rome and, shortly afterward, the official offer of the cardinalate had arrived, he wrote: "It is a wonderful termination, in God's good Providence, of my life. I have lived long enough to see a great marvel."[83] Yet he admitted that there were other aspects of this great honor. He thought it too high a dignity. Long ago he had prayed: "I promise . . . with Thy grace, that I will never set myself up, never seek pre-eminence, never court any great thing of the world, never prefer myself to others. I wish to bear insults meekly, and to return good for evil. I wish to humble myself in all things, and to be silent when I am ill-used, and to be patient when sorrow or pain is prolonged, and all for the love of Thee, and Thy cross."[84] No wonder, therefore, that the thought of a refusal should enter his mind. On the other hand, he knew that the Protestants would put a false interpretation on a possible refusal and consider him an indifferent son of the Church. Catholics too might be puzzled and unsettled as though he "were snubbing the Pope". He knew that anti-Catholics and some Protestant sects hoped that he would decline the offer.[85] His brother Frank also had strongly advised him not to accept the dignity.[86] But all things considered it was a pleasant duty to him to be grateful: "I used to say to myself, 'Time will set me right. I must be patient, for Time is on my side.' But the Pope has superseded Time. How should I not be most grateful to Him?" He felt especially grateful to St. Philip Neri. Never, since the Congregation had begun, had the Saint shown so great a mercy, surely an indication that Newman could leave the future of his House in his safekeeping.[87]

Marks of honor, love, respect and admiration poured in from all parts of the English-speaking world and from all ranks of society, and it is remarkable how spontaneous and warm and sincere they were. Protestants rejoiced as much as Catholics because they, too, loved Newman. They felt honored and they knew that the Pope wished to confer a mark of distinction on England itself.[88] A Protestant farmer, travelling with two Dominican Sisters, could not be silent about it and thumped his leg and exclaimed: "I am as pleased as if I were made Cardinal myself."[89] From all those proofs of affection, which after all were a burden and tired him out, Newman said: "I should be as hard as a stone, and as cruel as an hyena, and as ungrateful as a wild cat, if I did not welcome them; but they try me much. . . ."[90]

But in fact he was prepared for crosses. The sympathy and honors were so overpowering and the tenderness of the Holy Father had been such that something was bound to arise in the nature of a penance. The journey to Rome where he would receive the Cardinal's hat proved such a penance indeed. Snow and rain accompanied him. He caught a cold which developed into pneumonia. For six weeks he stayed in Rome and only on three occasions could he say Mass, and only with great difficulty and the utmost care was he able to endure the official ceremonies of the conferring of the hat.[91] At Leghorn, on the way home, he fell ill again and was even worse than he had been previously. On one particular night he was thought to be dying, and he regarded it as a special act of God's Providence that he came through. After a fortnight he was able to continue the homeward journey, accompanied by a doctor, who, however, forbade him to visit Maria Giberne, then at Autun as Sister Maria Pia, a bitter disappointment for both.[92]

Back in England he received congratulations from all kinds of people. His replies to the letters and addresses, all of them different from one another, all of them touching, all of them giving a glimpse of his inner life, reveal his deep gratitude toward God's Providence and his simplicity and humility. He appears wholly convinced of the exaggerations in the letters and addresses, and at the same time he thanks the writers and speakers for them because of the kindness and sincerity of their words: "Do you in your charity, my dear friends, pray for me," he wrote to a Jesuit community, "that I, an old man, may not fail Him who has never failed me; that I may not by my wilfulness and ingratitude lose His Divine Presence, His Sovereign protection, His love, and that, having been carried on by His undeserved mercy almost to the brink of eternity, I may be carried on safely into it."[93] And he repeated again and again: "Say a good prayer that I may please God in my thoughts and deeds under these new circumstances."[94]

Though he lived for more than ten years after this glorious event, he wore his Cardinal's robes and allowed public recognition of his station only once, namely, on his eightieth birthday.[95] He never wished to appear arrogant.

Even at his advanced age and although raised to such high rank, he remained true to his ideal of being an active minister of Christ. Because of this he wished very much to visit Döllinger, the German historian and theologian, whom he had known since 1847. During the Council the two men had exchanged letters, but later the correspondence ceased because Döllinger, to Newman's grief, left the Church. Through a mutual friend Newman was kept informed of Döllinger's state of mind. He had expressed his feelings of deep sympathy with the theologian but also his conviction that Döllinger's views were untenable and his actions irresponsible. "I am sincerely afflicted that so great a man should be lost us, though I feel the scandal and the reproach which it is to us, and though I am indignant at the way in which he has been treated and am much distressed in his distress, still I think he has taken a wrong course, and has got the Catholic world against him."[96] The news about Döllinger grew steadily worse, and at last Newman was even prepared to hear that he had lost his faith.[97] He had hoped to bring him back to the Church or at least to influence him, for he now had the authority, the power and the liberty to speak, which he had not possessed earlier. But the doctor had forbidden the fulfillment of this fervent wish.[98]

The long, elaborate letter he prepared in Rome for William Froude, brother of his long deceased friend Hurrell Froude, is a moving document. William Froude was a sceptic, but Newman had always hoped to see him become a Catholic like his wife and children. This was his final attempt to convince him, but the letter never reached Froude, who died before it was sent.[99] More touching still is the correspondence with Mark Pattison, once his pupil at Oxford, who from being a fervent adherent of the Oxford Movement had become an infidel and was now dangerously ill. In the winter of 1884 Newman risked his health and perhaps his life in order to visit him and to rescue him from his unbelief.[100] For the same reason and in the same manner he went to Tenby to his brother Charles, whom he had not seen for many years. It is said that Charles would not receive him, but this is certainly not true. In the private notes of Newman's constant companion in his last years, Father Neville, it is indicated that this visit may have been successful. This is also confirmed by Charles' letters to others, in which he always spoke well of John Henry while he often spoke harsh and bitter words about other relatives.[101]

But the most important work he did as a minister of Christ was to aid intellectuals who had difficulties regarding their faith. He did all he could to draw them nearer to the Church and nearer to God.[102] He felt especially concerned about young people, for he foresaw the trials which would attack them stemming from the infidelity surrounding them.[103] Now and again he tried to do some good by preaching in his church. But his Oratorians said in all kindness: "The poor Cardinal, we must not ask him to preach again; his preaching days are over."[104] He desired particularly to go to Rome to speak to the Pope and the high ecclesiastics about the religious problems of the times, but after the date had been fixed, he fell and broke two ribs, and the journey had to be postponed. Never again did the necessary health and strength return for such an undertaking.[105]

Notwithstanding stiffness and pain in his fingers, which caused him to lament that he wrote "nearly as slowly as a child", he continued writing, often with Father Neville's assistance. He published notes of a deceased friend, William Palmer, who in his Anglican years had paid a long visit to Russia to attempt union of the Russian Orthodox church with the Anglican church. He also wrote about the burning question of whether "the Bible had to be sacrificed on the altar of science and human reason". His short treatise "quieted the minds and consciences of many good and thoughtful men".[106] He also wrote a long article as an answer to a Scotch professor who thought Newman a secret sceptic, full of doubts about the Faith he defended. "For a long seventy years, amid mental trials sharp and heavy," Newman wrote in his defense, "I can in my place and in my measure adopt the words of St. Polycarp before his martyrdom: For fourscore years and six I have served my Lord, and He never did me harm, but much good; and can I leave Him now?"[107]

It was especially by means of a vast and uninterrupted correspondence that he continued to fulfill his apostolate. The number of letters he received was freqently so oppressive that he did not know how to answer them all. "You must excuse an old man, who sometimes gets quite bewildered by the number of unanswered letters which lie on his table."[108] His replies are often very lengthy, and sometimes they resemble small tracts. The subjects show a remarkable variety, but, of course, they are mostly on intellectual problems, either natural or supernatural. He had little time for gossip. He often needed a definite call to write a letter. These are perhaps the main reasons why many correspondents kept his letters as treasures. "All Newman's sayings are of gold", a priest wrote.[109] One of the subjects of the correspondence was that of the spiritual life, though he once said he could not believe that he was a good spiritual director. "Alas!" he wrote to a priest, "had I been fitted for it, you would willingly have put yourself under my guidance; you would have given me your confidence. . . . But I know my infirmities. . . ."[110] From his letters it appears that he gave advice in a spirit of humility, prayer and trust in God. His principles were solid and safe. Very cautiously he advised future converts. Wise were his injunctions as regards bodily penances. Carefully he tried to prevent attachment to spiritual consolations. He promoted devotion to Our Lady and the rosary. How valuable were his counsels on almsgiving, visitation of homes, conversion of young people! And lastly how discreet, dignified and affectionate was his treatment of the problems of women!

From the stacks of letters directed to him and preserved at the Birmingham Oratory, we can get an idea of the influence he exercised. An unknown person once wrote to him: "What a joy thrilled thro' me this morning as I discerned *your* hand on the cover of one of the letters that were delivered to me. Fluttering with mingled emotions I read it on my knees. . . ."[111] Another letter reads: "How much I owe to you for the help afforded by your writings, I cannot tell."[112] After the death of a friend a woman wrote: she "was devoted to you and to your writings. Her books were her treasure and those amongst them of your writing she prized most."[113] A schoolboy, who had read some works against the Church and now wished to study books defending her, asked him: "As I know no man in the whole of England for whom I have a greater respect and on whose judgment I have more reliance than you I should feel infinitely honored and proud if you could send . . . a list of books that I ought to commence my reading with."[114] Anthony Trollope, the novelist, thought it an honor that Newman had enjoyed some of his novels: "There is no man as to whom I can say that his good opinion would give me such gratification as your own."[115] Lord Ripon spoke in a letter about "Those who like myself owe to your teaching more than to any other earthly cause the blessing of being members of the Catholic

Church."[116] Alfred Tennyson, the Poet Laureate, "would deem it a great favour" if the Cardinal could pass a few days with him.[117] He even wished to visit Newman: "There are a hundred things on which we might differ, there is no man on this side of the grave, more worthy of honours and affection than yourself. . . . I feel that some day or other I ought to go to you."[118] A great many people asked for his autograph and a photograph, and even several Protestants asked for his blessing.[119] At an Anglican diocesan conference a few words were to be quoted from one of his sermons. As soon as his name was mentioned thunders of applause rattled through the theatre even before the words had been read.[120] "I wonder," wrote one of his Anglican godsons, "if you know how much you are loved by England. I wonder, if any man, at least of our times was ever so loved by England, by all religious-minded England. And even the enemies of the faith are softened by their feeling for you."[121] A Jesuit gave an account of the respect and sympathy Newman enjoyed in the Order: "I know from experience that the Jesuits to a man not only admire but love him; and when people, whose heat was greater than their light, threw out misgiving and suspicion, the Jesuits felt and sympathized" with him.[122] A Methodist informed him that hundreds of his coreligionists were grateful that he was still spared for them: "By the books you have written as well as by the known life you have lived you belong to us as a Country and as Christians for all time."[123] The University of Edinburgh wished to confer on him an honorary degree.[124] Trinity, the College of his undergraduate years, elected him Honorary Fellow and received him with the greatest marks of esteem.[125] A correspondent even ventured to call him the Patron Saint of the University City.[126]

In the last years of his life it became increasingly difficult for Newman to leave his Oratory: "You must make great allowance to the weakness of an old man", he wrote to the Duke of Norfolk, who had invited him to be present at the opening of the new Oratory church in London. He was very well if he stayed quietly at home, but journeys and large gatherings exhausted him.

On January 1, 1888, Pope Leo celebrated his golden jubilee as a priest. The Cardinal attended the service in honor of this feast, read the Epistle and the Gospel and preached his last sermon. Did he think of himself when he described the wonderful ways of Providence evident in the Pope's life? He thought it remarkable that the Pope should have lived so long yet have been so little employed until his elevation to the papacy. But he had often noticed a similar phenomenon in the course of history. Sometimes God chose aged people to carry out his work. Moses was eighty years old before he became the leader of the Israelites, while Saint John the Baptist was cut off at the beginning of his career. He saw this same inscrutable rule of Providence in the life of the Pope. During his pontificate he had accomplished that which no other man could have done, though the world at large had known nothing about him before his election. There had seemed little probability that he would ever leave Perugia, his small bishopric, but he was found by the special Providence and inspiration of God. In conclusion, the Cardinal thanked God that he was allowed to say a few words on that day and that by a special favor of God he himself had lived long enough to see such a man. [127]

Although he never suffered from chronic illness, Newman had lesser complaints to bear during the whole of his life. Apart from the three severe illnesses he experienced, one as a boy of fifteen, the other at the time of the examinations in 1827 and the third while in Sicily, he was often vexed with eye trouble, toothache, painful fingers and nervousness. More than once he was overworked, and he had frequent colds. He neither lived nor worked with the cooperation of his body, and as he became very old he grew increasingly frail. He had to restrict both visiting hours and the length of conversations. [128] When he heard that his brother-in-law's sister, Anne Mozley, had

had an accident, he wrote to her: "The news came home to me more sharply from the selfish reason that I am always slipping and tumbling myself, and, alas, without any warning, or, as I think, imprudence on my part. And I hear of so many parallel cases. We can only say that we are in God's Hands."[129]

At the end of October 1888 he experienced such a serious attack of weakness that the doctor thought it safer for him to receive the last sacraments. The Oratorians knelt at his bedside, and after the ceremonies he gave them his blessing. He himself remained silent until all was over, when, characteristically, he explained to the doctor, a Protestant, the meaning and aim of extreme unction. The following day he felt somewhat better and was able to receive the new Bishop of Birmingham who came to see him. He asked for the Bishop's blessing, and the manner of his receiving it deeply affected the prelate. In the evening of that day he was still exceedingly ill but cheerful, and he laughed over the way "he was bullied to take food". Among other things he declared: "You know what St. Philip said: 'At last one must die.' Death must come with its terrors; and it only shows how right it is to be always ready on the chance of its coming." One morning when he had taken a cup of milk and some meat and bread, which he ate well, Father Henry said: "Well done", and the Cardinal replied: "You should say: 'Thank God.' He has ever been good to me. My bread has always been sure."[130]

He recovered. And one day, during his recovery, he remarked that he had always had a great affection for Father Faber's hymn "The Eternal Years" and that he wished to have it sung to him when he came to die. So the Oratorians put a harmonium in the passage between his rooms and they sang for the Cardinal:

> How shalt thou bear the Cross that now
>   So dread a weight appears?
> Keep quietly to God and think
>   Upon the Eternal Years. . . .

Bear gently, suffer like a child,
   Nor be ashamed of tears.
Kiss the sweet Cross, and in thy heart
   Sing of the Eternal Years.

"Some people", he said afterward, "have liked my *Lead, Kindly Light*, and it is the voice of one in darkness, asking for help from Our Lord. But this is quite different; this is one with full light, rejoicing in suffering with Our Lord, so that mine compares unfavourably with it. This is what those who like *Lead, Kindly Light* have got to come to, they have to learn it." Then the Oratorians played and sang it over again. And he thanked them: "I thank you with all my heart. God bless you. I pray that when you go to Heaven, you may hear the Angels singing. . . ."[131]

By Christmas of 1889 he was strong enough to be present at High Mass. When he noticed that the preacher had not come, he even wanted to preach the sermon, but the Oratorians dissuaded him. This he almost regarded as a disappointment. To his great joy, however, he had been able to say Mass. For eight years this had gradually become more and more difficult. His sight had become so weak that he could only read by sunlight.[132] He was afraid, too, that he might become dizzy and drop the chalice. When on that Christmas morning he was wished a "Happy Feast", he sadly remarked with an allusion to his joy: "Never again, never again." He had made up his mind not to repeat the attempt to say Mass and to risk an accident. Every day, however, he said, wholly or in part, the prayers of the Mass of the Blessed Virgin or the Mass of the Dead, which he had learned by heart, with the appropriate ceremonies, hoping against hope that with more strength and the brighter days of spring he might be in a condition to offer up the Holy Sacrifice again. His preparation was the greatest happiness of each day.[133]

But the gradual loss of sight was a severe penance.[134] He was obliged to dictate his letters or else send a printed note to his correspondents saying that he was unable to answer. But every day he had the Epistles and Gospels read to him, while now and again he commented on them. From beginning to end his love of the Bible remained.[135]

It was obvious to both his friends and his spiritual children that he could not live much longer. A well-known Protestant author put into words what the threat of his coming death meant to them: "May I say that I hope it is some alleviation to you of the burdens of life, to know how it lightens the world to many of us, that you are still with us, and to know what a passionate grief it will cause to your most intimate friends, and how keen a pang to all who love you, when you leave us."[136] But in February 1890 he himself declared: "I am not capable of doing anything more. I am not wanted. Now mind what I say: It is not kind to keep me longer from God."[137]

It is remarkable to note that the old Cardinal was always busily engaged, even during the last four months before his death. He dictated his answers to correspondents to Father Neville, and with his help he corrected some essays for the printer. The Cardinal spent much time in prayer and loved to say the rosary, but because of the stiffness in his fingers he had to have larger and larger beads. At times he became depressed at being shut up in his room all day.[138] The old are very often sorely tried by the manners of the young, by their noise, thoughtlessness and lack of courtesy. But Newman never complained, never became querulous or lost his gentleness, though his strength failed and he had to endure a great number of deprivations.[139]

His mind remained clear to the last. Five days before his death he told Father Neville that he would like to leave Cardinal Macchi a little ivory piece to which he was greatly attached. This prelate had been extremely kind to him when he stayed in Rome ten years before. Father Neville had to put his name on it and to promise that he would tell Cardinal Macchi the story of the ivory. It was a present given Newman by Frederic Rogers, now Lord Blachford, who had been a close friend in the Oxford days. This friendship had come to an end at the time of Newman's conversion but much later was renewed, and Lord Blachford did not let an opportunity of showing his deep respect and affection go by, though his old aversion to Rome remained. When they did meet, both suffered on account of the wide gulf between them. Newman suffered especially because he realized that an old friend, both good and conscientious, would die without those blessings which had been bestowed on himself. Father Neville, to whom he spoke of his hope regarding Blachford, was deeply touched by both the beauty of his expression and the sweetness and sincerity of his tone.

Newman also spoke of other Cardinals to whom he wished souvenirs to be sent. Looking round his room, he exclaimed with regret and at the same time with surprise and amusement: "What is there that it would be respectful to send to a Cardinal?" His lack of suitable gifts was a disappointment, especially as he felt, in spite of what his doctors said, that he would die in two or three days.

Gratitude to the Pope also arose in his heart because the Holy Father had bestowed on him such a high honor: "Why should the Holy Father have done it? How came it about that he should have picked me out?" And looking to the little engraving the Pope had sent him in the first days of his pontificate, he asked Father Neville to take particular care of it because it was the first proof he had of Leo XIII's respect for him.[140]

This was on August 5, 1890. A few days later, on Saturday, August 9, Grace, the daughter of Newman's sister Harriett, visited the Cardinal. He felt happy about the visit and kept holding her hand in his. Grace was sorry that she had kept her gloves on. Did he think of his long-deceased sister whom he had loved so much and who had been so saddened by his departure from the Anglican church? Did he want to show that he was still full of affection for her? He told Grace that he had seen her once when she was three years old. He spoke about her son and asked about her father's books. Tom Mozley, her

father, had been his pupil at Oxford. Grace could not understand everything he said, but she noticed the gentle expression
in his eyes and his long thin fingers, so well known to her from
his portraits. Finally, he gave her his blessing.

The following night he woke Father Neville and an hour
later said he felt very bad. The usual remedies did not bring the
usual relief, and in the morning the doctor diagnosed pneumonia. At ten he felt a little better, and he asked Father Neville
to recite with him a portion of the breviary. But by twelve he
began to lose consciousness. With the exception of one short
period it did not return, and he was able to receive only
extreme unction.

The next day, Monday, August 11, at ten minutes to nine in
the evening, Cardinal Newman died, quietly, without any
struggle or pain, surrounded by his Oratorians.[141]

Then came the fulfillment of what he himself had foreseen and
spoken of in one of his most beautiful sermons describing the
state of "the loving soul on its separation from the body". He
was allowed to see the face of his Redeemer and to hear His
voice.

> O Saviour of men, I come to Thee though it be in order to be at
> once remanded from Thee; I come to Thee who art my Life and
> my All; I come to Thee on the thought of whom I have lived all
> my life long. To Thee I gave myself when first I had to take part
> in the world; I sought Thee for my chief good early, for early
> didst Thou teach me, that good elsewhere was none. Whom
> have I in heaven but Thee? whom have I desired on earth, whom
> have I had on earth, but Thee? . . . I will fear no ill, for Thou
> art with me. I have seen Thee this day face to face, and it
> sufficeth. . . . That eye of Thine shall be sunshine and comfort
> to my weary, longing soul; that voice of Thine shall be ever-
> lasting music in my ears. Nothing can harm me, nothing shall
> discompose me . . . till the end comes. . . .[142]

He had prayed long before,

What a day will that be when I am thoroughly cleansed from all impurity and sin . . . and am fit to draw near to my Incarnate God in His palace of light above! what a morning, when having done with all penal suffering, I see Thee for the first time with these very eyes of mine, I see Thy countenance, gaze upon Thy eyes and gracious lips. . . . What a day, a long day without ending, the day of eternity. . . . O my Lord, what a day when I shall have done once for all with all sins . . . and shall stand perfect and acceptable in Thy sight, able to bear Thy presence, nothing shrinking from Thy eye, not shrinking from the pure scrutiny of Angels and Archangels, when I stand in the midst and they around me. . . .[143]

On the day preceding the funeral, Cardinal Manning delivered the funeral oration in the London Oratory church, ending with the words:

Beyond the power of all books has been the example of his humble and unworldly life; always the same, in union with God, and in manifold charity to all who sought him. He was the centre of innumerable souls, drawn to him as Teacher, Guide and Comforter. . . . To them he was a spring of light and strength from a supernatural source. A noble and beautiful life is the most convincing and persuasive of all preaching, and we have all felt its power. . . . The history of our land will hereafter record the name of John Henry Newman among the greatest of our people, as a confessor for the faith, a great teacher of men, a preacher of justice, of piety and of compassion. May we all follow him in his life, and may our end be painless and peaceful like his.[144]

CHAPTER TWELVE

THE SOUL OF NEWMAN

No life known to me in the last century of our national history can for a moment compare with Newman's lonely and severe and saintly life. . . . It has been carved, as it were, out of one solid block of spiritual substance, and though there may be weak and wavering lines here and there in the carving, it is not easy to detect any flaw in the material upon which the long and indefatigable labour has been spent.[1]

There exist numerous pictures, paintings and photographs of Newman. But more often than not they reveal neither the real man nor his inner life. Many of them even give a false impression, suggesting despondency or irritation or a certain querulousness; others depict him as somewhat effeminate or as a dreamer.

When we study the descriptions of Newman's outward appearance, two things strike us at once. First, they often do not agree with the paintings and photographs; second, they almost always associate the inner Newman with his outward appearance. As early as his Oxford years, when he was the leader in the great reformation of the Anglican church, one of the students saw him as a man with the outward features and the soul of Julius Caesar. In both he discovered the same head and forehead, ears and nose, the same lines of the mouth. In both he respected "an original force of character which refused to be moulded by circumstances; a clearness of intellectual perception, a disdain for conventionalities". In both he revered the "gentleness, sweetness, singleness of heart and purpose" which accompanied "a temper, imperious and wilful".[2] Another student remembered his fast walk, with a very peculiar gait, as if he did not lift his heels; deep in thought, as if he pursued a purpose, not caring what impression he was making or what people thought about him.[3] Shortly after Newman's conversion to the Catholic Church, Manning wrote to Gladstone: "It would be unnatural not to say something of dear Newman. What do I not owe him? No living man has so powerfully affected me, and there is no mind I have so reverenced. It was so unlike those around him—so discerning, masculine, real, and self-controlled, such perfect absence of formation and artificial habits."[4] In the dark days of 1859 to 1864, a Master at the Oratory School who had known Newman during his happy years at Oxford wrote about him: "The air of deep abstraction with which he used to glide along the streets of Oxford was now in great measure exchanged for the look of preoccupation and anxiety about temporal affairs . . . but otherwise he seemed to be quite as vigorous and little older than I had last seen him at Oxford."[5] Fifteen years later a Canon came to see him and wrote about his visit: "I recall the swift sudden way in which I found him beside me. . . . I turned at the sound of the soft quick speech, and there he was—white, frail and wistful, for all the ruggedness of the actual features. I remembered at once the words of Furse about him, 'delicate as an old lady washed in milk'."[6] When Newman visited the Dominican Sisters of Stone they found that he looked old and feeble but full of brightness and sweeter than he had ever been.[7] And Father Joseph Bacchus, who lived with him during his last years, tells us that the Cardinal "carried the art of being ordinary to perfection. He was singular in nothing. He took his food, his recreation, went about his ordinary duties, conversed without any mannerisms whatsoever. He had no foibles, no crotchets. The best testimony to this is the absence of good stories about him" which there were about Manning and Ullathorne.[8]

Indeed, Newman had "the soul and manners of a king".[9] Each line of his own well-known description of a gentleman's qualities and ways can be rightly said of him. But whereas many an English gentleman cultivated them on natural grounds only, Newman saw and cultivated them for supernatural motives: "The Apostles were gentlemen," he once said, "not that they made a good bow, wore kid gloves, or spoke Attic Greek, but their minds and their hearts were refined. I have always maintained that St. Paul, as seen in his Epistles, was the first of gentlemen—and that, if you would look for precepts of that courtesy and grace, which the world so much admires, you must go to him for them."[10] It is a fact that one never finds a single vulgar word in Newman's books or letters. He rebuked Faber for using slang in the pulpit.[11] When he was compelled to speak strongly he was careful not to be abusive.[12] After a very severe letter to a spiritual child who deserved censure, she called him "gentleness itself".[13] And regarding the moral faults of others, he "was always extremely careful not to let anything that might give unnecessary offence or pain."[14]

If Newman was a gentleman, he was even more a friend of friends. Frederic Rogers called this capacity for friendship his most striking characteristic.[15] Innumerable are the proofs of his mysterious ability to win hearts and minds. Those who once came to know him felt influenced by his charm not only when he was a young curate at Oxford but in his last days when as a Cardinal the old man fascinated a Protestant girl who wished to become a Catholic.[16] Because of this magnetic attraction he received many invitations from his friends, and many gifts, among them such diverse and precious items as a violin, a pony, a brougham; and large sums of money were showered on him. John Bowden called Newman's friendship the most important thing in his life.[17] Many friends ascribed their happiness to him: "You must allow me to tell you", Lord Emily wrote, "that to you—to your writings—to an indescribable sort of feeling I have long had for you I attribute more than to any other human instrument my present happiness."[18] There were those who felt so intensely impressed by his personality that, with their hearts, they also gave him their possessions and their lives. Among these were Maria Giberne, Father Ambrose St. John, Mrs. Wootten and Father Caswall. Apparently God had made him what he was, a friend above all friends, in order to lead them to a profound spiritual life, to the Catholic religion and to eternal happiness. Hence we find a great many letters in which correspondents declare: "If I ever reach heaven, I owe it to you."

His friendship was deep, tender and unselfish. Pusey, at the time of his wife's death, wrote to Keble: "God has been very good to me. . . . He sent Newman . . . in the first hour of sorrow; and it was like the visit of an angel."[19] When Dalgairns was about to become a Catholic, Newman wrote to the young man's father: "I write from the great affection I have for your son, and my knowledge of your own heart and kind and indulgent character—and I assure you I feel very intimately both his distress and that of yourself and Mrs. Dalgairns—and most rejoiced should I be, if any word of mine could be the means of lessening it."[20] When Newman had joined the Catholic Church and his friends had left him, his love remained, so that in 1863 he could write to Keble: "Never have I doubted for one moment your affection for me, never have I been hurt at your silence. . . . You are always with me a thought of reverence and love, and there is nothing I love better than you, and Isaac and Copeland, and many others I could name, except Him whom I ought to love best of all and supremely. . . . None but He, can make up for the losses of those old familiar faces which haunt me continually."[21]

This deep affection sometimes went so far as to involve him in a kind of identification with his friends. There exists a letter referring to the illness of one of his Oratorians in 1858 in which it would appear that he himself suffered the disease with the sick priest.[22] This gift of identification explains how his introspective nature possessed also the precious quality of being able to enter into the minds of others with unparalleled clarity.

It also accounts for the fact that he could lament his egotism but was never boring: it was an egotism that had nothing of egoism in it. Thus he wrote to people in difficulties: "I know well how hard it is to bear trouble which we must keep to ourselves—and I am very glad, and think it very kind, that you have said what you have said to me. I can only give you what I can—but that is what everyone cannot give. I will, please God, give you a Mass for your intention once a week for some time to come."[23]

The supernatural foundation of his natural feelings of friendship is something that strikes one again and again. It was one of his foremost principles, and his sermons prove it. "We love because it is our nature to love," he once said in the pulpit, "and it is our nature because God the Holy Ghost has made it our nature. Love is the immediate fruit and the evidence of regeneration."[24] He considered that the commandment to love all men does not imply that it is against the spirit of the Gospel to have personal friends. In this Christ himself was the example. Newman thought that the best preparation for a general love is to cultivate an intimate friendship and affection toward those who are immediately about us. And the union with God, the "Unchangeable and the essentially Good", is perhaps a first condition in the making of indestructible friendships. Thus true friendship may be a proof of a profound love of God.[25] In this way such friendships become "realities and no worldly vicissitudes can sweep them away, not even death itself".[26] He prayed: "Let my life be spent in the presence of Thee and Thy dearest friends. . . . Because Thou hast blessed me so much and given to me friends, let me not depend or rely or throw myself in any way upon them but in Thee be my life. . . ."[27]

From his prayer we may conclude that he felt extremely grateful for the blessing of friends, who to his door unasked, unhoped had come", as he once wrote.[28] His gratitude is found in his poems, his letters, his autobiographical writings. He considered those friendships a special token of God's mercy.[29] Again and again he thanked his friends for their fidelity and patience, and God for this great favor.[30] Recalling his conversion, he told Anne Mozley: "In spite of the shock hearts have been true to me, and while I can only bless God that the pain of parting did not make me falter in my purpose, I thank them the more for their loving forbearance and tender mercy."[31]

There is another aspect of his friendships which explains the great number of his friends and his statement in the *Apologia*: "Never man had kinder or more indulgent friends than I have had."[32] It is the fact that he himself yearned for sympathy and love. He was sure that the Son of God Himself could not live on earth without the sympathy of others. For as long as thirty years He lived with Mary and Joseph, enjoying their company. They were "like three instruments absolutely in tune which all vibrate when one vibrates, and vibrate either one and the same note, or in perfect harmony."[33] When in Italy he wrote to a friend: "How I should have liked to have been with you, or others. . . . One loses half the pleasure by being alone."[34] He did discover some contradiction or inconsistency in his own feelings: "I have often been puzzled at myself, that I should be both particularly fond of being alone, and particularly fond of being with friends. Yet I know both the one and the other are true."[35] But in the main, he resembled Saint Paul, who had rest and peace in the love of man and was not satisfied without the love of men. He felt with them and for them; he was anxious about them; he gave them help, and in turn he looked for comfort from them.[36]

In spite of this, Newman is sometimes accused of disloyalty whenever friends could not agree with him. The truth is that he never withdrew his friendship from such intimates as Rogers, Pusey, Keble, Copeland and many others, although he disagreed with them in very important matters. He was being quite honest when he wrote: "I am the friend of persons from whom I differ in matters of faith; much more can I endure a Catholic from whom I differ in opinion and conduct."[37] Only when friends acted in such a manner as to lose his confidence did friendly intimacy stop, although love and affection remained. Even his brothers and sisters did not lose his love, although, since his conversion in 1845, he had fallen into disgrace with them.

An interesting confirmation of Newman's loyalty is a curiously moving document, preserved at the London Oratory. Newman describes in it how a Protestant friend treated him and how he reacted: "Once on a time a young man made his Senior a present in token of esteem for him. It was a Madonna, and that Senior put her over his bedstead, and whenever any one spoke of it, he used to say: 'John Walter gave me that picture.' And he never said so without thinking kindly of him. —And so years passed, and changes came with them, and at length there was a day when the young man made a speech before a whole county; and after speaking by name of that elderly man for whom he once had felt esteem, he said, that he wished that all who were such as that elderly man was, were kicked out of the kingdom. —What then could that elderly man do before he was kicked out, but send back to that young man, who once had an innocent conscience and a gentle heart, that same sweet Madonna, to plead with the dear Child whom she holds in her arms for him, and with her gentle look and calm eyes to soften him towards that elderly man to whom he once gave it and who had kept it so safely?"

This incident occurred in 1850 when at the Restoration of the Hierarchy John Walter had publicly spoken of kicking out the Catholics, or rather the converts, from the country.[38] Newman heard about the speech, asked Father Dalgairns' advice and sent the picture back with the above story. Walter replied: "It needed not the look of that sweet Madonna to soften the heart of that young man of whom you have spoken. . . . He hopes that the utterance of his Protestant remark may be forgiven him. . . ."[39]

This small event is an example of Newman's reactions when friends had offended him or otherwise deserved a rebuke and also when selfish motives were imputed to him or slanders circulated about him. More often than not he kept silence. But in special cases he thought it his duty to answer. Very often he first asked advice. Then his reaction followed, deliberately strong or sarcastic, angry or affectionate, as the case required, but always inspired by supernatural feelings and never by revenge. Thus, as an Anglican, he once reproached a woman who wished to become a Catholic with disobedience and self-will. His words fell on her heart like an iceberg, as she later wrote. She called him "cruel and hard-hearted". But in the same letter she said: "Oh, what would I give to find a Roman Catholic priest like you in mind and manner. . . . You meant it all to my good."[40] Two years later Newman treated her in a still more severe way when she called on him at Maryvale: "You seemed . . . a wooden image", she wrote. She was too frightened to cry. Before he left the room, however, he smiled, and the smile saved her from despair. But she saw that she needed such severity and thanked him for it.[41]

However, he did not always realize how painful his severe behavior could be. He once declared that he had never been severe to anyone personally with the exception of Achilli. He had only spoken "very keenly on tenets, modes of acting, traditions, and institutions, perhaps of historical characters".[42] But there are some words or acts of his by which unconsciously and against his intention he hurt his friends. This happened, for example, to Mrs. William Froude. She complained about hard words of his, and he answered: "I never can be hard upon you, whom I love so well, and it is a great shame you should say so. . . . Do not suppose I have not ever the kindest and most considerate and loving thoughts of you."[43] Whenever he noticed his unintentional stiffness or harshness he apologized for it, and he said he felt anxious that he had not shown the tenderness which really was in his heart and which he always wished to express.[44]

This aspect of Newman's character is closely connected with his sensitiveness. There are many who consider this quality as a flaw in his admirable personality. Thus Cardinal Manning, when an old man, wrote about him: "That Newman had a morbid sensitiveness is well-known." Manning also ascribed the disappearance of friendly relations between Newman on the one hand and Faber, Wiseman, the London Oratory, and so on, on the other, to that abnormal sensitiveness.[45] Once, when a Jesuit spoke about this character trait, Father Ambrose explained to him that it was not Newman who caused loss of friendship but the friends themselves, because they no longer inspired him with confidence. His biographer, Wilfrid Ward, was of the opinion that the root of this sensitiveness lay in his extraordinary acuteness of perception.[46] He saw more aspects of men and of matters than anyone else. Such penetration affected not only his intellect but his whole personality. Others could not enter into his many-sided views of persons and things; they felt estranged from him and left him. This happened particularly at his conversion. At first he took every opportunity and made every excuse to keep the many friends whom he loved so much. But in spite of his encouragement, many of them could not tolerate the Catholic atmosphere about him and showed their bewilderment, their suspicion, their abhorrence, their pain. Sometimes they did not answer his letters. That is how he lost many friends for a long time or for ever.[47]

One symptom of his "sensitiveness" is what he himself once called his "ingrained, contemptible shyness". As a boy he consoled himself by thinking of the shyness of Ulysses and Saint Paul.[48] He recounts in his *Apologia* how he was so embarrassed after his election as Fellow of Oriel College when he had to shake hands with Keble and the other Fellows that he felt "desirous of quite sinking into the ground".[49] When he was travelling he hated seeing new faces, making new acquaintances and "playing the agreeable".[50] Even as leader of the Oxford Movement he could blush at a mistake.[51] And as a Cardinal he still found it difficult to feel at ease with strangers.[52]

This sensitiveness cost him many tears. He wept during the funeral Mass sung for the Pope's confidential friend whom

Newman had loved while in Rome and who had been assassinated by an enemy of the Pope.[53] Memories, too, could make him cry. He could hardly think of his sister Mary and even of the house at Ham, where he had enjoyed the first years of his life, without tears.[54]

This sensitiveness often caused him to muse on the past. He mourned over past times as over a friend departed. In the same manner as he might recall that he had never been as kind to a deceased friend as he should have been, so he would reproach himself for not having used his time as he should have done. He was even tempted to say a *De Profundis* for these omissions.[55]

Another aspect of this trait was a tenderness of conscience, sometimes bordering on the scrupulous. He reminds us of the just man of the Bible who falls seven times a day, when he wrote:

> I'm ashamed of myself, of my tears and my tongue,
> So easily fretted, so often unstrung;
> Mad at trifles, to which a chance moment gives birth,
> Complaining of heaven, and complaining of earth.[56]

There were innumerable and various impulses and emotions which rose from his sensitive nature and which he ascribed to his great imperfection. Even his prayerful complaints, written down, as it were, in God's sight and on his knees, were sometimes considered by him as signs of ingratitude.[57] On one occasion after he had baptized someone, he became scrupulous about the validity of the baptism: "The water was exhausted out of the abominable shell before I made the three crosses. I do hope it was validly done."[58]

His "sensitiveness" was markedly revealed in his relations with his godson, Father Ignatius Ryder. Father Ignatius not only venerated and loved Newman but also praised him highly in his writings. Indeed, he had come to the Oratory to be near him, yet he seems to have been a considerable trial to his godfather. "His mind is so differently constructed from mine", Newman wrote. "I don't recollect his ever showing sympathy with any thing I have said or done; he is sure to take a contradicting view; he has never taken my side; it is his rule to trip me up. . . . I have borne this, and without showing my pain, for 25 years." Because of this incompatibility, he forbade his executors to show Father Ryder any of his papers after his death.[59] If we consider that Newman always saw many more sides of a question than others; that his weak nerves, his many trials and tasks could easily have made him irritable; that a small thing might make him downcast,[60] we come to the conclusion that, as he himself wrote to a friend, it is wonderful that he should never have lost his self-control or shown his pain! Neither in his writings nor in the records of his contemporaries can we find a single instance to prove that he was ever carried away by his feelings. We have only the evidence of his strong expressions in the early journals.[61] This surely proves that he never acted from irritation, anger or a desire for revenge. The calm, deliberate way in which he expressed himself when irritated or pained made his complaints and reproaches all the more real.

This great sensitiveness had also something to do with his self-depreciation, or rather with the absence of all self-sufficiency and self-complacency. A year before his death, for example, he said that he was unable to think highly of his works. Nevertheless he knew that they had received an intelligent welcome from men of judgment,[62] and a famous Oxford don had described him as the clearest-headed man he knew.[63] Sometimes he complained that he could not feel himself to be an authority in any field,[64] although a great contemporary historian declared that his mind was worldwide in its scope, that he was interested in everything that was going on in science, politics and literature; that he had studied modern thought and modern life in all its forms.[65] He often said that he was no theologian, although Gladstone called him "the first living theologian" and Dupanloup would have had him as his theologian at the Vatican Council.[66] In his *Grammar of Assent* he often asserts that he is no philosopher, although philosophers are anxious to know what he teaches on philosophical subjects. He was convinced that he lacked "the staidness or dignity necessary for a leader",[67] but a former friend and historian, who certainly could not be suspected of partiality, called him "the true chief of the Catholic revival".[68] He lamented his extreme incapacity as rector of a university,[69] although not only his administrative but his initiative, leadership and educational abilities were unparalleled.[70] In the same way he felt himself "unfitted . . . to be a Superior",[71] but the Oratory could not do without him, and one of the Fathers who left the Oratory spoke with profound veneration of his superhuman wisdom.[72] Again and again he reproached himself with all manner of faults: sluggishness, laziness, insolence, lack of self-confidence, unkindness, rudeness and many more vices, especially in his journals and written meditations. Nevertheless, many people saw a saint in him.

All this cannot be called "morbid sensitiveness" or even an inferiority complex. If one studies the circumstances under which he spoke these words of self-depreciation, one sees they are due to his keen intellect, his delicate mind, his many-sidedness, his genius and, last but not least, his high ideals. He realized to the full what he could be and should be and how far he was below his ideal. Thus he recognized the deficiencies in his written works because he knew there was no subject in which he was an expert in the full sense of the word. Hence he did not like to be called a theologian or a philosopher because he had never studied the great theological and philosophical systems, although he knew the works of many theologians and philosophers, Saint Thomas not excluded. According to his view he was a self-taught man or a dilettante. "He had to pick his way as he could over a road in a measure to him untrodden. . . . In the philosophical approaches to his subject he had need of more thought and more reading."[73] For the same reason he thought humbly of his book on human certitude and his psychological discovery, the illative sense. Concerning his leadership during the Oxford Movement, he observed that he led other people only through his ideas and not through his commands. He was a teacher, not a general.[74] As rector of the Catholic University of Dublin, he once mentioned the many things he ought to do and could not do.[75] In the same way he did not feel that he measured up to his own high ideal of a superior. He noticed that he gave way too much and that he prayed too little so that he was not a good example to his community.[76] Lastly, he had a high conception of the holiness required in a privileged person like himself, who out of thousands had been led to the one true Fold, had been made a priest and had been presented with great gifts. He compared himself with Saint Philip and other saints and saw the difference. If he had an inferiority complex, it was the inferiority complex of the saints, who always look up to the perfect. It was humility.

If it were true that Newman was "morbidly sensitive", his inner life would surely have lacked balance. But seldom have there been men as balanced of temperament and character as Newman was.

Everyone who attentively reads Newman's works will be struck by the harmony that appears in each and every part of them. Everywhere there is consistency, justness of proportion, balance of mind, equilibrium. From first to last we find delicacy of feelings, richness of imagination, strength of will, while the "imperial intellect" reigns supreme, creating harmony. He is matter-of-fact and at the same time poetic. He has a faculty for strict logic and at the same time he is the discoverer of the illative sense, which reaches absolute truth without applying the rules of logic. He is subtle and sublime and at the same time he remains simple and natural. He knows how to analyze an idea intellectually while not concealing the tenderness of his heart. He understands the old and the young, the learned and the unlearned, the conservatives and the modernists. He weighs the opinions and theories of opponents with admirable insight and objectivity, and he wisely makes use of their criticisms. He often states and explains their theories and arguments more clearly than they themselves do. He sees the unity of all branches of learning and their places in the whole. He sees the compatibility of faith and science, and the truths hidden in heresies. Writing on many subjects, he does so with a great inner freedom from compulsion and prejudice, while he remains true to revelation with the simplicity of a child. Yet his faith is an intellectual submission of his mind and not an unjustifiable leap in the dark. In him we see realized what he himself said of a man of liberal education: "Such an intellect cannot be exclusive, cannot be impetuous, cannot be at a loss, cannot but be patient, collected and majestically calm."[77]

It was his adherence to the real which in great measure supported his mental balance. "In this world of sense we have to do with things far more than with notions. We are solitary, left to the contemplation of our own thoughts and their legitimate developments."[78] For him life is real; we live in a concrete world, not in a world of abstractions. "We must take things as we find them" is a saying which he repeated a hundred times and on which he acted from his Oxford years till the end. Hence it is a mistake to speak of Newman as subjective. True, he often wrote about personal experiences and his own mental state, but always as realities, not as dreams and fantasies. He was continually both objective and concrete.

Wonderful, too, was the balance between his energy and activity on the one hand, and his sensitivity, affections and emotions on the other. As soon as he had confidence in his cause he was able to act courageously and perseveringly, without blind impetuosity. His sensitivity prevented him from hurting anyone unnecessarily, from any exaggeration in the execution of his plans or from indulging in willfulness or obstinacy. He was energetic and at the same time amenable. When he was forced to be fierce, harsh or sarcastic, he was so deliberately and with good reason. In other words, he always acted on his judgment, not on feelings, though he did take feelings into account.

He possessed a tempered manliness and strength. "Let him

obey or let him leave", he wrote to Faber about a young and self-willed Oratorian.[79] In the pulpit he was not afraid of "being a lion" and warning easygoing Catholics of the danger of hell.[80] He would remind his Oratorians of Saint Philip's words: "Never fear, don't be afraid." On the other hand, his heart was as tender as a woman's, so that many women found in him an understanding friend and spiritual father. He knew how to help and comfort them in a gentle, affectionate way. Although he lived a celibate life and gave his whole mind and heart to God, he never showed aversion or prudish reserve toward women. He did not decline their assistance, their respect, their sympathy and their affection. A remarkable instance of this is contained in his poem on the beauty of a lady's dress.[81] Some biographers have erroneously explained his sensitive nature as feminine, excluding manliness. His one-time pupil, Father Lockhart, knew better when he wrote: "He had, also, according to time and persons, a wonderful caressing way, which had in it nothing of softness, but which was felt to be a communication of strength from a strong soul."[82] And this is not the only testimony to his balanced nature.

There is another proof of his natural equilibrium in his well-developed sense of humor. Many authors imagine him as an exceedingly grave and rather melancholy person. They find this view confirmed by his photographs. Of course, the matters treated in his books and letters were of a serious nature, so that his humorous disposition could not show itself in them. However, one who knew him in his darkest days wrote about him: "There was at times in him a great vein of humour, and at times a certain playful way which he had of saying things which were full of meaning, and called to mind some passages in St. Paul's writings, suggesting, too, that there was in this, so also in other things, a certain likeness to the great Apostle who made himself all to all that he might gain all to God."[83] It was his ideal "to conceal seriousness under great cheerfulness, simplicity, modesty and humour", as Saint Philip did.[84] His books *Loss and Gain* and *The Present Position of Catholics in England*, concerning the prejudices of Protestants, are brimful of fine humor. It is amusing to read *The Undergraduate*, Newman's magazine, composed with John Bowden when he lived in a very strict way at Trinity College. It is full of fun, students' jokes and wit.[85] What good spirits he showed in the descriptions of his journeys![86] He describes with great humor the difficulties of a married parson.[87] Even after the catastrophe of Tract 90 and his resignation of Saint Mary's, he remained cheerful and showed it again and again in his letters.[88] After his conversion, we find him full of troubles, but at the same time he is joking and teasing, especially in the letters to Father Ambrose.[89] In Dublin, while many difficulties were pressing, his "gaiety of heart", said one of his professors, shed cheerfulness as a sunbeam sheds light.[90] And when Rodin painted him as a man full of sorrow, mourning for his Oxford days, the Oratorians were very much hurt and Newman himself wrote about it to a friend: "If you saw me and talked with me you never would consider me sad or distressed."[91]

When Bishop Clifford described Newman's character in his funeral sermon, he said: "His love of truth and his warm sympathising heart were chief among the traits of his character. He was void of personal ambition, most unselfish, and always ready to sacrifice himself for others. He was naturally of a retiring disposition and very sensitive."[92]

We have been trying to trace Newman's natural qualities and dispositions, starting from his outward appearance and gradually going on to the more inward features. Thus we have arrived at what his friend, Bishop Clifford, put first and foremost, namely his love of truth, a quality which people often denied or ignored in him while he lived. In the *Apologia* he himself spoke of the charge of "mysteriousness, shuffling and underhand dealing", which he could not properly meet because he never had any suspicion of his own honesty.[93] Not only his adversaries but his friends sometimes called him "artful". In his Anglican period, one of his spiritual children frankly told him: "I am not the only person who complains that your language is often ambiguous. . . . Do try, and be always explicit and plain."[94] As a Catholic he was accused of the same fault by an Oratorian, who complained of Newman's "diplomacy".[95] Ward stated in 1863 that no Catholic understood Newman because he never spoke out and always hinted at things.[96] At the time of Tract 90, Jemima formulated the deepest ground of this accusation: "You must be aware that to persons who have not been brought up with you, or long accustomed to your manner of thought, yours is a difficult character. There is something which seems almost paradoxical which they cannot understand."[97] Nevertheless, if ever a man loved and sought the truth it was John Henry Newman. His whole life had been a struggle for truth. He had neglected his own interests to find the truth. He had used his powerful and subtle intellect to discover the true relationship between man and his Maker.[98] So he could not understand the accusations of insincerity and untrustworthiness and lack of veracity. "Do not think me arrogant", he wrote as early as 1853, "when I say, that, with ten thousand failings, I have a witness within me to singleness of mind and purpose, and to a heart bared before my Maker and Judge."[99] His ideal was to mean what he said and to say what he meant.[100] One of the Oriel Fellows, a very intelligent and outspoken man, once praised him for his sincerity: "I like you, for you do not, as others, only agree with me, but you differ."[101] He has been called "the most transparent of men."[102]

What we have described of the distinctive traits in Newman's portrait, have been considered especially from the natural viewpoint. But the natural man in him formed a unity with the supernatural. We may even assert that the supernatural purified and elevated the natural in such a way that the supernatural could reign supreme.

In the *Autobiographical Writings* we find a curious document,

consisting of only one page. He began to write it in 1812 as a
schoolboy, and he finished it seventy-two years later. The first
lines are a boyish expression of his joy at the coming holidays.
Then he wrote down with long intermezzi where he was and
what he did. The last entry tells us in a few words that he has
been made a Cardinal. But there is one passage, the fifth and
the longest, that gives a touching picture of his whole life:

> And now in my rooms at Oriel College, a Tutor, a Parish Priest
> and Fellow, having suffered much, slowly advancing to what is
> good and holy, and led on by God's hand blindly, not knowing
> whither He is taking me. Even so, O Lord. September 7, 1829.
> Monday morning. ¼ past 10.[103]

This is a summary of his supernatural life, his life in the
invisible world, his life in God's presence, while he is led on by
the Almighty and surrenders himself to His will, expressing
his resignation in the biblical words: "Even so, O Lord", that
is, "Do Thou with me whatever Thou wilst, I abandon myself
to Thee."[104] These words could be used as the motto of his
life. They are the most profound explanation of his entire
personality.

Whoever starts reading Newman will be struck by his
intense awareness of the invisible world. He lived, so to speak,
his doctrine that material phenomena are both the types and
instruments of real things unseen. For him the world of sense
was less real than the world of the spirit: from the time when
he thought life might be a dream and he an angel[105] up to his
old age this remained one of his great principles. Hence he
scorned materialism with utter disgust and gave the impression
that he attributed no reality at all to material phenomena. For
him the outer world, whether in its beauty or its grandeur, was
the manifold but transient garb of the one eternal Being, the
voice of Him Who "worketh hitherto"[106] and had called him
as well. This belief led him to the prayer "Even so, O Lord"
and made him ask for the great gift of perfect obedience to
God's will.[107]

We often come across passages in his works where he expresses this idea, the so-called sacramental principle. Thus meals and feasts, wine and bread, not only rejoice the heart of man and strengthen him, he said, but they mean much more: they create social feelings; they are tokens of good will and kindness; they are, he says, "of a sacramental nature". They are not an end in themselves. We do not enjoy them in solitude. They are intended to open our hearts toward each other in love.[108] Joys and pleasant things are also a manifestation of this sacramental principle. All that is bright and beautiful he sees as a figure and promise of what is to be. He declares that "it is God's unusual mode of dealing with us in mercy to send the shadow before the substance, that we may take comfort in what is to be, before it comes."[109] In a sermon preached in the year 1880, he remembered how he once climbed Vesuvius and saw the hot lava. There is something very awful in the lava, he said. It is very slow but very sure and very destructive. It is a kind of type of the Almighty. The lava comes; it may not come today, it may not come tomorrow, but in its slow course it is sure to come. So it is with God's judgments: they are just as sure, though they are just as slow.[110]

These habitual thoughts of the transcendent reality of the invisible world declare the utter unworldliness which is so conspicuous in him. "All is vanity", he exclaimed in his last sermon as an Anglican. "And time and matter, and motion, and force, and the will of man, how vain are they all, except as instruments of the grace of God, blessing them and working with them! How vain are all our pains, our thought, our care, unless God uses them, unless God has inspired them! how worse than fruitless are they, unless directed to His glory, and given back to the Giver!"[111]

After all this we can easily understand how intensely Newman realized God's presence. From his earliest days he had become more and more aware of the fact that there were but two beings in the whole universe, he himself and God, Who had created him. Everything else vanished before the clear vision

he had, first of his own existence, next of the presence of the
Supreme Being, Who revealed Himself through his conscience.
His conscience was God's representative.[112] Thus he heard
God's voice in his heart when still a very small child. He
obeyed, except for a short time when as a wayward boy he
"loved to choose and see his path" and went astray. This voice
resembled the pillar of the cloud, the kindly light that led him
on. This voice was his great proof of God's existence, speaking
louder than the voice of the visible world.[113]

The divine presence gave him a great trust in Providence,
even in the most desperate circumstances. "Such is God's rule
in Scripture, to dispense His blessings silently and secretly."
God leads us forward by a way we know not of. So we should
have faith in what we cannot see, "the Presence of the Eternal
Son, ten times more glorious, more powerful than when He
trod the earth in our flesh".[114] Therefore he could write down
this hopeful statement: "When we get to heaven, if we are
worthy, we shall enjoy the sight of how, all our failures and
disappointments, if borne well, have been for God's glory and
our own salvation."[115] Therefore, too, he could trust in Providence after the three blows and the failures of the *Via Media*;
when he was harassed by the Achilli trial; when he suffered
from the deadlock in Catholic education; when he was misunderstood and suspected by Church authorities. He knew
that Providence would fight for him and set things right,
probably not in his lifetime, but most certainly when he had
gone. So at the end of his life he could say in all truth: "I have
lived a long life and can witness to His faithfulness. He is a true
friend, and the more you can trust Him, the more you will
gain from Him."[116]

God's presence also intensified his love of prayer. Since the
Almighty lived in his soul, he could not but converse with
Him. He prayed not only when he felt the joy of heavenly
consolations—which seems to have been not so very frequently
—but when he felt indifferent and cold, or when his mind was
wandering and distracted and affective prayer was almost

impossible. His journal of retreats shows clearly how hard and difficult it often was. When he became older he even felt a loss of confidence in his prayers.[117] In spite of this, he never left off praying. In the solitude at Littlemore where God's presence could be felt, he had prepared himself for the great sacrifice by prayers combined with fasting and study. He prayed not only in church, near the Blessed Sacrament, and at set times but in all circumstances and all places, during his walks, at sickbeds, before decisions of consequence and even when writing letters. "No wish really means anything, which is not a prayer too", he declared.[118] He did not understand how religious men could have an aversion to prayer, nor how a priest could be bored when he had to be alone for a long time.[119] He was convinced that God's presence could never become a reality without a life of prayer. "Is anyone then desirous . . . of bringing Christ's presence home to his very heart. . . ? Let him pray", he said as an Anglican. And as a Catholic he asked: "Shed over me the sweetness of Thy presence lest I faint by the way."[120]

The reverence he desired in his prayers made him anxious about "wandering thoughts". This was especially the case in his Anglican period, probably under the influence of his book of meditations, written by Bishop Wilson, who called it a crime to indulge in distractions.[121] So Newman wished to achieve attention in prayers by humble and tedious practice. He thought it "a most irreverent and presumptuous judgment" to attribute lack of feeling and inattention "to the arbitrary coming and going of God's Holy Spirit". Neither could the length of Church prayers be a reason for not keeping one's mind fixed upon them.[122] But he softens his severe remarks on "wandering thoughts" by adding: "Inattention to our prayers . . . should not surprise or frighten us . . . unless we acquiesce in it."[123]

He had an immense confidence in the efficacy of prayer. He never undertook a work of importance without much previous prayer, and when he had done his best in all respects for any object or person, he left the rest to prayer, with great comfort.

To hear that anyone had been praying for him and his interests touched him with deep gratitude, touched him more than anything else. High as were his intellectual gifts, they were absolutely secondary in his eyes compared with the gift of prayer, in the poor and ignorant as in others. Thus he could accept trials with great patience because they were left in God's hands by means of prayer.[124] In an eloquent way he tried to lead others to such confidence: "You can never have an idea of the worth and power of prayer, or of the great efficacy of your prayers . . . till you are in the unseen world. He does for us 'exceeding abundantly above all that we ask or think according to power that worketh in us'."[125] Even when apparently there was no answer to his prayers, he was convinced of the truth of his words: "It is certainly wonderful", he wrote to Sister Maria Pia, "that no one of your or my own family has been converted, considering how many prayers have been offered for them— but . . . your prayers most surely are not thrown away, not one of them is lost or fails."[126]

The above mainly concerns what spiritual authors call vocal prayer. But Newman was a man of mental prayer as well. He considered this kind of prayer a necessary part of his and everyone's spiritual life. Without it we easily prefer the visible world to the invisible. His sermons, preached as an Anglican, often exhort his congregation to apply themselves to mental prayer, to meditation. One of the main lessons of the *Grammar of Assent* is the necessity of meditation, so that notional assent to religious truths might be changed into real assent and certitude. In an Anglican sermon he asked why we are not moved by the Passion of Our Lord. He answered that it is because we do not meditate: "We have stony hearts, hearts as hard as the Highways; the history of Christ makes no impression on them. And yet, if we would be saved, we must have tender, sensitive, living hearts; our hearts must be broken, must be broken up like ground, and dug, and watered, and tended, and cultivated, till they become as gardens, gardens of Eden, acceptable to our God, gardens in which the Lord God may walk and dwell; filled, not with briars and thorns, but with all sweet-smelling and useful plants, with heavenly trees and flowers. . . . And how is this to be effected, under God's grace, but by godly and practical meditation through the day?"[127] Of course, he knew that it is only by slow degrees that meditation is able to soften our hearts. It will be like the unfolding of leaves in the spring. But gradually it will bring us to deep feelings of love and gratitude, self-reproach, earnest repentance and an eager longing after a new heart.[128] He admitted, however, that meditation was not very easy: "We are what we are—Englishmen; and for us who are active in our habits and social in our tempers, fasting and meditation have no such great attractions, and are of no such easy observance."[129] Nevertheless, he asked his hearers, Englishmen as himself: "Is God habitually in our thoughts? Do we think of Him, and of His Son our Saviour, through the day? . . . When we do things in themselves right, do we lift up our minds to Him, and desire to promote His glory . . . to know His will more exactly . . . and aiming at fulfilling it more completely and abundantly? Do we wait on His grace to enlighten, renew, strengthen us? . . . We are always with ourselves and God. . . ."[130]

Words such as these prove the reality of Newman's faith and show the background of his beautiful, unshakeable mental balance. They also prove a certain inner experience of the invisible world and his Creator, a perception effected not only by means of his intellect but of his entire personality. This perception helped him to bear his failures and troubles and also the weaknesses and shortsightedness of some ecclesiastical authorities. Though God acted so mysteriously regarding his special talents, his faith prevented the slightest doubt. He never feared for the future as far as the Almighty was concerned because he knew that God's hand was over him and that he acted under the patronage of the Blessed Virgin and the wonderworking Saint Philip.[131] He often experienced the reality of his good guardian angel.[132] That is why he could live in a wonderful stability and serenity of mind. While he was always extremely careful in his statements concerning secular matters, he spoke with a surprising boldness of speech about the dogmatic truths of revelation. Though he naturally shrank from troubles and difficulties, and though he could shudder at the pain his "sensitive skin" caused him, his faith conquered all, and unhesitatingly he followed the kindly light of God's will and God's revelation and became a Catholic.

If we consider that he seems to have enjoyed only very seldom, if at all, the experiential perception of God's presence and the palpable certitude of his union with "the Lover of his Soul" which is bestowed on the mystics, his faith must have been great indeed. For mystics it is easier, at least in a sense, to be magnanimous and heroic. Newman's most intimate bio-graphical writings, however, his most confidential letters, his most self-revealing sermons, do not contain a single passage that can be explained solely as a mystical experience in the strict sense of the word. We cannot suppose that he would have excluded such experience from the many things he wrote about his spiritual life. Of course, his life of pure faith was now and again brightened by great supernatural consolations. He wrote about "special visitations and comforts from the Spirit . . . yearnings after the life to come, or bright and pleasing gleams of God's eternal election". He thought about them and considered them a "choice encouragement to his soul".[133] He spoke about "a thick black veil" which is spread between this world and the next. Every now and then, however, "marvel-lous disclosures are made to us of what is behind it. . . . At times we seem to catch a glimpse of a Form which we shall hereafter see face to face. We approach, and in spite of the darkness, our hands, or our head, or our brow, or our lips become, as it were, sensible of the contact of something more than earthly. We know not where we are, but we have been bathing in water, and a voice tells us that it is blood. Or we have a mark signed upon our foreheads, and it spake of Calvary. Or we recollect a hand laid upon our heads, and surely it had the print of nails in it, and resembled His who

with a touch gave sight to the blind and raised the dead."[134]
This he taught in one of his sermons, convinced that "the
spiritual heart may see Him even upon earth".[135] But all these
statements can be explained quite apart from the mystical
works of Saint Teresa of Avila and Saint John of the Cross.

There are even some positive proofs which seem to show
that in his long life he seldom or never enjoyed God's presence
in this mystical way. When a meditation had seemed very long
to him he wrote down in his diary: "If an hour tries me, what
will serving and adoring for ever in heaven?"[136] Is it possible
that one who had real mystical experiences should say such a
thing? Moreover, his diaries, his meditations and devotions,
and the fact that the pages in the works of Saint John of the
Cross in his study have never been cut, raise the same question.
He himself seems to confirm this view explicitly when he
prays: "The Saints . . . who keep close to Thee, see visions,
and in many ways are brought into sensible perception of Thy
presence. But to a sinner such as I am, what is left but to
possess Thee without seeing Thee? . . . To live by faith is my
necessity, from my present state of being and from my sin; but
Thou hast pronounced a blessing on it. Thou hast said that I
am more blessed if I believe on Thee, than if I saw Thee. . . .
Enable me to believe as if I saw; let me have Thee always before
me as if Thou wert always bodily and sensibly present."[137]

The intense realization of God's presence and his own existence,
seen in connection with his introspective nature; his egotism,
which he considered "true modesty";[138] his great sensitiveness; his extremely personal view of things; his lifelong habit
of jotting down all kinds of autobiographical notes, and several
other proofs of interest in self, have led some authors to
consider him a man of a strongly marked individualism, a man
of self-centered feelings and conduct, even in his supernatural
life. Nothing could be less true. His whole soul went out to the
Church and to his fellowmen in an admirably unselfish way.

It would be easy to write a book on Newman's love of the

Church. How intensely he admired her! How tenderly he spoke about her! How wisely, justly and charitably he regarded the errors and sins of her representatives! And how strenuously and unselfishly he worked for her! As a young man he had recognized his Spiritual Mother by her "majestic movement".[139] His love for her never diminished. For him it was always the Church that mattered. Hence the Oxford Movement. His tremendous efforts were all on behalf of Christ's Church, though he had not yet seen her in her true light and mistook a shadow for the substance. As a Catholic he toiled and suffered for the Church. We may say that from 1828 onward his whole life was spent in fighting her greatest enemy, the Liberalism of the day, as he called it. This was the rationalistic spirit in religion, which threatened both Anglicanism and Catholicism.[140]

After his Evangelical period he had gradually become convinced that the Church must be a visible entity. She possesses sacraments and rites, the channels of invisible grace. This was the teaching of Scripture, of primitive Christianity and of the Anglican Church. He never changed this view.[141] Of course, he saw her human side as well as her divine aspect. He wrote striking pages on the sinful element within her and reminded his readers that the Gospel warned us against the expectation that vice and irreligion will be abolished on earth.[142] Therefore he prayed God to increase in him the habit of mind which made him look on the Church with sorrow indeed, but also with love, sorrow for the human deficiencies in her, love for the invisible beauty of grace. He said so when he was an Anglican; he repeated it in a prayer when he was a Catholic: "Let me never for an instant forget that Thou hast established on earth a Kingdom of Thy own, that the Church is Thy work, Thy establishment, Thy instrument; that we are under Thy rule, Thy laws and Thy eye—that when the Church speaks Thou dost speak. Let not familiarity with this wonderful truth lead me to be insensible to it—let not the weakness of Thy human representatives lead me to forget it is Thou who does speak and act through them."[143]

He wrote panegyrics on the Church, in beautiful phrases and majestic sentences, panegyrics on her wonderful origin, her independence, her universality, her indefectibility.[144] At the end of his Anglican ministry he addresses her as Mother of the saints, school of the wise, nurse of the heroic, "of whom went forth, in whom have dwelt, memorable names of old, to spread the truth abroad".[145] He called her a refuge and home for all nations, the head of an empire, exalted and established above all earthly power.[146] He considered her "a pledge and proof of God's never-dying love and power from age to age".[147] He was especially fascinated by her indefectibility. From the very beginning, on the day of Pentecost, the world has prophesied that this "ark for the salvation of souls" would not be seaworthy and would go to pieces and founder. But

who can say why so old a framework, put together eighteen hundred years ago, should have lasted, against all human calculation, even to this day; always going, and never gone; ever failing, yet ever managing to explore new seas and foreign coasts—except that He, who once said to the rowers, "It is I, be not afraid", and to the waters, "Peace," is still in His own ark which He has made, to direct and prosper her course?[148] . . . What an awful vitality is here! What a heavenly sustained sovereignty! What a self-evident divinity! . . . Her strength is in her God; her rule is over the souls of men; her glory is in their willing subjection and loving loyalty. She hopes and fears nothing from the world; it made her not, nor can destroy her. . . . She may be persecuted by it, but she thrives under the persecution. She may be ignored, she may be silenced and thrown into a corner, but she is thought of the more. Calumniate her, and her influence grows; ridicule her,—she does but smile upon you more awfully and persuasively. . . .[149] In the awful music of her doctrines, in the deep wisdom of her precepts, in the majesty of her Hierarchy, in the beauty of her Ritual, in the dazzling lustre of her Saints, in the consistent march of her policy, and in the manifold riches of her long history,—in all of these we recognize the Hand of the God of order, luminously, illustriously displayed.[150]

She was not only an external or visible unity in his eyes but a collection of souls,[151] the "poor strugglers with the flesh and the devil" and those who live in the City of the Living God, "pure from sin and rid of probation".[152] So if he worked for the Church, he did not work from the desire for the praise of earthly superiors or from the desire to live on the breath and to bask in the smile of man,[153] but he only wished to please God, living in the invisible community of saints, the Mystical Body of Christ.

These wonderful views were put into practice by an admirable habit of obedience. Both as an Anglican and as a Catholic, if he but knew his bishop's wish, he would have fulfilled it before the wish was uttered.[154] This obedience may even be called blind in the sense that he did not regard his own opinion when authority had spoken. In special circumstances he thought it necessary to reveal his own views on matters, even to the pope, but after explaining and defending his ideas, he always considered it his duty to submit.[155] Unlike some other reformers and leaders of movements in the Church, he laid it down as a rule that reform was not wrought by disobedience.[156] Nor was he ever conscious of having made charges against his superiors, publicly or in their absence.[157] How could he? Every bishop was a "lineal descendant of St. Peter and St. Paul". True, at various times bishops had forgotten their high rank and acted in a way unworthy of it. So had kings. Yet noble they were by blood in spite of their personal errors.[158]

Newman's love for the Church, not only in her rulers but in the other members of Christ's Mystical Body, also proves the absence of narrow-minded individualism. "The test of our being joined to Christ is love; the test of love towards Christ and His Church, is loving those whom we actually see", he preached.[159] Hence he unselfishly worked for the young men at Oxford, Littlemore and Dublin; for the young scholars connected with the *Rambler*; for the young Catholic generation that could not get a university education. One of these young men wrote about him after his death: "Newman had the power of so impressing your soul as to efface himself, and you thought only of that majestic soul that saw God. You felt it was God speaking to you." Newman planted in them a personal faith and knowledge of God, a sense of His presence, of their duty to Him, in all things. [160] And he always acted according to his principle: "One single soul, if but one, is precious enough for Christ's love and His Church's rearing." [161]

His Oratorians, too, enjoyed the fullness of his natural and supernatural affection. When Father Stanislaus was going to leave the Oratory, he wrote about Newman, his superior, that he had always been too lenient toward his many faults and infirmities; that he had always shown too great a confidence in him. Never since he knew him had Newman wounded or hurt his feelings, except once, and even that act was meant as an act of kindness. He knew his superior as few persons could know him, and he admired his great virtues, his self-denial and the wonderful sacrifices he had made for God, for the Church and for the Congregation. He declared that he had learned more from his discussions with him than he had ever learned from many books. He could not be sufficiently grateful. [162]

Father Neville remembered how on one occasion Newman, late at night, hurried to a dying man before any other Oratorian was roused, and, although the man lived at some distance, he instructed him, baptized him and prepared him for death. He remembered, too, how at another time Newman stayed at home for weeks, even months, expecting a lady to visit him. She wanted to discuss her desire to become a Catholic, but it was impossible for her to fix a definite time, and she was obliged to wait for an opportunity to present itself. The Oratorians remarked upon it: the fine weather was passing, he did not get the benefit of fresh air, and so on. At length in November she arrived. She was received into the Church and departed the next day. Three or four months later she died. [163]

It is often said that Newman remained unaware of the social problems of the time. We must not forget that he did not live in circumstances that enabled him to occupy himself with such problems. As his books were only written after a clear call—without a call, no time for a book—he did not fight against social injustice because he had no special call to do so. Moreover, his personal talents lay in the education of the young. He explained this himself in 1883 when he said: "It never has been my line to take up political or social questions, unless they came close to me as matters of personal duty."[164] We must not, however, imagine that he had no eye for the miserable condition of the poor. He once wrote: "Were it to my present purpose to attack the principles and proceedings of the world, of course it would be obvious for me to retort upon the cold, cruel, selfish system, which this supreme worship of comfort, decency, and social order necessarily introduces; to show you how the many are sacrificed to the few, the poor to the wealthy, how an oligarchical monopoly of enjoyment is established far and wide, and the claims of want and pain, and sorrow and affection, and guilt and misery, are practically forgotten."[165] Father Neville tells us that everything interested him: literature and politics, the circumstances of persons and places known to him, the thoughts of the simple and the lowly. Every day he read the newspapers as a lifelong habit,[166] and he enjoyed the social novels of Dickens. He clearly saw and described the conditions of the poor in the great industrial towns and wished to change them, not by demonstrations and similar activities, but by making people more religious.[167] In his sermons, too, he did not omit to speak about the poor and their misery. As he was a priest and apostle, he saw the great difficulties of the working classes especially in the light of faith, and wished to solve them in his own way, in a religious way.

Nor is it true that he never actively fought against social evils. During the Oxford Movement he wrote in protest to the plans of Lord Brougham, who proposed that social abuses could be corrected by acquainting the working classes with literature and physical science.[168] Newman wanted one of his pupils to take up the subject of the Poor Laws.[169] He requested Tracts concerning the poor.[170] He pleaded tenderness for the poorer classes[171] and did not like "to pass by God's little ones rudely as the world does". The voice of the widow and the orphan, the poor and the destitute, should reach our ears, he said. Our hearts should be open toward them, our word and deed befriend them. That is what he preached.[172] At Oxford, Littlemore and Alcester Street he put these views into practice. In Birmingham he and his Oratorians took care of the work-house, the hospital, the insane asylum, the jail and the schools. Among his sermons there are several sermons calling for charity, one "for distressed manufacturers", another "for the negroes". One of his first sermons was for "the starving silk-weavers".[173] "The Cardinal felt greatly for the poor, whether as masses or individually", wrote Father Neville. He was much concerned about the misery which the aged poor endured in the abominable workhouses. He followed with interest the great movement in London on behalf of the poor, and he said he half envied Cardinal Manning who could help them actively. "Indeed, our Cardinal's thought about the poor was, how much he could give them discreetly; and in some cases whether they were known to him personally or not, after learning well how things stood with them, he would give them five pounds, even ten pounds to one person at a time."[174] And among the poor of Dublin he was idolized.[175] A few months before his death he went personally to the owners of a great factory, the Cadbury Brothers, who forced Catholic girls employed by them to attend religious instruction given by Quakers. Though the gentlemen could not follow the Cardinal's argument, they were moved by the Christian spirit with which he defended his cause. In a few days the news came that his interference had been successful.[176]

The deepest foundation of all this was his love of Christ.

When we study Newman's spiritual life, we are struck by the high ideals which pervade it. This is especially evident in his sermons. As an Anglican he described the true Christian state: it was "not perfect joy and certainty in heaven, but a deep resignation to God's will, a surrender of ourselves, soul and body to Him; hoping indeed, that we shall be saved, but fixing our eyes more earnestly on Him than on ourselves; that is, acting for His glory, seeking to please Him, devoting ourselves to Him in all manly obedience."[177] In the same way he sketched a picture of the real Christian: "He has a devoted love of God, high faith, holy hope, overflowing charity, a noble self-command, a strict conscientiousness, humility never absent, gentleness in speech, simplicity, modesty, and unaffectedness, an unconsciousness of what his endowments are, and what they make him in God's sight."[178] And as a Catholic he spoke in the same vein: "They . . . watch and wait for their Lord, who are tender and sensitive in their devotion towards Him; who feed on the thought of Him, hang on His words; live in His smile, and thrive and grow under His Hand. They are eager for His approval, quick in catching His meaning, jealous of His honour. They see Him in all things, except Him in all events, and amid all the cares, the interests, and the pursuits of this life, still would feel an awful joy, not a disappointment, did they hear He was on the point of coming."[179] And in his darkest days he expressed his ideals in a beautiful wish, spoken at the funeral of a friend: "God in his great mercy . . . grant us, with unselfish hearts and pure love of Him, ever to aim at His glory, and to seek His will, and to ask for His grace, and to obey His word, labouring according to our strength, labouring to the end . . . in humility, diligence and love."[180]

These high ideals had a strong foundation in his deep humility. Newman was humble, "one of the most humble and lovable men I have ever met", Father Dominic declared.[181] Living in God's presence, he always was aware of the immense distance between God's infinite sanctity and his own spiritual poverty. "What am I but a parcel of dead bones, a feeble, tottering, miserable being, compared with Thee. . . . I acknowledge and feel, not only as a matter of faith but of experience, that I cannot have one good thought or do one good act without Thee. I know, that if I attempt anything good in my own strength, I shall to a certainty fail. I have bitter

experience of this."[182] He was convinced that only saints could
be really humble because they see God. This makes them
hideous to themselves because the infinite glory of the All-
holy, the All-beautiful, makes them sink into the earth with
self-contempt and self-abhorrence.[183] There was nothing morbid, nothing unbalanced, nothing exaggerated in this humble
view of himself: "Though full of imperfections, full of miseries,
I trust that I may say in my measure after the Apostle, 'I have
lived in all good conscience before God unto this day. . . .' I
have followed His guidance, and He has not disappointed me;
I have put myself into His hands, and He has given me what I
sought."[184] .

In many ways he showed that he himself acted according to
these high views. When he became a Catholic he said again and
again that he had not come to criticize but to learn, therefore he
did not wish to defend himself against false accusations.[185]
When Father Dalgairns left the Birmingham Oratory, Newman
humbly asked his forgiveness for all acts of inconsiderateness
or unkindness.[186] One of his servants has left behind a letter
saying that now and again Newman took a walk with him and
gave him valuable instruction, and the man added: "Though I
was a servant you never treated me as such."[187] As a Cardinal
he once visited an ex-Oratorian, who wrote to Father Neville:
"I cannot tell you how much I feel thankful to the Cardinal for
his visit. What humility, what charity, what loving condescension."[188] Whenever he had feelings of resentment toward
those who had thwarted or pained him, he conquered them by
humility: "Almighty God has done much for us and would
have done much more. And when, having contemplated our
sin, we think next of what He did for us, . . . can we then have
those feelings of resentment, a desire of retaliation, a smarting
under injuries? . . . That is true humility when we think 'I am
not worthy of the least of these Thy mercies.' "[189] Though he
possessed a prophet's foresight and could often tell beforehand
what was going to happen (there are numerous attestations to
this), he could never bring himself to say: "Listen to me, for I

have something great to tell you, which no one else knows, but of which there is no manner of doubt."[190] It was humility, too, which made him always pray for the grace of final perseverance and to ask others to pray for it. He commenced this practice when he was fifteen, and even in his old age and as a Cardinal he continued it. When a young girl visited him in 1887 and asked him to say something that she would remember all her life, to make her good, he gave the one word "perseverance".[191]

This profound humility was not only the foundation of his high ideals, it gained him spiritual benefits without number. His intellect was illuminated by the light of the Holy Spirit so that he clearly saw the credibility of everything taught by the Church. He perceived no difficulty whatsoever in believing all her doctrines. He received such supernatural strength for his will that he became the magnanimous priest we know, the man who generously surrendered his entire being to the Almighty, the Lover of his soul, by giving his inner liberty wholly and unreservedly.

There are innumerable passages in his writings which prove Newman's greatest desire "to do God's will under all circumstances". To please God was all in all. "How could we be happy but in obeying Thee?" he asked.[192] He called perfect obedience the standard of Gospel holiness.[193] Obeying God's will in all things would train our hearts into the fullness of a Christian spirit.[194] He deliberately wished to prefer God's service to everything else and to give up all for Him.[195] He thought nothing nobler or more elevating and transporting, he said, than the generosity of heart which risked everything on God's word.[196]

Once he preached an entire sermon on the frightening example of one who refused to do God's will.[197] "God's Will, the End of Life" and "Surrender to God" are among his most beautiful sermons.[198] And Bishop Clifford testified at his funeral: "He always felt himself to be in the presence of God and doing His will was prominent to all other thoughts."[199]

And therefore Newman prayed: "O Emmanuel, O Sapientia,

I give myself to Thee. I trust Thee wholly. Thou art wiser than I—more loving to me than I myself. Deign to fulfil Thy high purposes in me whatever they be—work in me and through me. . . . Let me be Thy blind instrument. I ask not to see—I ask not to know—I ask simply to be used. . . . And as Thou has loved me from the beginning, so make me to love Thee unto the end."[200]

This prayer was answered. He knew how to bear all his adversities and disappointments as the "servant of a crucified Lord".[201] Sometimes he repeated in his own words the prayer of Our Lord in the Garden of Olives: "Visit me not, O my loving Lord—if it be not wrong so to pray—visit me not with those trying visitations which saints only can bear. . . . Still I leave all in Thy hands, my dear Saviour—I bargain for nothing —only, if Thou shalt bring heavier trials on me, give me more grace. . . ."[202] And whenever such visitations came upon him, he bowed his head and accepted them.

This constant desire to give his will to God without any reserve made him great in the little things of life. Thus he never criticized others in a merely negative way, but always built up what he had pulled down. When he had to defend himself or others, he was never aggressive. He never thought of his own reputation but of God's honor. He never cherished a feeling of resentment. Keble's brother once had hurt him considerably by a letter. Newman said nothing about it except that he could not understand parts of it, and then he sent him some money for the poor of his parish.[203] After the Achilli trial he was so utterly free from feelings of resentment that in his dreams he fancied he was falling on his accuser's neck and embracing him.[204] It is moving to read the kind letters he sent to the Bishop of Newport, who had denounced him in Rome and been the cause of much pain.[205] In conversation he would speak of a kind action done him by those who often had treated him badly. It was his natural disposition to do so. It is understandable, then, that after his death his Oratorians were highly surprised when they came to know about the painful antagonism between him and Manning. He had never told them.[206] His patient way of forgiving and forgetting injuries deeply impressed outsiders, and a man who had followed Newman's life for years said at the end of Newman's career: "His life was a most stormy one and no man ever had to face more criticism or was less understood. . . . I have watched him pass through trial after trial, and I have never heard him complain. . . . His silence and patience have been to me a lasting and ever-present lesson."[207] No wonder, then, that Ward, who could not sympathize with Newman's ideas, once exclaimed: "I am more struck than I can express at all times with your wonderful disinterestedness",[208] and Dr. Russell, the saintly president of Maynooth, put it in still stronger terms: "I have never ceased to admire your humble sincerity, your loyal love of truth, and your entire and self-sacrificing devotedness for the sake of duty and conscience."[209]

All this magnanimity had its source in his intense love of God. "What is perfectly clear to any one who can appreciate Cardinal Newman at all, is that from beginning to the end of his career he has been penetrated by a fervent love of God", wrote a Protestant biographer.[210] His early sermons reveal that he had made it his highest ideal to live from love toward God. He observed that it is possible to obey, not from love of God and man, but from a sort of conscientiousness short of love; however, love must be the ruling principle; we should learn, not merely to obey, but to love.[211] The truest obedience is indisputably that which stems from love of God, without measuring the magnitude or nature of the sacrifice involved in it.[212]

This love as an ideal was not inspired by fear of hell. True, now and again he dwells on this subject, and in one of his sermons he described the horrible misery of a lost soul.[213] He often mused on the eternity of hellfire and tried to make the idea less awful to the imagination. He never had any doubt about the doctrine, but he could not always agree with the explanations.[214] But nowhere in his writing is there the slightest trace of a scrupulous or unjustifiable fear of hell. He was convinced that perseverance is a special grace. He prayed for it and wanted others to pray for it. But at the same time, he was full of trust in God's mercy, so that he could confidently surrender himself to the Almighty.

Some passages from his writings might suggest that the desire of the greatest possible happiness in heaven is the deepest motive of his love of God. The place of honor about God's throne is given to those who have loved and served Him, as he asserted in one of his sermons.[215] Indeed, he spoke more of heaven than of hell. An often recurring thought of his is that to attain heaven we should prepare ourselves by acquiring the habit of an intimate relationship with God. He rejoiced because of the light, the order, the stillness of heaven, but more because there we shall have incorruptible, spiritual, glorified bodies as our Lord has. The devil will no longer have any power over us. "We shall have nothing to fear, nothing to be perplexed at, for the Lord God shall enlighten us and encompass us, and we shall be in perfect security and peace. . . . And this one thought will be upon us, that this blessedness is to last for ever. . . . Our happiness and peace will be founded in the infinite blessedness and peace of God, and as He is eternal and happy, so shall we be."[216]

But it was not heaven that could be called the mainspring of his love of God. It was the awareness of God as the Being of beings, as the Infinite, as the Only Uncreated One, as the Supreme Good, the sovereign and transcendent beauty, the immeasurable Love in all His indescribable attributes. They made him speak of love as the highest motive of surrender to God.

He saw God's infinite amiability first and foremost in the great gifts of love He bestowed on man. There is nothing that can be done for us which God has not done and will not do.[217] In His treasure-house He has a store of favors. He makes His sun to rise on the unjust as well as on the just. He disperses His favors variously and indiscriminately, but nobody can number the benefits which he bestows on each one of us.[218] Newman saw God's unspeakable love in His creation and His redemption of humanity. "He is the God of love; He brought us all into existence, because He found satisfaction in surrounding Himself with happy creatures: He made us innocent, holy, upright and happy. And when Adam fell into sin and his descendants after him, then ever since He has been imploring us to return to Him."[219] Newman could not find earthly images which might fully express the gracious truth that God became the Son of Man. This condescension is an indescribable and ineffable mystery of love.[220] Moreover, without first asking any gifts from us, God has from our infancy taken us in charge and freely given us "all things that pertain unto life and godliness". The fullness of God's grace anticipated the first movements of pride and lust in us.[221] Especially in Christ's Passion and death, amazing proofs of God's infinite love are supplied. One moment of His agony, one stroke of the scourge would have been sufficient to satisfy for our sins. He gave the whole treasure of His blood, to the last drop. "He shed His whole life for us. . . . He left His throne on high; He gave up His home on earth; He parted with His Mother; He gave His strength and His toil, He gave His body and soul, He offered up His passion, His crucifixion and His death, that man should not be bought for nothing." It was as if He delighted in sufferings. It was a prodigality of charity.[222] This infinitude of love is continued and perpetuated by the gift of the sacraments, keys that open the treasure-house of grace, showing God's present favor, the certainty that He is reconciled to us.[223] We should be singularly grateful for the Eucharist, says Newman, because it means "a condescension on the part of Almighty God which would be quite overwhelming, were it not withal so very gracious". We should be full of reverence for it, but at the same time full of "exulting joy and grateful affection".[224]

It is not surprising, then, that Newman should have had a special devotion to the Sacred Heart. His sensitive, affectionate nature must have been drawn by this symbol of God's human and divine love. He said that it affected him more powerfully than any other devotion.[225] Even as a leader of the Oxford Movement he could not bring himself to say anything against it,[226] although it was so particularly a Catholic devotion. As a Catholic he preached: "Oh think of the Heart of Our Lord and Saviour, Jesus Christ; think how loving He was, how merciful; think how He looked with such infinite interest, and loving interest on every soul that came before Him, even on those who would not obey Him and turned away from Him, He looked with loving eyes. . . ."[227]

So one of the most striking reasons why Newman considered a practical love of God as his highest ideal was the infinitude of God's love itself. But this is not all. Bishop Clifford expressed it perfectly when he said in the funeral oration: Newman "had from his childhood a great idea of the majesty and greatness of God".[228] He wrote wonderful pages on this subject, pages which betray how profoundly he meditated on the Supreme Being, how habitually he must have lived in His presence and how he found the source of his spiritual life in the deepest depth of His loving heart. In his *Idea of a University*, he wrote:

I mean then by the Supreme Being One who is simply self-dependent, and the only Being who is such; moreover that He is without beginning or Eternal, or the only Eternal; that in consequence He has lived a whole eternity by Himself; and hence that He is all-sufficient, sufficient for His own blessedness, and all-blessed, and ever-blessed. Further, I mean a Being, who, having these prerogatives, has the Supreme Good, or rather is the Supreme Good, or has all the attributes of Good in infinite intenseness; all wisdom, all truth, all justice, all love, all holiness, all beautifulness; who is omnipotent, omniscient, omnipresent; ineffably one, absolutely perfect; and such, that what we do not know and cannot even imagine of Him, is far more wonderful than what we do and can. I mean One who is sovereign over His own will and actions, though always according to the eternal Rule of right and wrong, which is Himself. I mean, moreover, that He created all things out of nothing, and preserves them every moment, and could destroy them as easily as He made them. . . .[229] Look out even upon the material world. . . . He has traced out many of His attributes upon it, His immensity, His wisdom, His power, His loving-kindness, and His skill; but more than all, its very face is illuminated with the glory and beauty of His external excellence. . . . We can, as creatures, recognise and rejoice in the brightness, harmony, and serenity, which is their resulting excellence. . . .[230] Such is the Creator in His Eternal, Uncreated Beauty, that, were it given to us to behold it, we should die of very rapture of the sight.[231]

And therefore Newman prayed:

The more, O my dear Lord, I meditate on Thy words, works, actions, and sufferings in the Gospel, the more wonderfully glorious and beautiful I see Thee to be. And therefore, O my dear Lord, since I perceive Thee to be so beautiful, I love Thee, and desire to love Thee more and more. Since Thou art the One Goodness, Beautifulness, Gloriousness, in the whole world of being, and there is nothing like Thee, but Thou art infinitely more glorious and good than even the most beautiful of creatures, therefore I love Thee with a singular love, a one, only, sovereign love. . . . And I would lose everything whatever rather than lose Thee. For Thou, O my Lord, art my supreme and only Lord and Love.[232]

NOTES

Since this book was written, many letters which I saw in the Oratory Archives have been published in *Letters and Diaries*. For those interested, the dates of my notes will help them to find the printed text. But letters, etc., written between January 1838 and October 1845 are not yet published. A table of Abbreviations of Sources follows the Notes.

CHAPTER ONE

[1] Par. Pl. S., 8 (serm. 8): 110–11.

[2] S. O'F., 1–6.

[3] From a flyleaf of a book at the Birmingham Oratory, given as a present. The baptism took place on Holy Saturday, 1830.

[4] Vers., 4:13; June 27, 1826.

[5] Ibid., 14.

[6] Mozl., 1:80.

[7] Lett. D., Aug. 17, 1825.

[8] Ibid., passim.

[9] Ibid., Nov. 23, 1821; Maisie W., 12–13.

[10] Lett. J. M., May 21, 1836.

[11] Lett. D., Jan. 30, 1832; June 26, 1836; Maisie W., 280.

[12] Lett. D., Oct. 27, 1821; Aug. 26, 1824.

[13] Ibid., Aug. 30, 1822.

[14] Keble, 394; Contr., 3, 6–7.

[15] Aut. Wr., 81–82. The reliability of Newman's autobiographical writings has often been doubted but unjustly. See my articles in the *Irish Ecclesiastical Record*, Nov. 1956, 297–305; Jan. 1957, 25–37.

[16] Fam. L., Aug. 17, 1825; Contr., 6.

[17] Card. C., B.1.1.

[18] Gramm., 109.

[19] From an unpublished manuscript by Fr. Henry Tristram; Keble, 394 and Lett. D., May 12, 1825.

[20] From Fam. L., formerly in the possession of Miss Dorothy Mozley, and Aut. Wr., 150.

[21] Aut. Wr., 223.

[22] Ap., 2.

[23] Par. Pl. S., 2:65.

[24] Gramm., 112–13, 115.

[25] *John H. Newman: The Philosophical Notebook*, edited by E. J. Sillem

(Louvain, 1970), 2:50. The story was in the *Westminster Review*, Oct. 1860, 535.

[26] Gramm., 112.

[27] Ibid., 108.

[28] Mozl., 1:14.

[29] Ward, 2:340.

[30] From a margin note by Newman in an old children's book: *An Easy Introduction of the Arts and Sciences*.

[31] Addr., 125.

[32] From a book at the Oratory which Newman used at Ealing. He wrote on the title page: "I must have had this in 1808 or 1809. I was in the little school at the time, and I was out of it by June 1809."

[33] Aut. Wr., 29; Card. C., B.1.1.

[34] Contr., 3–5; Card. C., B.1.1.; Ward, 2:399; Mozl., 1:16.

[35] From the book mentioned in note 32.

[36] Card. C., B.1.1.

[37] Cf. Psalm 24 (23): 3–4.

[38] Keble, 314.

[39] Aut. Wr., 250.

[40] Ibid., 268.

[41] Ap., 3.

[42] Aut. Wr., 169.

[43] Med., 2: (1), 6. On the autobiographical value of this book, see H. Tristram's study: *John Henry Newman: Centenary Essays*, 123.

[44] Med., 14: (2), 2.

[45] Keble, 113, 114, 116, 394–95.

[46] Par. Pl. S., 1 (sermon 16): 220ff.; 8 (sermon 18): 260; Mix., Disc. 1:8–13; Occ., 1:9–12; Idea, Disc. 6:132.

CHAPTER TWO

[1] Med., 14: (2), 2.

[2] Aut. Wr., 268, 150.

[3] Keble, 113–14.

[4] Mozl., 1:19.

[5] Aut. Wr., 165.

[6] Ibid., 80.

[7] Idea, Disc. 2:28.

[8] Ap., 4.

[9] Ibid.

[10] Aut. Wr., 81.

[11] Ap., 49.

[12] Ap., 4.

[13] Aut. Wr., 147–248.

[14] Ap., 4.

[15] Aut. Wr., 150–151.

[16] Ibid., 179, 181.

[17] Ibid., 149.

[18] Ibid., 151. This was written in Latin.

[19] Ibid., 153.

[20] Ap., 7.

[21] From the rough draft of the *Apologia*, published by L. Bouyer in: *Newman: Sa vie. Sa spiritualité*, 44. See also the cancelled passage on p. 160.

[22] Keble, 114–116.

[23] Aut. Wr., 152, 154.

[24] Mozl., 1:179; Ap., 4, 5, 6.

[25] Keble, 112.

[26] Vers., 3.

[27] Aut. Wr., 156–157.

[28] *John H. Newman: The Philosophical Notebook*, edited by E. J. Sillem, 2:195–196. Ward, 2:341.

[29] Ap., 25.

[30] Aut. Wr., 38, 89.

[31] Ibid., 30–31, 42–44, 37. Or. L., Nov. 12, 1857.

[32] Keble, 322.

[33] Mozl., 1:30, footnote.

[34] Aut. Wr., 36.

[35] Ibid., 157–58. The date of his success was May 18, 1818.

[36] Ibid., 159.

[37] Fam. L. (to Walter Mayers), Sept. 12, 1820.

[38] Aut. Wr., 46, 160.

[39] Ibid., 46–47, 51–53.

[40] Ibid., 48, 181.

[41] Fam. L., Jan. 19, 1822.

[42] Aut. Wr., 48.

[43] Ibid., 180, 182.

[44] Ibid., 55, 167–69.

[45] Ibid., 249–50.

[46] Ibid., 180. According to his Autobiographical Memoir, this happened in the course of 1821. (See Aut. Wr., 49.) Probably he had made up his mind in 1821 but not yet told anybody.

[47] Ibid., 87, 192.

[48] Ibid., 188.

[49] Par. Pl. S., 1 (sermon 4): 47.

[50] Aut. Wr., 165–66, 174, 178, 188.

[51] Ibid., 175, 186, 188–89, etc.

[52] Ibid., 174, 184.

[53] Ibid., 174, 194, etc.

[54] Ibid., 175, 189, 188.

[55] Ibid., 186, 189.

[56] Ibid., 180.

[57] Ibid., 175, 184, 187, 188–89, 194, etc.

[58] Ibid., 186.

[59] Ibid., 177, 184, 186, 187.

[60] Ibid., 176.

[61] Ibid., 175.

[62] Ibid., 165–66, 187.

[63] Ibid., 175.

[64] Ibid., 166–67.

[65] Ibid., 176, 177, 187, 196.

[66] Ibid., 196, Feb. 9, 1824; 194, Nov. 4, 1823.

[67] Ibid., 181.

[68] Ibid., 174, 175, 192.

[69] Ibid., 177.

[70] Ibid., 195.

[71] The text, not yet published in English, is in the Card. C.

[72] Aut. Wr., 82, 179–80.

[73] Ibid., 82.

[74] Ibid., 186, 194; Mozl., 1:72.

[75] Aut. Wr., 182.

[76] Ibid., 178.

[77] Ibid., 75–76, 190–91, 197–98.

[78] Ibid., 194.

[79] Ibid., 49, 54.

[80] Ibid., 55–56.

[81] Ibid., 177.

[82] Ibid., 182–83.

[83] Ibid., 185.

[84] Ibid., 61, 185–86; Lidd., 1:369.

[85] Aut. Wr., 186.

[86] Ibid., 186.

[87] Ibid., 187.

[88] Ibid., 63.

CHAPTER THREE

1 Card. C., A.10.4. From a book of prayers, written by Newman as a boy.
2 Aut. Wr., 71.
3 Ibid., 192.
4 Ibid., 199.
5 Ibid., 198–99.
6 Ibid., 196.
7 Ibid., 200.
8 Ibid., 199.
9 Ibid., 200.
10 Ibid., 200; Diff., 1:81.
11 Mozl., 1:3–4; Card. C., A.12.3.
12 Mozl., 2:41.
13 Card. C., A.12.3.
14 Chron., July 17, 1824.
15 Mozl., 2:48; 1:75–76.
16 Published by Sir J. Stonhouse, Bart. M.D. Oxford 1822.
17 Card. C., A.10.4.
18 Priv. D., 1824–1825, passim.
19 Clem., i.v. Edgington.
20 Priv. D., Aug. 4, 20, 1824.
21 Ibid., Oct. 31, 1824, appendix.
22 Clem., i.v. Oldcroft.
23 Aut. Wr., 202.
24 Priv. D., July 24, 1824; May 29, 1825.
25 Priv. D., and Aut. Wr., passim.
26 Mozl., 1:76.
27 Clem., and Priv. D., passim.
28 Priv. D., 1824, passim; Clem., i.v. Swell.
29 Priv. D., Mrs. Pattenson, Dec. 1824, appendix.
30 Clem., i.v. Edgington.
31 Mozl., 1:82.
32 Ibid., 1:85. Card. C., A.12.3. has an angry letter from a parishioner on the subject.
33 Priv. D., appendix, Aug. 1824; Clem., i.v. Oldcroft.
34 Aut. Wr., 204–5.
35 Mozl., 1:84.
36 Aut. Wr., 206; July 17, 1825.
37 Ibid., 205.
38 S. O'F., 53.
39 Priv. D., Sept. 25, 1824; Loss, 155.
40 Mozl., 1:77; Aut. Wr., 175.

[41] Mozl., 1:79; Aut. Wr., 202–3; Chron., Sept. 25, 1824.

[42] Mozl., 2:57; Aut. Wr., 208.

[43] Mozl., 1:149, 114, 157; Aut. Wr., 202; Family Adventures, passim. It is a well-founded tradition in the Mozley family and at the Birmingham Oratory that Harriett's little stories faithfully describe the Newman family. Indeed, one easily recognizes the brothers and sisters. John Henry is called Henry; Harriett Elizabeth is called Bessie; Charles Robert goes by the name Robert; Francis William by the name Willie; while Jemima Charlotte bears the name Alice.

[44] Fam. L., Dec. 12, 1823; May 12, Dec. 6, 1825; Aut. Wr., 192–93.

[45] From a memorandum written by Newman and added to the copies of Fam. L., May 1874, and from Card. C., A.38.3.

[46] Card. C., A.4.2. This item consists of 8 copybooks.

[47] Ibid., March 3, 1825.

[48] Ibid., Aug. 12, 1825.

[49] Ibid., April 14, 1825.

[50] Ibid., Aug. 19, 1830.

[51] Priv. D., May 29, 1825.

[52] Ibid., May 29, 1825.

[53] Aut. Wr., passim, and 202.

[54] Ibid., 205.

[55] Ibid., 207.

[56] Ibid., 106: *scholares tutelae suae commissos probis moribus instruat, et in probatis auctoribus instituat, et maxime in rudimentis religionis et doctrinae articulis.*

[57] Ibid., 87–88.

[58] Ibid., 209.

[59] Ibid., 89.

[60] Rem., 1:181; Aut. Wr., 90.

[61] Aut. Wr., 259.

[62] Ibid., 194, 201.

[63] Ibid., 203.

[64] Card. C., A.11.8. Sermon preached at Deddington. Sept. 19, 1825.

[65] Aut. Wr., 208; Mozl., 1:189–90.

[66] Ap., 5.

[67] Ibid., 13–14; 288–89; Eccl. M., 28–39, 30, 32, 37, 38; against the Primitive Church, 39, 41, 42, 77; popish miracles, 57, 66, 79 footnote.

[68] Ap., 14.

[69] Mozl., 1:151–52; Aut. Wr., 211–13.

[70] Fam. L., passim; Priv. D., Aug. 24, 1824.

[71] Family Adventures. See Maisie W., 11–15.

[72] Aut. Wr., 207, 196.

[73] Fam. L., Dec. 10, 1829.

[74] Mozl., 1:69; Fam. L., Feb. 6, 1828.

[75] Fam. L., Nov. 19, 1835.
[76] Vers., 9:28.
[77] Ibid., 10:29–32.
[78] Aut. Wr., 213.
[79] Mozl., 1:163.
[80] Ibid., 1:170–71.
[81] Aut. Wr., 211.
[82] Vers., 9:26.
[83] Fam. L., June 8, 1828.
[84] Ap., 118.
[85] Ibid., 7.
[86] Ibid., 25.
[87] Ibid., 9.
[88] Mozl., 1:118.
[89] Ap., 25.

CHAPTER FOUR

[1] Vers., 90:156, June 16, 1833.
[2] Card. C., A.50.2.
[3] Un. S., 3:51.
[4] Mozl., 1:177–80.
[5] Par. Pl. S., 2 (sermon 16): 181.
[6] Mozl., 1:209.
[7] Par. Pl. S., 8 (sermon 5): 63–65.
[8] Card. C., B.2.9.
[9] Par. Pl. S., 1 (sermon 29): 311–12.
[10] Un. S., 4:67–68.
[11] Ibid., 72.
[12] Ibid., 6:103–4.
[13] Card. C., A.50, Dec. 18, 1831.
[14] Un. S., 9:174–75.
[15] Mozl., 1:175, 179, 181.
[16] Ibid., 177.
[17] Via M., 2:3; Mozl., 1:189.
[18] Via M., 2:10–12.
[19] Ibid., 15.
[20] Mozl., 1:196.
[21] Ibid., 198.
[22] Chron., Nov. 7, 1830; Mozl., 1:207.
[23] Aut. Wr., 208; Mozl., 1:200.
[24] Pers. C., Pope. Aug. 15, 1830; Ap., 10.

[25] Contr., 6.

[26] Card. C., A.26.13.

[27] S. O'F., 158–59; Mozl., 1:209.

[28] Pers. C., F. Newman, Aug. 21, 1826.

[29] Chron., Jan. 1829; Pers. C., F. Newman, 1830. See S. O'F., 141–43.

[30] Pers. C., F. Newman, Nov. 23, 1835.

[31] Card. C., A.9.1., Feb. 13, 1827.

[32] Ibid., B.11.5.

[33] M. F. Glancey, *The Press on Cardinal Newman*, 85, 178.

[34] The *Irish Ecclesiastical Record*, Oct. 1890, article by Fr. Lockhart.

[35] Short Studies IV, Letter III.

[36] Par. Pl. S., 7 (sermon 5): 58.

[37] Principal Shairp, Card. C., A.12.9.

[38] The *Irish Ecclesiastical Record*, Oct. 1890, 869–70.

[39] Par. Pl. S., 1 (sermon 24): 323.

[40] Ibid., 8 (sermon 7): 108–9.

[41] Ibid. (sermon 13): 199.

[42] Ibid., 1 (sermon 14): 180.

[43] Aut. Wr., 105–6.

[44] Ap., 8–9.

[45] Aut. Wr., 101, 103.

[46] Var. C., Oriel Tutorship.

[47] Mozl., 1:240–43, 248–378.

[48] He published 85 of them in *Verses on Various Occasions*. Some others are to be found in Anne Mozley's volumes. One cannot doubt their autobiographical character. Newman did not sublimate his thoughts and emotions; his verses exclude all pose. He applied the principle that great value should be attached to words as the expression of thought. A word meant to him a precious gem which should never be misused for concealing poverty of ideas. It has to cover thought as perfectly as possible. This autobiographical character is confirmed by two concrete data. First, in his later works he now and again refers to these poems in order to describe his feelings at the time. See, for example, Ap., 119, Ward, 1:188, 575. And secondly, when rereading his *Verses on Various Occasions* for a new edition, he changed a word or a sentence here and there but said: "In this and other alterations in these compositions care has been taken not to introduce ideas foreign to the Author's sentiment at the time of writing" (p. 71). This implies that he considered these poems to be the exact reflection of his inner life.

[49] Mozl., 1:319, 327, 297; Ap., 33.

[50] Mozl., 1:295–96.

[51] Vers., 82:143, June 4, 1833.

[52] Vers., 49:98, Dec. 25, 1832.

53 Vers., 81:141, June 3, 1833.

54 Vers., 83:144, June 5, 1833.

55 Vers., 106:181, June 23, 1833.

56 Ap., 32–35.

57 Mozl., 1:315.

58 Ibid., 325.

59 Ibid., 329–30.

60 Ibid., 338.

61 Ibid., 310.

62 Par. Pl. S., 2 (sermon 10): 115.

63 Mozl., 1:220.

64 Ibid., 237.

65 Ap., 34–35.

66 Mozl., 1:250.

67 Ibid., 269–70.

68 Ibid., 299.

69 Ibid., 349–51.

70 Psalm 121 (Auth. Version), Mozl., 1:351.

71 Aut. Wr., 121–27.

72 Mozl., 1:312.

73 Ibid., 266.

74 Ibid., 288.

75 Ibid., 266, 312.

76 Ibid., 318.

77 Ibid., 361.

78 Vers., 87:153, June 13, 1833.

79 Mozl., 1:361.

80 Vers., 109:185, June 24, 1833.

81 Ibid., 81:141, June 3, 1833.

82 Ibid., 110:186, June 24, 1833.

83 Ibid., 31:73, Dec. 3, 1832.

84 Ibid., 78:136, April 29, 1833.

85 Ibid., 90:156, June 16, 1833.

86 Ibid., 97:168, June 20, 1833.

87 Ibid., 79:138, June 1, 1833.

88 Ibid., 74:132, March 28, 1833.

89 Ibid., 64:121, Jan. 19, 1833.

90 Ibid., 47:95, Dec. 23, 1832.

91 Ibid., 59:112, Jan. 10, 1833.

92 Ibid., 37:82, Dec. 13, 1832; 84:132, March 28, 1833; 89:155, June 14, 1833; 110:156, June 16, 1833.

93 Ibid., 31:73, Dec. 3, 1832.

94 Ibid., 64:121, Jan. 19, 1833.
95 Ibid., 107:182, June 23, 1833.
96 Ibid., 110:156, June 16, 1833.

CHAPTER FIVE

1 Par. Pl. S., 3 (sermon 13): 188–89; June 8, 1834.
2 Ap., 35.
3 Mozl., 1:379–81.
4 Ap., 39.
5 Mozl., 1:399.
6 Ibid., 389.
7 Ibid., 429.
8 Ibid., 419.
9 Rem., 1:316.
10 Mozl., 2:192.
11 Ibid., 250.
12 Ap., 75–76; Ess. Cr., 1:263–66; Rem., 1:406–8; Mozl., 2:165, 186.
13 Vers., 15:46, Oct. 20, 1829.
14 Keble, 315.
15 Ap., 23–25.
16 Pers. C., J. W. Bowden, Oct. 6, 1837.
17 Mozl., 2:424.
18 Ibid., 1:135; Ap., 289.
19 Ap., 18.
20 C. Dawson, *The Spirit of the Oxford Movement*, 16–26.
21 Ap., 17.
22 Ibid., 161–62.
23 Mozl., 2:172.
24 Card. C., A.36.4.
25 H. Tristram, *Newman and His Friends*, 52.
26 Ibid., passim, especially 124.
27 Mozl., 2:242.
28 Ibid., 176.
29 Par. Pl. S., 5 (sermon 20): 298.
30 Mozl., 2:passim.
31 Ibid., 31 and passim.
32 Ibid., 49–56.
33 Lidd., 2:58.
34 Mozl., 2:50.
35 Lidd., 1:382–83.
36 Par. Pl. S., 8 (sermon 11): 162.

[37] Mozl., 2:155–56.

[38] Par. Pl. S., 4 (sermon 20): 303–4.

[39] Mozl., 2:160, 67 (footnote); Par. Pl. S., 2 (sermon 18): 214.

[40] Pers. C., F. Newman, Nov. 23, 1835. Note in the margin of Fam. L., part 2, 92.

[41] Apology for myself, 1874 memorandum in the copied Fam. L.; ibid., Feb. 12, 1834; April 12, 1836; Mozl., 2:176.

[42] Fam. L., May 16, 1836; Mozl., 2:173.

[43] Fam. L., May 17, 1836.

[44] Mozl., 2:175, 176.

[45] *Newman at Oxford*, by Middleton, 134–35.

[46] Via M., 2:256.

[47] Mozl., 2:230.

[48] Ibid., 231.

[49] Lidd., 2:58. See also Ap., 187.

[50] Mozl., 2:233; Aug. 17, 1838.

[51] Ibid., 234–35.

[52] Ibid., 247; Lidd., 2:62.

[53] Ap., 74.

[54] Pers. C., Keble, Nov. 28, 1838.

[55] Mozl., 2:243.

[56] Ibid., 240.

[57] Ibid., 311.

[58] Ap., 46–48.

[59] Pers. C., J. Bowden, Aug. 8, 1833.

[60] Mozl., 1:399.

[61] Card. C., A.27.9.

[62] Mozl., 2:229.

[63] Par. Pl. S., 5 (sermon 21): 307, 308, 309; 3 (sermon 11): 143, 147–50, 151.

[64] Ibid., 2 (sermon 18): 215–16.

[65] Ibid., 3 (sermon 18): 270.

[66] Ibid., 5 (sermon 19): 283, 270, 271.

[67] Card. C., A.50.5., Dec. 8, 1833.

[68] Par. Pl. S., 6 (sermon 25): 367, 368.

[69] Ibid., 6 (sermon 8): 103.

[70] Pers. C., John Bowden, Jan. 30, 1834.

[71] Ibid. Cf. Ap., 61.

[72] Mozl., 2:143–45.

[73] Ibid., 1:422.

[74] Card. C., B.11.8., Aug. 1, 1833.

[75] Cop. L., Jan. 1, 1834.

[76] Pers. C., H. Wilberforce, April 25, 1836.

[77] Rem., 1:396; chapter 62.

[78] Par. Pl. S., 6 (sermon 20): 321–23.
[79] Ibid., 5 (sermon 15): 214–15.
[80] Ibid., 5 (sermon 4): 53–54.
[81] Pers. C., Pope, April 5, 1830.
[82] Chron., June 30, 1834.
[83] Par. Pl. S., 3 (sermon 22): 332; Oct. 26, 1834.
[84] Ibid., 3 (sermon 21): 301.
[85] See preface, 1.
[86] Chron., Jan. 9, 1837.
[87] Pers. C., H. Wilberforce, March 14, 1837.
[88] Card. C., A.10.4., July 10, 1837.
[89] Par. Pl. S., 4 (sermon 15): 234.
[90] Ibid., (sermon 14): 223.
[91] Card. C., A.50.5., Dec. 8, 1833.
[92] Vers., 119:200.
[93] Pers. C., Pusey, 1834, no precise date.
[94] Par. Pl. S., 3 (sermon 15): 210–11.
[95] Pers. C., Pusey, 1834, no precise date.
[96] Par. Pl. S., 4 (sermon 1): 4.
[97] Ibid., 2 (sermon 6): 67.
[98] Ibid., 4 (sermon 1): 4.
[99] Ibid., 3 (sermon 22): 321.
[100] Ibid., 2 (sermon 14): 153.
[101] Card. C., A.50.5. No date but probably written between 1833–1839.
[102] Par. Pl. S., 3 (sermon 17): 246.
[103] Ibid., 2 (sermon 3): 38.
[104] Ibid. (sermon 19): 217.
[105] Ibid., 3 (sermon 10): 128.
[106] Ibid., 2 (sermon 22): 260–61.
[107] Ibid., 3 (sermon 9): 126.
[108] Ibid., 5 (sermon 21): 271.
[109] Ibid., 4 (sermon 8): 121–31.
[110] Ibid., 5 (sermon 6): 84.

CHAPTER SIX

[1] Med., 14: (2) 2.
[2] Ap., 92–93.
[3] Par. Pl. S., 5 (sermon 6): 85. Sept. 22, 1838.
[4] Ap., 119.
[5] Ibid., 114–15; Keble, 9; G. H. Harper, *Cardinal Newman and William Froude*, 44–45.

[6] Ap., 116–17.
[7] Pers. C., M. Giberne, Oct. 15, 1870.
[8] Ap., 117.
[9] Ibid., 162.
[10] Keble, 14; Mozl., 2:256–57; from the *Dublin Review*, April 1869.
[11] Keble, 220–21.
[12] Ibid., 14.
[13] Ap., 119.
[14] Ibid., 215–16; Keble, 346.
[15] Ap., 119.
[16] Pers. C., Robert Williams, Nov. 10, 1839.
[17] Ap., 129, 123.
[18] Ibid., 129.
[19] Mozl., 2:266–67.
[20] Ibid., 268.
[21] Ap., 128, 129.
[22] Ibid., 78, 129–30.
[23] Par. Pl. S., 5 (sermon 24): 343, 347, 348.
[24] Mozl., 2:269–71.
[25] Ap., 131; Pers. C., Wood, March 17, 1840.
[26] Pers. C., Miss Holmes, Oct. 19, 1840.
[27] Pers. C., Pusey, Jan. 1, 1841.
[28] Mozl., 2:292–98; Ap., 89.
[29] Ap., 88–89.
[30] Via M., 2:365–93.
[31] Mozl., 2:296–97. Via M., 2:363.
[32] Par. Pl. S., 8 (sermon 10): 145–46.
[33] Fam. L., March 16, 1841.
[34] Ap., 187.
[35] Lidd., 2:185.
[36] Ibid., 187.
[37] Ibid., 188–89.
[38] Ibid., 190.
[39] Ibid., 195; Ap., 89–90, 208.
[40] Ap., 90, 139.
[41] Via M., 2:424.
[42] Ap., 139.
[43] Ibid., 139–40; Pers. C., Copeland, July 1, 1868.
[44] Ap., 141.
[45] Mozl., 2:315–16; Ap., 141–44.
[46] Ap., 143.
[47] Mozl., 2:318.
[48] Ibid., 321.

[49] Ibid., 338.

[50] Ibid., 312; Pers. C., Holmes, Aug. 15, 1841.

[51] Sub. D., sermon 21, 318–19.

[52] Ibid., 322.

[53] Ibid., sermon 22, 348–56.

[54] Ibid., sermon 24, 367ff.

[55] Ap., 156.

[56] Pers. C., Robert Wilberforce, Dec. 9, 1841.

[57] Ibid., Jan. 29, 1842; partly Ap., 162.

[58] Keble, 311–12.

[59] Ap., 171–72.

[60] Ibid., 172–74.

[61] Ibid., 176.

[62] Chron.

[63] Par. Pl. S., 5 (sermon 23): 337.

[64] Aut. Wr., 219–21; Notes at the end of Newman's Ecclesiastical Almanac for 1842; letter by Dalgairns, Sept. 12, 1842; Pers. C., M. Giberne. Feb. 28, 1843; April 13, 1842. Ibid., H. Wilberforce, April 25, 1842.

[65] Var. C., Movement toward Rome. Jan. 25, 1842.

[66] Pers. C., H. Wilberforce, Feb. 12, 1842.

[67] Cop. L., March 8, 1842.

[68] Sub. D., sermon 25, 384–85.

[69] Pers. C., Phillippe de Lisle, Feb. 10, 1843; Misc. L., Fr. Pagani, in a Latin letter, feria IV infra hebd. II Quadr.

[70] Misc. L., March 16, 1843.

[71] Mozl., 2:365–66.

[72] Ap., 132; Keble, 210–13.

[73] Aut. Wr., 221–22; Pers. C., M. Giberne, Feb. 28, 1843.

[74] Card. C., A.11.6.

[75] Aut. Wr., 222–38, passim.

[76] Ibid., 223, 226.

[77] Pers. C., Miss Holmes, May 18, 1843.

[78] Var. C., Littlemore, Easter Eve, 1845.

[79] Keble, 216; cf. ibid., 212.

[80] Ibid., 217, May 4, 1843.

[81] Ibid., 219–20, May 4, 1843.

[82] Ibid., 222–25, May 14, 1843.

[83] Ibid., 225–29.

[84] Ibid., 231–32.

[85] Ibid., 243.

[86] On Aug. 1, 1843. Ibid., 245.

[87] Aut. Wr., 242–45. Only this part has been preserved. Keble, 267.

[88] Mozl., 2:403.

[89] Ibid., 373; Keble, 250–51.

[90] Mozl., 2:378.

[91] Keble, 255.

[92] Mozl., 2:376, 377.

[93] Ibid., 381.

[94] Keble, 262–63.

[95] Chron., Sept. 25, 1843.

[96] Memorials of Mr. Serjeant Bellasis, 59.

[97] Lidd., 2:375.

[98] Sub. D., sermon 26, 408–9.

[99] Keble, 219.

[100] Cf. Loss, 344–47.

[101] Ap., 174, 198, 222; Keble, 269.

[102] Keble, 342.

[103] Passim from many unpublished letters.

[104] Cop. L., to Edward Coleridge, Nov. 12, 1844.

[105] Mozl., 2:398.

[106] G. H. Harper, *Cardinal Newman and William Froude* (1933), 50–51.

[107] Keble, 347.

[108] Aut. Wr., 228–33.

[109] Keble, 296.

[110] Mozl., 2:387.

[111] Ibid., 391.

[112] Ibid., 392.

[113] Ibid., 396.

[114] Pers. C., Mrs. Bowden. Oct. 8, 1844.

[115] Mozl., 2:398.

[116] Manuscript letter in the possession of Miss D. Mozley (now deceased). March 11, 1841.

[117] Mozl., 2:403.

[118] Ibid., 404.

[119] Ibid., 403.

[120] Keble, 314–18.

[121] Ibid., 318–19.

[122] Ibid., 122.

[123] Mozl., 2:399.

[124] Keble, 349–50.

[125] Mozl., 2:406–7.

[126] Ap., 228.

[127] Keble, 381.

[128] Fam. L., Jan. 21, 1844.

[129] Pers. C., Mrs. Bowden, April 4, 1845.

[130] Fam. L., Aug. 1845.

[131] Ibid., May 1, 1845.

[132] Ibid., Jan. 9, 1845.

[133] Fam. L., March 15, 1845; published in part by Mozl., 2:410ff.

[134] Pers. C., H. Wilberforce, April 27, 1845.

[135] Harper (see note 106), 67; June 1, 1845.

[136] Cop. L., July 3, 1845.

[137] Ess. Dev., xi.

[138] Ibid., 445.

[139] Henry Tristram, *Father Dominic and Cardinal Newman*, in: *Homage to Newman* 1845–1945, 34.

[140] Un. S., 92.

[141] R. D. Middleton, *Newman and Bloxam*, 118–19.

[142] Pers. C., Mrs. Bowden, Oct. 8, 1845.

[143] Ward, 1:94–95 footnote.

[144] For the details of this event see the article of footnote 139, esp. 32, and Ward 1:94–95 footnote.

[145] Ap., 238.

CHAPTER SEVEN

[1] Med., Novena of St. Philip, sixth day.

[2] Mix., 9:189, 1849.

[3] Pers. C., Mrs. Bowden, March 22, 1846. See also Ward, 1:112–13.

[4] From a letter by Dalgairns, Oct. 22, 1845.

[5] Mozl., 2:423.

[6] Lidd., 2:460–62, 508–14.

[7] From an unpublished manuscript by Fr. Tristram.

[8] Card. C., A.38.3., Feb. 5, 1846.

[9] Diff., 2:3.

[10] Ward, 1:241.

[11] Lett. D., 11:16–17.

[12] Ward, 1:98–99.

[13] Lett. D., 11:28–30.

[14] From an unpublished manuscript by Fr. Tristram.

[15] Ap., 236. Lett. D., 11:120.

[16] Ward, 1:116, 117.

[17] Lett. D., 11:131.

[18] Card. C., A.15.7.

[19] Memorials of J. H. Newman by Miss Bowles. Card. C., A.15.18.

[20] Aut. Wr., 255.

[21] Ibid., 255.

[22] Lett. D., 11:105.

23 Ward, 1:143.
24 Lett. D., 11:226–27. Ward, 1:144, 153.
25 Lett. D., 11:233–34.
26 Ibid., 254.
27 Ward, 1:139, 141–42.
28 Lett. D., 11:272–73.
29 Ibid., 294.
30 Ward, 1:154–56. Card. C., B.13.10.
31 Lett. D., 11, 12, passim.
32 Ward, 1:172–74.
33 Lett. D., 12:13, 14.
34 Ibid., 11:286; 12:12. Pers. C., M. Giberne, 1846.
35 Var. C., Rome, 1847.
36 Ward, 1:169–70.
37 Card. C., A.32.6.
38 Ibid., B.9.2.
39 Ward, 1:176–81. Card. C., B.9.2.
40 Lett. D., 12:15.
41 Aut. Wr., 239–42, 245–48.
42 Mix., 138.
43 W. F. Stockley, *Newman, Education and Ireland*, 12–13.
44 Loss, 327–28.
45 Med., 2: (2), 13.
46 Chapt., Dec. 11, 1850.
47 Ibid., Dec. 22, 1852.
48 From Alma Mater, Collegio Urbano de Propaganda Fide, Rome, 1947; 41–47.
49 Aut. Wr., 256.
50 Card. C., A.18.18.
51 Chapt., Jan. 19, 1853.
52 Lett. D., 12:143.
53 Ibid.
54 Chron., Lett. D., 12:226, footnote.
55 Lett. D., 12:177–78.
56 Ibid., 12, passim.
57 Chapt., June 30, 1848.
58 Or. L., Oct. 27, 1847.
59 Ibid., passim.
60 Lett. D., 12:348.
61 Ibid., 403.
62 Ibid., 312.
63 Ibid., 302–3, 338, 316.
64 Ibid., 349.

[65] Ibid., 352–53.

[66] Ibid., 358.

[67] Card. C., B.13.10.

[68] See Wilfrid Ward, *William George Ward and the Catholic Revival*, 16.

[69] See Wilfrid Ward, *The Life and Times of Cardinal Wiseman*, 1:448.

[70] Lett. D., 12:340.

[71] Pers. C., Ullathorne.

[72] Card. C., B.13.6.

[73] Ap., 370.

[74] Card. C., B.13.10.

[75] Ibid., B.13.6.

[76] Lett. D., 12:345.

[77] Ibid., passim. Card. C., B.13.10. Ward, 2:345–46.

[78] Aut. Wr., 249.

[79] Pers. C., Ambrose St. John, June 13, 1858.

[80] Mix., Disc. 7:13.

[81] Med., Fourth Prayer to St. Philip.

[82] Lett. D., 12:264–65. Chron., Mix., Disc. 1:6.

[83] Mix., Disc. 8:162–63.

[84] Ibid., Disc. 6:115–16.

[85] Ibid., Disc. 2:41.

[86] Lett. D., 3:286.

[87] The London Oratory, 1849–1949, 6.

[88] Lett. D., 13:254, 294, 299, 352.

[89] Ward, 1:203–4.

[90] Lett. D., 13:31, 32.

[91] Or. L., April 26, 1849.

[92] Lett. D., 13:130–31.

[93] Wilfrid Ward, *The Life and Times of Cardinal Wiseman*, 1:464–65.

[94] Lett. D., 13:38–134, passim.

[95] Ibid., 94–95.

[96] Ibid., 114.

[97] Or. L., April 16, 1849.

[98] Lett. D., 13, passim, esp. 242–43, 150–51, 154–55.

[99] Ibid., 208–9.

[100] Ap., 370.

[101] Lett. D., 13:378; Card. C., B.13.10.

[102] Lett. D., 13:285, 286, 330, 400.

[103] Ibid., 332–33, 229–353, passim.

[104] Ibid., 432.

[105] Ibid., 14:77.

[106] Ibid., 50.

[107] Ibid., 77.

[108] Ibid., 152.
[109] Ibid., November, passim.
[110] Pres. P., 394.
[111] Chapt., 1854.
[112] Ibid.

CHAPTER EIGHT

[1] Lett. D., 18:438.
[2] Pres. P., IX.
[3] Chapt., Feb. 2, 1853.
[4] Lett. D., 14:320. See Pres. P., 207ff. Ward, 1:279.
[5] Lett. D., 14:439–40.
[6] Ibid., 438.
[7] Ibid., 373, 441.
[8] Ibid., 437.
[9] Ibid., 438 footnote.
[10] Ibid., 451.
[11] Ibid., 15:7.
[12] Ibid., 50, 44, 155; Pers. C., H. Wilberforce, April 4, 1861.
[13] Archives Birmingham. Rough drafts of University Matters, in album.
[14] Lett. D., 15:98.
[15] Ibid., 100.
[16] Ibid., 103.
[17] Ibid., 292.
[18] Ibid., 103–23, 278–97.
[19] Ibid., 107.
[20] Ibid., 125, 127.
[21] Ibid., 14:79.
[22] Card. C., A.38.3. Letter to T. Mozley, Feb. 5, 1846.
[23] Lett. D., 14:47.
[24] Ibid., 15:127.
[25] Note appended to letter from Mrs. Bowden, July 20, 1852.
[26] Chapt., Feb. 2, 1853. Lett. D., 15:114.
[27] Ibid., 139–42.
[28] Ibid., 210.
[29] Ibid., 246, 248.
[30] Ibid., 253.
[31] Ibid., 247, 248.
[32] Chapt., Dec. 22, 1852.
[33] Ibid., Feb. 2, 1853.
[34] Lett. D., 15:285, 278. Ward, 1:300–301.

[35] Card. C., A.41.4.

[36] Lett. D., 15:310–11; 316–17, 335; Aut. Wr., 299–300.

[37] Camp., 76.

[38] Lett. D., 322.

[39] From a Memorandum by J. H. Newman, Aug. 11, 1863.

[40] Lett. D., 15:433–34.

[41] Ibid., 434–35.

[42] Ibid., 440–41.

[43] Ibid., 446 footnote.

[44] Ibid., 447, 448.

[45] Ibid., 448–49.

[46] Ibid., 450, 451–52.

[47] Memorandum on Fr. Dalgairns, Aug. 31, 1856.

[48] Lett. D., 15:514–15.

[49] McGrath, 220–24.

[50] Ibid., 236–37.

[51] Ibid., 238–44.

[52] Ibid., 258–59.

[53] Ibid., passim, esp. 256–58.

[54] Ibid., 261.

[55] Lett. D., 16:58.

[56] Ibid., 78.

[57] Ibid., 131.

[58] Ibid., 94.

[59] Ibid., 62–63.

[60] Ibid., 154.

[61] Ibid., 150.

[62] Card. C., A.3.10.

[63] McGrath, 244, 246, 250, 313–15.

[64] See letters to the Oratorians in Lett. D., passim.

[65] Lett. D., 16:472; 18:69.

[66] Ibid., passim; esp. 554–57.

[67] Ibid., 388.

[68] McGrath, 358–59.

[69] Card. C., A.15.7.

[70] McGrath, passim.

[71] Lett. D., 16:420.

[72] Ibid., 352.

[73] Ibid., 535.

[74] Ibid., 17:260–61.

[75] Ibid., 270.

[76] Ibid., 9.

[77] See Var. C., London Oratory, 1856. Introduction. This preface is

evidently written by somebody strongly in favor of the London Oratory. See also Purcell (1895), 2:5ff.

[78] Lett. D., 17:11. The whole story is concisely told in Lett. D., 17:41–51.
[79] Ibid., 10, and passim.
[80] Ibid., 43–46.
[81] Var. C., London Oratory, 1856. Introduction. Misc. L., Dec. 20, 1860. Lett. D., 17:51, footnote 59.
[82] Ibid., 17:13–14.
[83] Card. C., B.9.2. Remarks on the Oratorian vocation.
[84] Lett. D., 17:13.
[85] Ibid., 38–39.
[86] Ibid., 38–39, 171.
[87] Ibid., 59–60.
[88] Ibid., 65–66.
[89] Ibid., 268–69.
[90] Ibid., 38–39, 71.
[91] Ibid., 73.
[92] Or. L., March 2, 1856.
[93] Lett. D., 17:103.
[94] Ibid., 74, 121, 126, 129.
[95] Or. L., Feb. 3, 1856.
[96] Lett. D., 17:53.
[97] Ibid., 104–43, passim.
[98] Var. C., Visit to Rome, Jan. 25, 1856.
[99] Lett. D., 17:135, 137.
[100] Ibid., 135, 137, 139.
[101] Ibid., 145.
[102] Ibid., 163, 169–74.
[103] Ibid., 234–35.
[104] Ibid., 236, 274.
[105] Ibid., 273.
[106] Ibid., 248–49.
[107] Ibid., 254.
[108] Ibid., 270.
[109] Ibid., 307.
[110] Lett. D., passim; 17:560–61; Pers. C., Holmes, April 19, 1859.
[111] See, e.g., ibidem and Fr. Neville's private papers: Card. C., B.13.10.
[112] Lett. D., 17:157.
[113] Ibid., 16:393.
[114] Ibid., 17:216.
[115] Ibid., 514.
[116] Ibid., 18:220.
[117] Ibid., 17:178–79.

[118] Camp., 154.
[119] Lett. D., 17:378.
[120] Ibid., 361, 371.
[121] Ibid., 418–19.
[122] Ibid., 426.
[123] Ibid., 444–45.
[124] Ibid., 18:75–76, 92–93.
[125] Ibid., 17:420.
[126] Ibid., 519, 524.
[127] Ibid., 18:3–9.
[128] Ibid., 41.
[129] Ibid., 17:513–14.
[130] Ibid., 419.
[131] Ibid., 460.
[132] Ibid., 18:34.
[133] Ibid., 112–15.
[134] Ibid., 116.
[135] Ibid., 483–84; Aut. Wr., 327.
[136] Lett. D., 18:501.
[137] Ibid., 225, footnote.
[138] Ibid., 248.
[139] Compare McGrath, 488–89.
[140] Cop. L., Ornsby, Oct. 26, 1858.
[141] Or. L., Feb. 14, 1857.
[142] Aut. Wr., 320.
[143] Ward, 1:449–50.
[144] Or. L., Jan.–April 1858, passim. Lett. D., 18:236–342, passim.
[145] Gen 15:1.
[146] Lett. D., 342, 271.
[147] Card. C., A.36.1., Sept. 29, 1858.
[148] Lett. D., 18:351.
[149] Ibid., 377.

CHAPTER NINE

[1] Aut. Wr., 271.
[2] Ward, 1:420.
[3] Ibid., 423.
[4] Lett. D., 18:128–29, 162.
[5] Ibid., 134.
[6] Ibid., 423.
[7] Ibid., 425–28. Trev., 2:169–73.

[8] Aut. Wr., 256; see 254–57.

[9] E.g., Var. C., Oratory School, April 30, 1857.

[10] Lett. D., 18:489.

[11] Chapt., Dec. 20, 1858. Placid Murray, O.S.B., *Newman the Oratorian*, 380, 383.

[12] Cop. L., Aug. 8, 1859.

[13] Var. C., Oratory School, Dec. 28, 1861.

[14] Pers. C., Ornsby, Dec. 27, 1863.

[15] Ward, 1:437–38; Lett. D., 18:29–30.

[16] Ibid., 479–80.

[17] Ibid., 480–81.

[18] Lett. D., 18:522. Pers. C., Ornsby, March 25, 1859.

[19] Ibid., H. Wilberforce, March 31, 1859.

[20] Cop. L., May 15, 1859.

[21] Ward, 1:487–88. Lett. D., 19:51–52.

[22] Ward, 1:494–800; Pers. C., Allies, Jan. 20, 1864.

[23] Lett. D., 19:289–90; Ward, 1:503–4; 2:171 footnote; Aut. Wr., 253.

[24] Lett. D., XV, 165.

[25] Ward, 2:170.

[26] From a paper by Fr. Neville, Card. C., B.13.11.

[27] Aut. Wr., 249–75.

[28] Ibid., 249–51.

[29] Ibid., 251.

[30] Ibid., 252.

[31] Ibid., 253–60.

[32] Ibid., 249, 252, 275.

[33] Ibid., 252, 253.

[34] Ibid., 258–59.

[35] Ibid., 256.

[36] Mix., 6:111–12, 122.

[37] Pers. C., Ornsby, June 16, 1861.

[38] Ibid., Mrs. Bowden, Dec. 31, 1862. Lett. D., 18:376–77.

[39] Par. Pl. S., 5:79–80.

[40] Pers. C., Holmes, April 28, 1863.

[41] Lett. D., 19:273.

[42] Ibid., 19:325.

[43] Ibid., 455.

[44] Ibid., 235–36.

[45] Or. L., Dec. 3, 1861.

[46] Pers. C., Monsell. Jan. 5, 1862.

[47] Aut. Wr., 254; Or. L., Fr. Ambrose, July 18, 26, 29, 1861.

[48] Aut. Wr., 254; Ward, 1:594; Trev., 2:240–45; Chron.

[49] Or. L., Aug. 11, 1861.

[50] Ibid., July 18, 1861.

[51] Aut. Wr., 254.

[52] Lett. D., 19:447.

[53] Var. C., Oratory School. 1861–1862. The whole story is taken from this file unless otherwise indicated. Trev., 2:248–84.

[54] Pers. C., H. Wilberforce, Jan. 26, 1862; ibid., Ullathorne, Jan. 12, 1862.

[55] Var. C., Oratory School. 1861–1862, Oct. 16, 1865.

[56] Or. L., Aug. 18, 1862.

[57] Ibid., Oct. 25, 1862.

[58] Card. C., A.15.18; an account by Miss Bowles.

[59] Ward, 1:546.

[60] Ward, 1:544–45; Oct. 24, 25, 1862.

[61] Ibid., 544–45.

[62] Ibid., 524.

[63] Pers. C., Ornsby, Dec. 21, 1861.

[64] Ward, 1:565–67.

[65] Pers. C., Ornsby, July 11, 1861; Card. C., A.15.18., Jan. 8, 1867; Cop. L., Sept. 20, 1862; Nov. 28, 1862.

[66] Or. L., Memorandum, Jan. 1, 1859.

[67] Lett. D., 19:5.

[68] Notes for a statement presented to Propaganda. March 30, 1867.

[69] Card. C., A.15.18.

[70] Ward, 1:579–82.

[71] Cop. L., July 6, 1864; Ward, 2:43; Or. L., Aug. 15, 1863.

[72] Card. C., B.13.7.

[73] Cop. L., July 6, 1864; Ward, 2:43.

[74] Original *Apologia*, first pamphlet; Ed. W. 5–12. Var. C., *Apologia*, Feb. 12, 1864.

[75] Var. C., *Apologia*, Feb. 10, 1864.

[76] Ed. W., 25–62, passim.

[77] Pers. C., Copeland, March 31, 1864.

[78] Var. C., *Apologia*, March 8, 1864.

[79] Original *Apologia*, 179–80; Ed. W., 191.

[80] Ed. W., 80.

[81] Ibid., 81.

[82] Ap., 1.

[83] Chron.

[84] Card. C., A.15.7., March 30, 1889.

[85] Ed. W., 101.

[86] Ibid., 100–101.

[87] Ibid., 81.

[88] Ibid., 82.

[89] Ap., 283.

[90] Ibid., 284.

[91] Card. C., A.15.18.

[92] Ap., 368–79.

[93] Quoted by Culler in *The Imperial Intellect*, VIII.

[94] Ward, 2:45; Aut. Wr., 25.

CHAPTER TEN

[1] Aut. Wr., 275.

[2] Ibid., 260–61.

[3] Purc., 2:86.

[4] Keble, 280.

[5] Ibid., 282–90.

[6] Ibid., 290–93.

[7] Ibid., 290–93; Purc., 2:346–51.

[8] Camp., 23.

[9] Pers. C., Manning, Oct. 20, 1857.

[10] Cop. L., Jan. 10, 1862.

[11] Lett. D., 20:254.

[12] Cop. L., Memorandum, Dec. 19, 1864.

[13] Lett. D., 20:506.

[14] Card. C., Philosophical Papers, 20; Nov. 18, 1864; June 25, 1874.

[15] Cop. L., Memorandum by Fr. Ambrose, April 13, 1865.

[16] Pers. C., Monsell, May 28, 1865.

[17] Purc., 1, 2, passim.

[18] Cop. L., June 8, 1865.

[19] Purc., 2:317–18; Ward, 2:146–47; for these considerations I am greatly indebted to an essay by Fr. Ignatius Ryder, printed in his *Essays*, edited by Fr. Francis Baccus (1911), 271–302.

[20] Card. C., B.13.9.

[21] To Dr. Ullathorne, Aug. 12, 1866.

[22] Var. C., Memoranda, June 9, 1875.

[23] Cf. Ward, 2:149–50.

[24] Or. L., Sept. 2, 1864.

[25] Card. C., B.13.10.

[26] Pers. C., Monsell, Jan. 12, 1865.

[27] Ward, 2:61.

[28] Purc., 2:296–97.

[29] Ward, 2:63.

[30] Lord Charles Thynne to Newman, Dec. 13, 1864. Cop. L.

[31] Ward, 2:66–67, 540–42.

[32] Purc., 2:291.

33 Cop. L., Memorandum, Dec. 19, 1864.

34 Letter to Dr. Ullathorne, Aug. 12, 1866.

35 See note 33.

36 Ward, 2:67–68.

37 Pers. C., Monsell, Feb. 5, 1865.

38 Ward, 2:71.

39 Ibid., 67.

40 Cop. L., Feb. 10, 1865.

41 Diff., 2:113–14.

42 Ward, 2:213.

43 Diff., 2:20; Ward, 2:100; Aut. Wr., 273.

44 Ap., 194.

45 Ibid., 165. See Par. Pl. S., 2:127ff.

46 Lett. D., 19:346–47; Var. C., Movement toward Rome, 1, nr. 30. Note on a letter of Dec. 1839.

47 Ward, 1:99.

48 Quoted in W. Ward, *William Ward and the Anglican Revival*, 16. March 11, 1849. Lett. D., 13:83.

49 Lett. D., 16:336.

50 June 28, 1864.

51 Pers. C., Giberne, Aug. 28, 1861.

52 See the Catholic sermons at the Birmingham Oratory, taken down by others in shorthand and not yet printed; the sermons on the Glories of Mary in Mix. Disc. 17, 18; further, the sermon notes, published posthumously; lastly the Catholic sermons, published by Fr. Dessain, sermon 7, March 26, 1848.

53 Diff., 2:117–18.

54 Ward, 2:100–102.

55 Letter to Pusey, 1–8.

56 Ibid., 116.

57 Ibid., 90–91.

58 Ibid., 96.

59 Aut. Wr., Jan. 16, 1866.

60 Account by Fr. Neville. Card. C., B.13.11; Or. L., Jan. 17, 1867; Trev., 2:272–73.

61 Var. C., Oxford Question, Jan. 7, 1867; Ward, 2:124.

62 Ward, 2:127, 142.

63 Var. C., Oxford Question, May 17, 1867.

64 Cop. L., Dec. 21, 1866. See Ward, 2:124–25.

65 From Manning's *Temporal Power* (1861), 219, 55–56, xxxviii; Purc., 2:161.

66 Occ., 281ff.

67 Ibid., 286–87.

68 Ibid., 306–12.

[69] Card. C., A.15.18., Nov. 11, 1866; Ward, 2:127–28, leaves this passage out.

[70] Cop. L., Oct. 20, 1870.

[71] Or. L., May 19, 1867.

[72] Purc., 2:350–51.

[73] Chron., March 25, 1866.

[74] Cop. L., Memorandum, March 26, 1866.

[75] Chron., June 8, 1866; Card. C., B.4.3.

[76] Cop. L., May 27, 1866.

[77] Ward, 2:121–22, April 29, 1866.

[78] Ibid., 130.

[79] Pers. C., Ullathorne, July 24, 1866.

[80] To Ullathorne, July 26, 1866.

[81] Cop. L., Aug. 12, 1866; Ward, 2:121–22.

[82] Cop. L., April 1867. The permission arrived Dec. 18, 1866. Newman received a copy without the secret instruction on Dec. 25.

[83] Card. C., A.15.18., April 15, 1867.

[84] Ward, 2:129; Jan. 8, 1867.

[85] To Dr. Ullathorne, April 17, 1867.

[86] Cop. L., March 21, 1867.

[87] See note 84.

[88] Neve to Ullathorne, April 5, 1867.

[89] Or. L., to Fr. Ambrose, Aug. 20, 1867.

[90] Card. C., A.15.18., Jan. 8, 1872.

[91] Aut. Wr., 273–74.

[92] Card. C., A.25.5., March 30, 1867.

[93] Cop. L., Dec. 13, 1867; Ward, 2:543–44.

[94] Memorandum, Cop. L., April 10, 1867.

[95] Memorandum by Fr. Ambrose, Cop. L., 1867, Jan. April.

[96] Ward, 2:139–40.

[97] Memorandum, Cop. L., April 10, 1867.

[98] Ibid., projected answer.

[99] Cop. L., April 6, 1867.

[100] Ibid., April 7, 1867.

[101] Ward, 2: passim, 160–80.

[102] Ibid., 184.

[103] Or. L., to Fr. Ambrose, Aug. 16, 1867.

[104] Memorials of J. H. Newman by Miss Bowles. Card. C., A.15.18.

[105] To Miss Bowles, Jan. 8, 1872.

[106] Card. C., A.41.4. To Miss Aungier, April 24, 1867.

[107] Card. C., A.15.7. Notes by Fr. Ignatius Ryder.

[108] Ward, 2:191–92.

[109] Ibid., 545; Heb 13:17.

[110] Aut. Wr., 262–63.

[111] Purc., 2:329.

[112] Ibid., 327.

[113] Ibid., 330.

[114] Ibid., 331.

[115] Ibid., 332–34.

[116] Ibid., 334–39.

[117] Ibid., 331.

[118] Ibid., 341.

[119] Ibid., 345–46.

[120] Ward, 2:81.

[121] Ibid., 182.

[122] Ibid., 81; 301–2; Diff., 2:280.

[123] Purc., 2:273–74.

[124] Ibid., 160.

[125] Var. C., Memoranda, Dec. 12, 1869.

[126] G. H. Harper, *Cardinal Newman and William Froude* (1933), 193–95.

[127] Var. C., Prospective Convert, Aug. 30, 1869.

[128] Card. C., A.15.18. Ward gives several more examples of Newman's comfort to people in distress: 2:556–59.

[129] Card. C., B.13.10. Var. C., Memoranda, Oct. 14, 1868.

[130] Ward, 2:270.

[131] Ibid., 282–98; Diff., 2:300.

[132] Ward, 2:287–89.

[133] Ibid., 291.

[134] Pers. C., Giberne, Aug. 7, 1867.

[135] Ward, 2:303, 306.

[136] Diff., 2:301.

[137] Or. L., Aug. 13, 1870.

[138] See Cross, 171, Nov. 25, 1871.

[139] Purc., 2:457.

CHAPTER ELEVEN

[1] Aut. Wr., 271.

[2] Purc., 2:500.

[3] Pers. C., Fr. Hogan, Oct. 10, 1876.

[4] *Westminster Gazette*, Nov. 20, 1869, 483.

[5] Card. C., A.15.18. Memorials, 81.

[6] See Dr. Zeno, *John Henry Newman. Our Way to Certitude* (Leiden, 1957), 6–13.

[7] Aut. Wr., 269–70.

8 Ward, 2:252. Var. C., Vatican Council, April 22, 1869.

9 E.g., Or. L., to Fr. William, Aug. 12, 1866.

10 Ward, 2:253.

11 Card. C., A.15.18., Dec. 26, 1871.

12 Med., 12: (1), 2; written between 1855 and 1857.

13 See the Newman-Meynell correspondence in Dr. Zeno, *John Henry Newman, Our Way to Certitude*, 236, 238.

14 Cop. L., Aug. 17, 1869. Cf. Or. L., to Fr. Ambrose, April 15, 1869.

15 Dr. Zeno, 247.

16 Ibid., 247–48.

17 Ibid., 249.

18 Cop. L., Fr. Whitty, Dec. 20, 1878.

19 Spec. S., Vat. Council I, April 22, 1869; Chron.

20 Gramm., 491.

21 Ward, 2:262.

22 Pers. C., G. M. Hopkins, Feb. 23, 1883.

23 Card. C., A.15.18.

24 Via M., 1:x.

25 Ward, 2:396.

26 Chron., passim, 1870–1879.

27 Aut. Wr., 29–107.

28 Ibid., 24–25; Mozl. 1:3, introduction.

29 Pers. C., Blachford, Sept. 17, 1885.

30 From an anonymous article in the *Birmingham Daily Mail*, April 8, 1872.

31 Preached Nov. 19, 1876.

32 Diff., 2:77.

33 Ward, 2:559–660.

34 Pers. C., Fullerton, Nov. 10, 1874.

35 Aut. Wr., 273.

36 Ward, 2:560, Dec. 8, 1874.

37 Pers. C., Monsell, Nov. 23, 1874; Dec. 31, 1874.

38 Addr., 173, Aug. 15, 1879.

39 Ward, 2:560–65.

40 Ibid., 405–7.

41 Ibid., 408.

42 Shane Leslie, *Life of Manning*, 124–25.

43 Lett. D., 19:385.

44 Vers., 2:5, Feb. 21, 1819.

45 E.g., Lett. D., 13:111; memorandum no. 14, Oct. 8, 1868.

46 Cop. L., Feb. 8, 1839; no name.

47 Med., 7: (3), 2.

48 Ibid., 13: (4), 1.

49 Med., Tristram edition (Longmans, Green and Co., 1953), 347–48.

[50] Encycl. Brit., i.v. Newman.

[51] Several letters at the Oratory prove this fact. As to the title, Newman had read, in the *Dialogues of St. Gregory the Great*, bk. 4, chap. 26, a dream about death, dreamed by a monk called Gerontius. This seems to have given him the idea of its name.

[52] Cop. L., March 31, 1868.

[53] Fr. H. Tristram, *Newman and his Friends*, 103–4; Card. C., B.8.7.

[54] Letter to Anne Mozley, in the Anne Mozley file, Oct. 29, 1872; Pers. C., Lady Herbert of Lee, May 3, 1873.

[55] Occ., 279–80.

[56] This account by Fr. Neville to Sr. Pia, Misc., July 2, 1875, explodes the legend in Ward, 1:22, that Newman threw himself on the bed by the corpse and spent the night there. There is another account about this night in Card. C., C.3.9., confirming my narrative.

[57] Pers. C., Sr. Pia, June 4, 1875; Ward, 2:410–12.

[58] Card. C., C.3.9.

[59] Spec. S., Littlemore, file 60, April 8, 1845.

[60] Card. C., A.35.4.; letter by Edward Bellasis.

[61] Ward, 2:412.

[62] Card. C., A.15.18., Jan. 22, 1876; by mistake the date given is 1875.

[63] Ward, 2:411.

[64] Cop. L., to John H. Pollen, Sept. 5, 1875.

[65] Pers. C., M. Giberne, March 8, 1877.

[66] Ward, 2:410.

[67] Card. C., A.8.6.; A.11.10.; A.29.3.

[68] *The Philosophical Notebook*, edited at the Birmingham Oratory. 2:185.

[69] Pers. C., Anne Mozley, April 25, 1876.

[70] Purc., 2:556–57; 555–56.

[71] Ward, 2:436–38.

[72] Addr., 311–12.

[73] Ward, 2:440–42.

[74] Trev., 2:554.

[75] Purc., 2:560.

[76] Ward, 2:442.

[77] Ibid., 582.

[78] Addr., 1; Ward, 2:443; Trev., 556.

[79] Ward, 2:449.

[80] Cuthbert Butler, *Life and Times of Bishop Ullathorne*, 2:121, 159–60.

[81] Ward, 2:446.

[82] Fam. L., March 1, 1879, to Anne Mozley.

[83] Ward, 2:451–52.

[84] Med., 5:3.

[85] Addr., 8–9.

[86] Pers. C., Francis Newman, Feb. 27, 1879.

[87] Ward, 2:456. Misc. L., to Sr. Catharine, Jan. 1, 1884.

[88] Addr., 275, 71–72, 63.

[89] From Newman letters at the Brompton Oratory, bk. 10, 101.

[90] Addr., 319 footnote.

[91] Pers. C., Ullathorne, July 3, 1879; Addr., 18 footnote.

[92] Addr., 18–20.

[93] Ibid., 3–4.

[94] Pers. C., G. Ryder, March 20, 1879.

[95] Fr. Neville, in printed file labelled: Later Years.

[96] Cross, 172.

[97] Ibid., 175–76; Oct. 6, 1874.

[98] Addr., 312–13.

[99] Ward, 2:586–92.

[100] Ibid., 481–83.

[101] Card. C., B.13.10; Misc. L., 1884.

[102] Ward, 2:475–76.

[103] Card. C., B.13.10.

[104] Ibid.

[105] Ward, 2:476.

[106] See *Stray Essays* by Cardinal Newman, passim; and *Cardinal Newman's Doctrine on Holy Scripture*, by Seynave, 76–84; and Ward, 2:502ff.

[107] Stray Essays, 69–70ff.

[108] Cop. L., to Mrs. Keon, Nov. 27, 1878.

[109] Cop. L., May 21, 1870.

[110] Lett. D., 13:131–32.

[111] Misc. L., 1859, no further date.

[112] Ibid., Dec. 7, 1876.

[113] Ibid., April 4, 1877.

[114] Ibid., Feb. 24, 1878.

[115] Ibid., Oct. 27. See *Letters of A. Trollope* (Oxford, 1951), 494–95.

[116] Ibid., Feb. 20, 1879.

[117] Ibid., Aug. 17, 1882.

[118] Ibid., Aug. 20, 1882.

[119] Ibid., passim.

[120] Ibid., Oct. 31, 1878.

[121] Ibid., Nov. 6, 1879.

[122] Ibid., July 1880, nr. 8.

[123] Ibid., Dec. 30, 1882.

[124] Ibid., Feb. 27, 1884.

[125] Ward, 2:425–32; Ap., 390–91.

[126] Misc. L., G. Fitzgerald, 1882.

[127] Card. C., A.39.1.

[128] Letters 1880–1890, passim.

[129] Fam. L., Sept. 14, 1885.

[130] Or. L., Oct. 31, 1888.

[131] From E. Bellasis, *Coram Cardinali*, 47–48.

[132] Misc. L., March 22, 1882; Pers. C., Allies, May 27, 1887.

[133] From private papers by Frs. William Neville and Denis Sheil; Ward, 2:532–33; Centenary Essays, 125–26.

[134] Misc. L., July 21, 1889.

[135] Card. C., B.13.10.

[136] Pers. C., Hutton, May 10, 1884.

[137] Card. C., B.13.11.

[138] Misc. L., March 23, 1890; Maisie Ward, *The Wilfrid Wards*, 191.

[139] From Walter de la Mare, *The Eighteen-Eighties*, 71.

[140] Card. C., A.36.4.

[141] From an account by Mrs. Langord (Grace Mozley); a letter by Fr. Neville, Aug. 12, 1890, in the possession of Miss D. Mozley (now deceased); the funeral sermon by Bishop Clifford, Card. C., A.41.8., and an account by Fr. Denis Sheil, who was present at the Cardinal's death.

[142] Mix., 81–82.

[143] Med., 6: (2), 2.

[144] Purc., 2:751–52.

CHAPTER TWELVE

[1] Richard H. Hutton, *Cardinal Newman* (1890), 250.

[2] James Anthony Froude, IV, "Short Studies on Great Subjects", in: *The Oxford Counter-Reformation*, Letter III.

[3] William Lockhart, *Cardinal Newman. A Retrospect of Fifty Years*, in: *The Irish Ecclesiastical Record*, Oct. 1890, 868.

[4] Pers. C., Manning, Oct. 29, 1845.

[5] Thomas Arnold, *Passages in a Wandering Life*, 160.

[6] Ward, 2:369.

[7] London Oratory Newman Letters, bk. 2, 100; Feb. 1878.

[8] Walter de la Mare, *The Eighteen-Eighties* (1930), 71.

[9] Card. C., D.4.3. Patterson to Fr. Neville.

[10] Cop. L., June 27, 1873; cf. Occ. S., 116 on St. Paul as a gentleman.

[11] Lett. D., 13:145.

[12] Ibid., 12:159.

[13] Var. C., History of a Conversion, June 20, 1849.

[14] Card. C., A.12.10. Private Notes by H. J. Coleridge.

[15] Card. C., A.41.8., Lord Blachford's Reminiscences.

[16] Misc. L., Aug. 16, 1887.

[17] Pers. C., Mrs. Bowden, May 6, 1845.
[18] Pers. C., Monsell, Dec. 13, 1850.
[19] Keble, 141 footnote; Lidd. 2:100, 101.
[20] Var. C., Littlemore, Feb. 18, 1845.
[21] Lett. D., 20:503.
[22] Ibid., 18:264–66.
[23] Pers. C., Miss Bowden, May 24, 1866.
[24] Par. Pl. S., 4:310.
[25] Ibid., 2:59.
[26] Mozl., 2:134.
[27] Med., 2: (2), 8.
[28] Vers., 46; Aut. Wr., 258.
[29] Lett. D., 19:304.
[30] Ward, 2:516; Vers., 45–47.
[31] Fam. L., to Anne Mozley, Dec. 30, 1874.
[32] Ap., 15.
[33] Med., 2: (2) 2.
[34] Pers. C., Wood, March 17, 1833.
[35] Pers. C., Capes, March 16, 1868.
[36] Occ., S. 8:114.
[37] Lett. D., 17:472.
[38] London Oratory Newman Correspondence, bk. 12.M.115.
[39] Lett. D., 14:152–53, 159–60.
[40] Var. C., History of a Conversion, March 6, 1844.
[41] Pers. C., Holmes, April 4, 1846.
[42] Lett. D., 20:364–65.
[43] Harp., 89–91.
[44] See, e.g., Lett. D., 11:204.
[45] Purc., 2:351.
[46] Man and Matters, 279.
[47] See, e.g., Lett. D., 13:452.
[48] Ibid., 18:271.
[49] Ap., 15.
[50] Fam. L., Aug. 25, 1832.
[51] Mozl., 2:394.
[52] Card. C., B.13.10.
[53] Lett. D., 12:360–61.
[54] Pers. C., H. Wilberforce, June 8, 1840.
[55] Card. C., A.36.1. Address to the Union of Pious Sisters. Sept. 29, 1858.
[56] Vers., 314.
[57] Lett. D., 16:352; Aut. Wr., 275.
[58] Lett. D., 18:378.
[59] Card. C., A.29.3.; Aut. Wr., 266.

[60] Lett. D., 16:166.

[61] Aut. Wr., 149–213 passim.

[62] Card. C., B.13.10.; to Lord Emly.

[63] Aut. Wr., 66.

[64] Pers. C., Hutton, Feb. 25, 27, 1869.

[65] As in footnote 2.

[66] The Echo, Nov. 25, 1874; Cop. L., to Ward, Feb. 18, 1886.

[67] Ap., 59.

[68] As in footnote 2, letter 2.

[69] Lett. D., 18:41.

[70] McGrath, passim.

[71] Lett. D., 13:25.

[72] Or. L., Aug. 1862.

[73] Memorandum on the Essay of Development, July 15, 1846.

[74] Ap., 219.

[75] Lett. D., 16:535.

[76] Ibid., 16:131.

[77] Idea, 138.

[78] Gramm., 277.

[79] Lett. D., 13:357.

[80] Ibid., 13:341.

[81] Vers., 33.

[82] See note 4, p. 4.

[83] Ibid.

[84] Lett. D., 12:113.

[85] Card. C., A.18.8.

[86] Ibid., A.3.5.

[87] Maisie W., 277.

[88] See, e.g., Keble, 162, 321; Mozl., 2:295, 387.

[89] Lett. D., 11, 12 passim.

[90] Cop. L., J. H. Pollen to Fr. Goldie, Aug. 1890.

[91] Var. C., file 112, Jan. 20, 1875; Pers. C., Blachford, March 10, 1877.

[92] Card. C., A.41.8.

[93] Ap., 165.

[94] Var. C., History of a Conversion, June 22, 1844.

[95] Lett. D., 14:143.

[96] Lett. D., 20:388.

[97] Keble, 108, April 9, 1841.

[98] See footnote 2, letter 5.

[99] Lett. D., 15:398.

[100] Par. Pl. S., 5:45.

[101] Lett. D., 15:178.

[102] See footnote 2, letter 3.

103 Aut. Wr., 5.

104 See Mt 11:26, Authorised Version.

105 Ap., 2.

106 Jn 15:17.

107 Card. C., A.10.11.; an account by Fr. Eaglesim, who lived with Newman during his later years. That Newman admitted the reality of material phenomena is shown in Dr. Zeno, *John Henry Newman, Our Way to Certitude*, 60–63.

108 Sub. D., 28–29.

109 Par. Pl. S., 6:92.

110 Card. C., A.43.8.

111 Sub. D., 398.

112 Par. Pl. S., 1:20–21.

113 Gramm. 389ff.

114 Par. Pl. S., 4:257, 261, 265.

115 Lett. D., 20:437.

116 Cop. L., to Morris, Jan. 4, 1885.

117 Aut. Wr., 222–48, passim, esp. 247.

118 Pers. C., Ornsby, Jan. 16, 1879.

119 Lett. D., 18:198.

120 Par. Pl. S., 3:348; Med. 12: (3), 3.

121 See *Private Meditations, Devotions and Prayers*, esp. the chapter "On Devotion and Prayer".

122 Par. Pl. S., 1:142–43.

123 Ibid., 145.

124 Card. C., B.13.10.

125 Pers. C., Giberne, Oct. 10, 1876.

126 Ibid.

127 Par. Pl. S., 6:41–42.

128 Ibid., 43, 40.

129 Ibid., 4:75.

130 Ibid., 7:212–13.

131 Murray, 231.

132 Ward, 2:346.

133 Par. Pl. S., 2:226.

134 Ibid., 5:10–11.

135 Ibid., 4:252.

136 Aut. Wr., 229.

137 Med., 7: (2), 1, 2.

138 Gramm., 384.

139 Ap., 31.

140 Addr., 64.

141 Ap., 49.

142 Gramm., 454–56.
143 Med., 12: (1), 1.
144 E.g., Mix., 247–49; 252–54, 279–81.
145 Sub. D., 406–7.
146 Ibid., 218.
147 Par. Pl. S., 3:246.
148 Occ., 123.
149 Ibid., 137–38.
150 Ibid., 189.
151 Ibid., 57.
152 Par. Pl. S., 4:180.
153 Occ., 57.
154 Card. C., B.13.10.; Ap., 370.
155 See Lett. D., 20:568.
156 Occ., 217.
157 Pers. C., Hawkins, Dec. 1835.
158 Par. Pl. S., 3:247.
159 Ibid., 4:184.
160 Lockhart, 26.
161 Par. Pl. S., 3:332.
162 Or. L., to Fr. Caswall, Aug. 1862.
163 Pers. C., Fr. Neville, Later Years, 43.
164 Affirmation Bill file. Letter to MacColl, April 28, 1883.
165 Diff., 1:252.
166 Ward, 2:352, 354.
167 Lett. D., 12:37–39.
168 Dis., 254ff.
169 Keble, 35.
170 Mozl., 1:417.
171 Un. S., 169.
172 Par. Pl. S., 5:309.
173 Contr., 16–17.
174 Card. C., B.13.9.
175 Wilfrid Ward, *W. G. Ward and the Catholic Revival*, 450.
176 Ward, 2:534–35.
177 Par. Pl. S., 1:324.
178 Ibid., 4:159.
179 Occ., 35.
180 Ibid., 262.
181 *Homage to Newman*, 33.
182 Med., 21:3; 14: (1), 2.
183 Occ., 26–27.
184 Ibid., 258–59.

[185] Lett. D., 12:77–78.

[186] Ibid., 17:356.

[187] Misc. L., Sept. 1, 1884.

[188] Ibid. (in box 1885), June 8, 1888.

[189] Card. C., A.29.4., Oct. 26, 1879.

[190] Diff., 1:154.

[191] *A Torchbearer: Memoirs of Emily C. Fortey*, 20.

[192] Med., 4: (1), 1.

[193] Par. Pl. S., 8:204.

[194] Ibid., 1:233.

[195] Ibid., 1:180.

[196] Ibid., 2:215.

[197] Un. S., 9.

[198] Mix., Disc. 6; Catholic Sermons, 5.

[199] Card. C., A.41.8.

[200] Med., 1: (2), 3; 1: (3), 3.

[201] Par. Pl. S., 3:154.

[202] Med., 12: (2), 3.

[203] Mozl., 2:239.

[204] Card. C., C.5.5.

[205] Cop. L., Sept. 29, Nov. 3, 1869; April 8, 1870.

[206] Card. C., B.13.10.

[207] Letter by Hugh Pope, O.P., May 3, 1913; from a trunk in the Oratory Archivium.

[208] *W. G. Ward and the Catholic Revival*, 202.

[209] Cop. L., April 18, 1867.

[210] R. H. Hutton, *Cardinal Newman*, 2.

[211] Par. Pl. S., 5:327, 331, 333.

[212] Ibid., 2:171.

[213] Mix., 38ff.

[214] Gramm., Note 3:501ff.

[215] Par. Pl. S., 2:320–22.

[216] Catholic Sermons, 90–91.

[217] Par. Pl. S., 4:55.

[218] Ibid., 4:20–21.

[219] Ibid., 7:192.

[220] Ibid., 8:233.

[221] Ibid., 7:148.

[222] Mix., 307–8.

[223] Par. Pl. S., 3:291.

[224] Centenary Essays, 110; from Newman's Advertisement to Ch. Sutton's *Godly Meditations*.

[225] Pers. C., Fr. Neville, Later Years.

[226] Var. C., Movement toward Rome, Dec. 1839, letter 30.
[227] Card. C., A.43.8.
[228] Ibid., A.41.8.
[229] Idea, 62.
[230] Mix., 295.
[231] Ibid., 297.
[232] Med., 3: (3), 1, 2.

ABBREVIATIONS OF SOURCES

Unpublished sources will be mentioned as such.

Works without a date, published by Newman, refer to the Standard Editions of Longmans, Green and Co.

The letters all belong to the Birmingham Oratory, unless indicated otherwise. They were copied with the permission of the archivist before the publication of *The Letters and Diaries* was begun.

Addr.	*Addresses to Cardinal Newman with his Replies*, 1879–1881, edited by the Rev. W. P. Neville (Longmans, 1905).
Ap.	*Apologia pro Vita Sua*, by John Henry Cardinal Newman.
Aut. Wr.	*John Henry Newman. Autobiographical Writings*, edited by Henry Tristram (Sheed and Ward, 1956).
Cal.	*Callista. A Tale of the Third Century*, by John Henry Cardinal Newman.
Camp.	*My Campaign in Ireland*, Part I. Printed for private circulation only (1896).
Card. C.	This refers to the four cupboards in the Cardinal's study. Labelled A, B, C and D, they respectively contain 54, 13, 7 and 18 pigeonholes, each filled with many items, most of them not published. The cupboards are indicated in the references by the letters A, B, C, D; then follows the number of the pigeonhole, and in the third place the number of the special item.
Chapt.	A book containing many discourses Newman held for the Oratorian Chapters. Published in: *Newman the Oratorian*, by Placid Murray, O.S.B. (Dublin, 1969).
Chron.	*Chronological Notes*, an abbreviated survey of

Newman's *Private Diaries*, giving dates. Not published. See infra *Priv. Diary*.

Clem.   *John Henry Newman. St. Clement's 1824*. "A record of the persons I attended in sickness, principally in St. Clement's." (Not published; in Cardinal's cupboards A.10.3).

Contr.   *Contributions Chiefly to the Early History of Cardinal Newman*, by his brother F. W. Newman (London, 1891).

Cop. L.   *Copied Letters*. Twenty-two large boxes of a very great number of Newman letters, copied by Fr. W. P. Neville from the originals, lent to him by the owners. Most of them not published.

Cross   *John Henry Newman*, by Frank Leslie Cross (1933).

Diff.   *Certain Difficulties felt by Anglicans in Catholic Teaching*, by John Henry Cardinal Newman. In 2 vols.

Dis.   *Discussion and Arguments*, by John Henry Cardinal Newman.

Eccl. M.   *Two Essays on Biblical and Ecclesiastical Miracles*, by John Henry Cardinal Newman, being vol. 2 of the *Essays*.

Ed. W.   *Apologia pro Vita Sua*. Full text, edited by Wilfrid Ward (1913).

Ess. Cr.   *Essays Critical and Historical*. In 2 vols., being vols. 3 and 4 of the *Essays*.

Ess. Dev.   *An Essay on the Development of Christian Doctrine*, by John Henry Cardinal Newman.

Fam. L.   *Family Letters*. Some belong to the *Personal Collections* of the Oratory Archivium, others to typewritten collections. Some are originals, or copies from originals, done by Newman himself. The originals are in the possession either of the Birmingham Oratory or of the Mozley family. Most of them have not been published.

Gramm.   *An Essay in aid of a Grammar of Assent*, by John Henry Cardinal Newman.

Harp.   *Cardinal Newman and William Froude*, by Gordon Huntington Harper (Baltimore, 1933).

Idea   *The Idea of a University*, by John Henry Cardinal Newman.

Just.   *Lectures on the Doctrine of Justification*, by John Henry Newman.

Keble   *Correspondence of John Henry Newman with John Keble and Others*, edited at the Birmingham Oratory (Longmans, Green and Co., 1917).

Lett. D.   *The Letters and Diaries of John Henry Newman*, edited at the Birmingham Oratory.

Lett. J. M.   *Letters of the Rev. J. B. Mozley*, edited by Anne Mozley (1885).

Lett. N.   *A Letter Addressed to His Grace the Duke of Norfolk on occasion of Mr. Gladstone's recent expostulation*. In vol. 2 of *Diff. Angl.*

Lett. P.   *A Letter Addressed to the Rev. E. B. Pusey, D.D., on occasion of his Eirenicon*. In vol. 2 of *Diff. Angl.*

Lidd.   *Life of Edward Bouverie Pusey*, by H. P. Liddon, in 4 vols. (1894).

Lockhart   *Cardinal Newman: Reminiscences of fifty years since* (1891).

Lond. O. L.   Letters from or to Newman or connected with Newman at the London Oratory, beautifully collected in several books. Not published.

Loss   *Loss and Gain: The Story of a Convert*, by J. H. Cardinal Newman.

Maisie W.   *Young Mr. Newman*, by Maisie Ward (London, 1848).

McGrath	*Newman's University: Idea and Reality*, by Fergal McGrath, S.J. (1951).
Med.	*Meditations and Devotions*, by John Henry Newman (Longmans, Green and Co., 1953).
Misc. L.	*Miscellaneous Letters*, Sixty-eight boxes of letters to and from different correspondents, arranged according to the dates.
Mix.	*Discourses addressed to Mixed Congregations*, by J. H. Cardinal Newman.
Mozl.	*Letters and Correspondence of John Henry Newman*, edited by Anne Mozley. In 2 vols. New impression (Longmans, Green and Co., 1911).
Occ.	*Sermons Preached on Various Occasions*, by John Henry Cardinal Newman.
Or. L.	*Oratory Letters*. About sixty files of letters referring to Oratory matters. Published in *Letters and Diaries*.
Par. Pl. S.	*Parochial and Plain Sermons*, by John Henry Newman, B. D. In 8 vols.
Pers. C.	*Personal Collections*. Between 170 and 180 files of personal letters from or to Newman, arranged according to the names of the correspondents.
Pres, P.	*Lectures on the Present Position of Catholics in England*, by John Henry Newman.
Priv. D.	*Private Diary*. A series of books (in the Cardinal's cupboards) bought each year for the purpose of recording daily the events, great and small, Newman wished to remember. He started them in 1824 and kept using them till his old age. The *Chronological Notes* are an abridgement from them.
Purc.	*Life of Cardinal Manning*, by E. S. Purcell. In 2 vols. (1895).
Rem.	*Reminiscences*, chiefly of Oriel College and the Oxford Movement by T. Mozley. 2 vols. Second edition (1882).

Serm. N.   *Sermon Notes of John Henry Cardinal Newman*,
                  edited by the Fathers of the Birmingham
                  Oratory (1913).

S. O'F.   *Newman's Way*, by Sean O'Faolain (London,
                  1952).

Spec. S.   *Special Subjects*. Some files of letters on sub-
                  jects such as the *Vatican Council*, etc.

Stray Essays   *Stray Essays on Controversial Points*, by Cardinal
                  Newman (Privately published, 1890).

Sub. D.   *Sermons Bearing on Subjects of the Day*, by John
                  Henry Newman, B.D.

Trev.   *Newman. The Pillar of the Cloud*, by Meriol
                  Trevor (London, 1962). *Newman. Light in
                  Winter*, by the same (London, 1962).

Un. S.   *Fifteen Sermons Preached before the University of
                  Oxford*, by John Henry Newman.

Var. C.   *Various Collections*. Between 70 and 80 files of
                  letters, referring to outstanding events in
                  Newman's life.

Vers.   *Verses on Various Occasions*, by John Henry
                  Cardinal Newman.

Via M.   *The Via Media of the Anglican Church*, by
                  John Henry Cardinal Newman. In 2 vols.

Ward   *The Life of John Henry Cardinal Newman*, by
                  Wilfrid Ward. 2 vols. New impression (1913).